FAMILY MEDIATION PRACTICE

John Allen Lemmon

THE FREE PRESS
A Division of Macmillan, Inc.
NEW YORK

Collier Macmillan Publishers
LONDON

The Free Press
A Division of Macmillan, Inc.
866 Third Avenue, New York, N.Y. 10022

Collier Macmillan Canada, Inc.

Printed in the United States of America

printing number

1 2 3 4 5 6 7 8 9 10

Library of Congress Cataloging in Publication Data

Lemmon, John.
  Family mediation practice.

  Bibliography: p.
  Includes index.
  1. Family mediation. 2. Conflict management.
3. Mediation. I. Title.
HQ10.L44 1985   306.8'5   85-7032
ISBN 0-02-918550-5

for
Michael Belon Lemmon

Contents

Acknowledgments

MY PARENTS AND BROTHERS shaped the values that make me want to help others to continue relationships with their families. Sharing the care of my son, Michael, with his mother makes my own practice of the principles in this book vital.

Christina L. Zoppel consulted on the role-play section of the text and helped care for Michael. Provost Lawrence Ianni, Director David Shipp, and my colleagues at the Department of Social Work Education at San Francisco State University supported my sabbatical.

John Haynes, Joan Berlin Kelly, and other board members of the Academy of Family Mediators suggested I establish *Mediation Quarterly*, and contributors to MQ provided a number of ideas that I describe in this volume.

Laura Wolff and George Rowland at The Free Press, and copyeditors Madeleine Sann Birns and Jane Herman, suggested changes that improved the text. Robin Davey transcribed drafts of several chapters and typed the final manuscript. Alicia Valdivia inspired me to finish this book.

John Allen Lemmon

November 1984

CHAPTER 1

Family Mediation's Scope

FAMILY MEDIATION PRACTICE describes mediation as a method and demonstrates the techniques used to mediate various types of disputes. Families with problems who seek professional help may decide that mediation offers them the best assistance when this approach is explained to them. For the reader interested in becoming a mediator or considering hiring one to help resolve a dispute, this chapter provides a basic understanding of how mediation works.

Chapter Two, "The Mediation Process: Typical Stages and Techniques," demonstrates what actually happens in mediation sessions. Examples illustrate how the mediator sets the tone for open communication and encourages the disputants to focus on reaching an agreement rather than stressing their grievances. The reader learns how the mediator typically guides the disputants through a series of stages toward settling their conflict.

Chapter Three, "Mastering the Mediation Method: Art and Technology," discusses ways for the mediator to develop a personal mediating style by acquiring language skills that can be applied in a range of mediating contexts. Specific techniques, such as humor, story-telling, and role-playing are explained here. Using a personal computer and video taping can enhance the mediator's practice through procedures that are described in this chapter.

The creative, individualized nature of mediation makes it particularly effective in negotiating divorce settlements. The "Divorce Mediation" chapter stresses the importance of considering all family members' emotional and financial needs during mediation. Particularly when children are involved, the mediator is sensitive to the parties' complex, often unspoken fears and anger, and considers the interrelationships between the legal, psychological, and financial aspects of any settlement. "Mediation Throughout the Family Life Cycle" discusses the disputes which often arise as individuals in families grow and age. Conflicts between elderly parents and grown children, and between teenagers and parents require flexible, creative settlements. In "Mediation Between Neighbors or Unmarried Cohabitants," principles of family mediation are applied to disputants who are unrelated. In any ongoing relationship, conflicts can develop similar to those common in families, and mediation can help to settle them. Business and professional associates often have a close family-like relationship, and Chapter Seven discusses how the mediator can be effective in settling business-related disputes within the context of the working and personal relationships between the disputants.

Mediation is becoming a new profession, developed to meet the needs of people in a changing society, and its practice raises both legal and ethical questions. Chapter Eight discusses these issues, and reproduces the 1984 standards of family mediation approved by the American Bar Association and the 1984 interdisciplinary standards for family mediation developed by representatives of thirty law and mental health professional organizations. The final chapter, "Becoming a Family Mediator," provides advice and information on education, training, setting up an office, and establishing a successful practice. The appendixes contain the Domestic Relations Tax Reform Act of 1984, landmark cases on mediation, and information on the Academy of Family Mediators, a national organization offering services to five categories of members from students to experienced practitioners.

You Have a Dispute

You might be reading this book because you are trying to decide whether to ask a family mediator for help with a problem. Maybe you are facing a divorce or the breakup of another important relationship. You may feel as though you have lost control of your teenage children, while trying to come up with even the minimum payment for the credit cards each month and having to think about the fact that your brother and sister are threatening to take you and each other to court to settle whether or not to sell your late parents' house.

Psychotherapist

You have been a psychotherapist for a number of years. You planned to do marriage counseling, but your experience has been that many of the people you see are in transition to a divorce. If they do go through that procedure, you have felt powerless to help them while they tell about their pain in defining their future relationship with their children. Their lawyer says this will happen, their spouse says no, the court will do that, and there simply isn't enough money for two households. Who will get the house, or will it be sold? You have heard that mediation offers you the skills to assist them in making their own decisions by talking to each other with your guidance. How can you expand your work to include mediation and avoid the unauthorized practice of law? What do you need to know about family law and financial planning? How is mediation different from psychotherapy?

Family Lawyer

You might be an attorney who has established a successful practice in matrimonial law, which you know paradoxically means helping people get divorced, not married. However, you have always tried to reconcile being a vigorous advocate for your client and obtaining the result they ask for (before they change their mind yet again) with reaching workable agreements that consider any children involved. You do not want to become a family therapist, and are more comfortable valuing a high-tech company that may go public in the next year than talking with parents about the details of child custody. Still, the bar association has sponsored national and state conferences on family mediation, and it sounds appropriate for a number of your cases. How is it done? What guidelines will permit you to be both a mediator and a litigator in terms of your state bar's version of the Code of Professional Responsibility?

Graduate Student

You may be a graduate student in one of the mental health professions. Family mediation is an elective that appears to combine the family therapy techniques you have been practicing with knowledge of law and financial planning to help family members to reach written agreements with each other to resolve conflicts. Many of the recent articles on divorce and remarriage as well as conflicts throughout the family life cycle have discussed mediation and you are curious.

Law Student

Perhaps you are a law student. Your family law professor also offers a family mediation seminar that features the application of tactics of alternative dispute settlement to resolving divorce and other domestic conflicts out of court. You may be learning about mediation as one of the possible roles for an attorney in a course on lawyers as negotiators or a general introduction to alternative dispute resolution.

A Day in the Life of a Family Mediator

Since the Treadwells' appointment is at a quarter to eight this morning and traffic from your children's school is slow, you decide to skip the cappuccino. Both Ralph and Miranda Treadwell work downtown, so they prefer early morning appointments. Their divorce is moving from the "We're the best of friends" stage to snarling at each other. You have gone from being their enlightened guide as mediator to proof that all men are against women in Miranda's eyes and one of the cads likely to make a play for his soon-to-be ex-wife in Ralph's view. They are embarrassed and angry that they can't seem to maintain civilized manners as specific financial planning forces them to face the reality of separation. Today you are going to discuss how they might share custody of their daughter, Vanessa, a subject they have been avoiding. They probably will have done the homework you talked about last week, but even so, it will be a painful two hours. Still, they both were relieved when you told them that you had shared custody of your children for the past five years. "Maybe you do know something about this divorce business after all."

You are consulting this afternoon at one of the largest computer firms in the Bay Area. They are considering adding an "Agreement to Mediate" clause to their contracts with others in the industry. They have been impressed with the material you gave them about the movement toward getting quick and relatively low-cost resolution of disputes without risking company secrets in the legal discovery process. They became your clients when family mediation was added to their Employee Assistance Program, which already offered family counseling. A survey showed that many of the problems involved divorce, conflicts with adolescents or an elderly parent in the home, or financial troubles, all of which may be appropriate for mediation. When you helped to resolve a number of employee grievances that were the hidden agenda in training sessions and supervisor referrals, the need for mediation with other companies was expressed by the vice president for finance.

Your Family Mediation class at the university is considering the scope of divorce mediation tonight. In the past, the law students have tended to focus on resolving the money issues, while the social work students emphasized the psychological effect of divorce on children. Two of the family therapists who are experienced practitioners enrolled in your seminar through continuing education have been supporting your notion that, in real life, property settlement, spousal support, child support, and child custody are legally as well as psychologically linked. The doubting students should have seen the Treadwells relate living in the family residence to visitation and support schedules for Vanessa this morning. Maybe they will, since the Treadwells have given their consent for you to share videotapes of the sessions with the class.

Family Mediation Defined

Mediation is the practice of resolving disputes with the aid of an impartial third person. Conflicts happen no matter how hard we try to avoid them. In the past, people who could no longer tolerate unpleasant family situations might ask older family members, clergy, or community leaders to help. Today, the family may live far away, the disputants may not have religious affiliations, and they may not feel enough sense of community to ask their neighbors for help.

With the weakening of traditional sources for dispute resolution, people turned increasingly to the courts. Today we have reached the point where settling financial aspects of a divorce may take years of litigation. One court had to work out shared custody of the couple's treasured dog. A judge was asked by a daughter to make her father pay for college although he objected to her living with her boyfriend.

Crowded courts where judges apply general rules of law are not good places to work out the particular needs of people troubled by family or other interpersonal conflicts. The legal process costs too much, takes too long, and does not allow the people with the problem to talk to each other and to work out a solution they can live with.

The Advantage of Mediation over Arbitration and Adjudication

If you and a person you are in conflict with could agree on a neutral third party to help you talk about the problem without fear of consequences if neither of you are satisfied with any proposed agreement, you would be in mediation. This process is different from negotiating for yourself with no one else present, or having a representative, usually a lawyer, but maybe your mother, talk for you. Mediation also differs from arbitration, because to arbitrate means to decide if the disputants cannot agree for themselves. You may behave differently if you know that the third person you asked to referee your dispute will make a binding decision if an agreement is not reached. This sounds more like adjudication, a decision by a judge, except you may get to choose the arbitrator.

California has mandatory mediation of child custody disputes. However, some judges there instruct court-based mediators to make a recommendation as to which parent should live with the children if mediation is not successful. As a result, lawyers have advised clients to be cautious during the mandatory sessions and not to reveal unflattering information. In true mediation, a parent is free to say that she was intent on building her career for the next few years and would be willing to share custody without jeopardizing her position in court if no such agreement can be worked out. It would be up to the court-appointed child custody investigator, who is not a mediator, to discover this fact and report it to the judge with a recommendation.

Who Can Benefit from Family Mediation?

What is a family today? The Family Service Association of America defines a family as people who provide each other with emotional and economic support, protect one another, and intend to continue to do so permanently. This is a broader view than traditional notions of family ties being created only by marriage or birth. We will stretch this idea even further to include neighbors and colleagues at work to define who we may mediate.

Divorce Mediation

Divorce breaks up families. Mediation has proven particularly helpful with families through this painful period. The emotional connection between the spouses and the possibility that they may need to continue contact after divorce because they have children makes mediation a good choice. If you have heard of mediation with families it probably was divorce mediation. While I am going to devote part of this book to divorce mediation, I am also going to focus on mediating other personal relationships. First, though, a preview of two controversies facing divorce mediators.

Children and Money: Who Should Decide?

Divorce mediation is offered by courts in an increasing number of states. However, only child custody and visitation disputes can be mediated in most of these programs. Yet we know that all four issues to be decided when parents divorce—property settlement, spousal support, child support, and child custody and visitation—are emotionally and legally linked. Remember the Treadwells at the beginning of this chapter?

Whether or not mediation should be comprehensive or limited to child custody is related to the second controversy about divorce mediation. Who should mediate? Social workers, psychologists, and others with graduate degrees trained in family therapy may only talk about children because they are working in a court-based program. Mediators in private practice with these credentials may feel they do not know enough about law or financial planning to resolve money matters. Mental health mediators may fear being charged with the unauthorized practice of law if they help to settle financial aspects of the divorce. Attorneys who also mediate are concerned about possible conflict with the state bar's provisions for the practice of law if they are mediating impartially rather than representing only one of the divorcing parents in an adversarial manner.

Shared Custody

The greatest benefit of divorce mediation may be that parents who are going through a terrible time in their lives can be helped to preserve their relationships with their children. Sharing custody of children after divorcing is not easy. It is worth doing. Research suggests it may be the best decision you can make for children. States tend to pass a joint custody law first and legislation offering mediation later. If mediation is provided first, parents have a guide to help them at the time they need expert assistance most.

Family mediation can help parents reach an agreement to share caring for their children that has a good chance of lasting. There are problems with sharing custody that need discussing at the time of divorce. Other problems come with remarriage of one or both parents or the possibility of one of them moving beyond commuting distance. Sometimes sharing the rights and responsibilities of parenting after divorce just will not work for a particular couple.

Mediation After Divorce

Child custody and visitation may change any time after the divorce until the children are eighteen. This change may evolve gradually and informally to meet the needs of all members of the divorced family. However, if the parents cannot talk to each other well enough to work out these adjustments, the unmet needs may result in a costly court battle, years after the divorce, seeking to formally amend the marital settlement agreement by shifting legal custody to the other parent or providing for different visitation. Then the loser begins to gather information for the next round in court. How can you stop this cycle?

Successful mediation agreements assume that raising children is a process. The future needs of both the parents and children will indicate changes must be made in the arrangements made at the time of divorce. Parents are probably not thinking about private schools or bar mitzvahs when they divorce with a one-year-old, even if the mediator tries to introduce planning for these future decisions. One or both parents may swear that they will never marry again, so the mediator's stating that 75% of women and 80% of men remarry within six years after divorce, half of them within three years, may provoke incredulous comments.

Courts retain the power to change the amount of child support for children after the divorce. Parents cannot make any agreement that forfeits this right of the court. Child support all too often is set too low at the time of divorce. Worse, many parents, usually fathers, stop paying child support within a year or two after the divorce. Even when payments are made, they seldom increase to account for inflation or the greater expenses for older children. Remarriage or loss of a job affects the amount of money available to the children.

A good mediator teaches parents techniques for settling future custody and financial issues themselves. This good mediator also assumes that the parents may not be able to work out all future disputes. The parents may again need to consult with a third person sometime in the future in order to keep talking to each other and avoid resorting to court to solve problems they know most about. A good time to tell parents this is when they are happy about having worked out their initial custody and financial arrangements while divorcing.

The draft of their agreement may include an agreement to mediate future conflicts, although this plan is not binding. Still, signing an agreement to mediate inclines many of us to keep our word unless the changed circumstances preclude mediation. I will give examples of how to tell parents to consider mediation in the future. Situations where parents should not feel bound by such agreements to mediate are also described.

Mediation After Remarriage

Divorced people often remarry. New spouses as well as ex-spouses may have painful reactions to the complicated roles they must play if children are involved. The new wife may either urge her husband to take sole custody of his children from a former marriage—"I'm a better mother to them than she is"—or encourage him to think of his children with her as his real family. "That is your past. We are your family now." Either choice can lead to a return to court. The mother of children from a previous marriage will fight competition from the stepmother and any attempt to change custody or even visitation for that reason. Stepfathers may say, "I'm head of *this* family. Talk to me, not *my* wife." Fathers who begin to think of their latest brood as their real family may stop paying child support, which could also lead to court. Since we know all this may happen, how can mediation help to prevent it?

Nobody has a good name for remarried families, who may have his, hers, and ours children. Reconstituted sounds more like orange juice than home life. Stepfamilies have a bad reputation all the way back to fairy tales. Blended has possibilities but still has a cooking connotation. Family arrangements without a clear positive name may reflect society's ambivalence about the idea. These parents and children may lack guidelines for how to relate to one another as they work out living in different households.

Stepfamilies—at least we all know what this name means—can learn that mediation offers a forum for developing rules for living tailored to the needs of their particular situation. Emily and John Visher, whose book and Stepfamily Association provide help for stepfamilies, have noted the unique features of these families. Different expectations are based on previous parent-child relationships. Children may be living in two or more households on a frequent and continuing basis. Legal relationships either do not exist or are unclear. Do stepparents have a right to visitation? Do they have a duty to support stepchildren?

Mediation has the power to enable people to fulfill their expectations of what should be done when law and custom do not provide a model. I will offer examples of when mediation could help remarried families with children to resolve common causes of conflict.

Mediation with Intact Families

I do not even know what to call *these* families any more. How about ongoing families? The irony is that the reason they may need mediation could be that the problems they face are so troubling that they may break up.

Emotional problems lead some family members to consult with a third person. Neighbors, friends, and hair stylists know when a relationship is troubled. Some problems are present in every family. Some of these problems can be solved within the family. Others can be tolerated. If a family member feels compelled to make changes and enlists the help of a third person, how is mediation different from psychotherapy?

Parent-child mediation has been successful when the child is a teenager. Neither psychotherapy nor a command voice may work well for a single mother of a 6-foot-2-inch, 180-pound lad. Fathers who rule corporations have despaired at trying to prevent their daughters from seeing the "wrong" boys. Mediation recognizes that both persons in conflict have power, an essential point in working with adolescents.

When parents cannot control their children a community member may refer the children to juvenile court. Sometimes the parents themselves bring the child in, saying, "Make him behave!" or "You keep him, judge, I can't do a thing with him." Several juvenile courts have experimented with mediating these cases. Does mediation protect the child's rights? What would a model program look like?

Mediation is also useful when termination of parental rights becomes necessary. This approach can help biological parents adjust to and support the adoption of their children (Mayer, 1984). Would mediation techniques differ in such situations from those used in other types of family mediation? Who would pay the mediator?

Some women's groups have stated that mediation should never be considered when domestic violence is alleged. They feel that mediating this kind of dispute condones violence between family members. They also worry that mediation would fail to protect the victim.

Battering wives, children, parents, or anyone else is intolerable. The power of the law can halt this behavior. However, mediation in conjunction with court action has worked well in stopping family violence. We will review the recommendations of mediators involved with programs to stop domestic violence.

There are two reasons why mediation augments legislation barring violence against family members. One has to do with the reason for the violence. If the batterer suffers from the Billy Budd syndrome and resorts to physical threats because he cannot say what he means during family fights, being told to "stop that" does not give him a chance to tell his story.

The problem for the victim is that a "peace bond" telling a man to stay away from his spouse is not the powerful deterrent it's generally thought to be. Such a court order does not mean two large deputies sit in front of her home and follow her to work to prevent him from accosting her. He may still harass her in person and by telephone. Mediation may give him a chance to tell his story. His dignity can be preserved. Court orders prohibit behavior. They do not typically provide a plan for what should be done. Mediation can help the disputants work out detailed behavior for the future.

Courts are hesitant to interfere in family life without compelling evidence of need. This is exasperating to potential victims, who are told by the police, "We can't act until he does something." Even after one family member hurts another, can it be proved in court? Child abuse cases demonstrate this difficulty even when the goal is to protect infants who have suspicious marks. Can a judge be persuaded that a husband's threats against his wife go beyond normal family tiffs?

Mediation may prevent further physical or emotional violence. A safe place to talk with a mediator who models new ways to solve problems without threats to each other has promise. Written plans that are then signed are significant to many people, even if such behavioral contracts are not legally enforceable. Any agreement might be submitted to the court with the permission of the parties.

Contraindications for Mediation Between Family Members

This a good time to say when mediation should not be continued or even attempted. I do not recommend mediation for all problems that family members cannot solve themselves.

Some family members are so dangerous they can no longer be with their loved ones. Boundaries must be set and backed by the law. A husband may threaten his wife every time they see each other or talk by phone. He will not calm down. He drinks a quart of whiskey every day and has started carrying his pistol. She is so frightened she wishes he did not know how to contact her. Unless the mediator can control the process when all three meet and assure her that the negotiations are not making her plight worse the rest of the time, mediation should not be attempted.

Some people hear voices that most of us do not. They think we are out to get them. Sometimes they are right, but usually they are what one of my colleagues calls "nervous." That's his label for even the most serious mentally disordered behavior. These people do not respond well to a bossy mediator spouting rules.

Violent or crazy disputants may act that way partly because they take drugs. Maybe such self-medication masks the pain of their conflict, or maybe abusing substances is unrelated to the problem being considered for mediation. Mediation will not create binding agreements with chemically impaired clients. Workable settlements require alert participants.

A disputant may be under the influence of drugs both during and between mediation sessions and still be thought of by the other participants as being his usual self, or at least the way they have to deal with him most of the time. The mediator must make a judgment about whether to proceed if violence, irrational behavior, or drug abuse appear to be interfering with the process.

Mediation of Relationships
Between Unmarried Cohabitants

More couples are living together without being married than ever before (Blumstein and Schwartz, 1983). Some are rehearsing marriage. Others reject marriage. Homosexual couples cannot legally marry. Whatever the reason, living together intimately often leads to sharing leases, stereos, and big dogs. Disputes may occur in these ongoing relationships that could benefit from mediation, especially if the decision not to marry was based on avoiding the general legal requirements imposed by marriage.

Just as marriage sometimes ends in divorce, a relationship outside marriage may end despite initial expectations of permanency. Decisions made together while things were going well may have created a legacy of shared property and feelings that needs disentangling. Without the guidance provided by divorce laws, unmarried cohabitants have no clear legal rules for making such a division.

Mediation can create a forum for the disputants to decide privately what is fair. What laws apply in such situations if the conflict cannot be settled out of court? Does the application of these laws depend upon whether or not the disputants have an intimate relationship or are simply roommates? Does it matter in mediation?

Community Mediation

Neighbors may know almost as much about us as our family does. A feud with a neighbor can sour being at home. Viewers of Judge Wapner's "People's Court" on television may not get the attention they expect if they file a small claim locally.

Community board programs, such as the pioneering work by Ray Shonholtz in San Francisco, have trained neighborhood people as mediators to assist in resolving local disputes. They have heard about blocked driveways, barking dogs, and overhanging trees. They have helped neighbors in conflict to work out opening a day care center on a street where most of the residents are old and fearful of increased traffic and tricycles. What problems are appropriate for a community board mediation? What training is needed? We will describe how it works.

Business and Professional Applications

A successful family mediator will find opportunities to practice in organizations. Two types of mediation occur. Family mediation may be sponsored by the organization. The other sort of mediation ranges beyond family problems to disputes concerning the organization.

Family mediation is a logical addition to an Employee Assistance Program (EAP) sponsored by an organization. These programs have evolved from alcoholism treatment to assessment and aid for family problems such as divorce, parent-child relationships, and financial difficulties. Mental health professionals are increasingly practicing in industrial settings or under contract with an organization.

The brief, results-oriented mediation process impresses management as a cost-effective benefit. Employees may view mediation as less stigmatic than psychotherapy. How can you make an effective presentation to receive referrals to mediate from an existing EAP? What would persuade an organization without an EAP to refer family problems to you for mediation?

Two kinds of disputes concern organizations directly. One has to do with internal conflicts. Management and employees may differ about salaries. Colleagues at the same level of the organization may argue about cigar smoking in a shared office.

Mediation has a successful history in resolving disputes in labor relations. I will give examples of how mediation may also be preferred as an alternative to grievance hearings that are choking many organizations without providing relief to the complainants.

What does a family mediator know about labor relations or quasi-judicial grievance hearings? if you have been providing family mediation for members of an organization you may come to know about the personality and life cycle of the organization itself. Knowledge of the values and mission of the organization as well as the needs of its members may be the most important factor in resolving internal disputes out of court.

Using mediation and other alternatives to court in settling disputes between organizations has captured the interest of major corporations. They are weary of paying the salaries of their in-house counsel, the fees of outside lawyers who specialize in the particular problem, and court costs, often for years without a decision as each side buries the other in legal documents.

The chief executive officer of each company may agree to meet with a mediator for a limited time to attempt to reach a settlement. This procedure has succeeded after years of litigation. Unlike family mediation, where knowledge of family therapy and relevant law provides guidance to the mediator, a business dispute may involve unfamiliar facts and allegations. How can objective criteria be established? Do they matter if the parties are happy to settle?

The family mediator may find that disputes within major companies resemble the conflicts that family members have. The roles may even be familiar, with the authoritarian father, nurturing mother, and jealous brothers and sisters all represented. These roles may especially characterize family-owned businesses. When the boss is also a relative, good business practice may conflict with personal relationships. What techniques from family therapy could the mediator use to help in this situation?

Business partners need to trust one another and have a way to solve problems that inevitably come up. Members of law firms may devote much more time to selecting future partners at work than spouses at home. Many business partnerships last longer than a marriage.

Similarities between a business partnership and a marriage include the fact that financial decisions made by either a partner or spouse may be binding on the other person. If your partner is believed to be acting for the partnership when making a financial commitment, the creditors may be able to seek payment from your personal funds if the commitment is not met.

Business partners may also know valuable or embarrassing information about one another. Such a personal relationship calls out for the private ordering mediation provides when settling conflicts. What do you need to know about valuing the type of business under dispute in order to mediate effectively? What are the indications that tell you to refer the disputants to specialists?

Mental health professionals may find the sort of hearings mandated by the Education for All Handicapped Children Act familiar. This federal law provides that parents of children who have been assessed as needing special education may appeal the decision. A hearing that features due process protections must be held if the parents so choose.

Gallant's (1982) pioneering work suggests that mediation of special education disputes between parents and school officials is more effective than an adversarial hearing. The parents do not feel that the school personnel are ganging up on them. The people who know the child best, the parents and teachers, talk about a workable educational plan.

Peer review in mental health and legal professional associations often takes the form of mediation. The tension between protecting the public from incompetent practitioners and avoiding publicity that would damage all members of the group leads to a search for a private solution. The San Francisco Bar Association recently began a mediation service for clients and attorneys involved in fee disputes. Should such mediators be lawyers themselves in order to fully understand the issues? Should there be a rule against attorneys mediating the fee disputes of their colleagues with lay clients?

Family mediators may act as consultants and trainers. Sometimes the topic is mediation. Often the subject is unrelated to mediation. In either case, I have sometimes found that the reason I am asked to consult or train has to do with a hidden agenda. Somebody hopes that I will resolve a dispute.

Mediation is hard enough when all the parties acknowledge the dispute and agree to conform to certain rules. How do you determine that you are expected to mediate although hired as a consultant or trainer? When do you get the conflict out on the table? When is it better to try to improve the situation without acknowledging the dispute? When should you carry on without addressing the secret problem?

Can You Mediate Between Unequal Strangers?

We have expanded the range of family mediation to business, community, and professional applications. Just as with some kinds of family disputes, there are other categories of conflicts that may be difficult to mediate. Auerbach (1983) suggests that unequal strangers who disagree may require the courts to balance the power enough to reach a fair resolution.

Do the disputants know each other? Are they apt to continue their relationship? Do they share values? Are they reasonably equal in power? The more of these questions that must be answered "no," the less effective mediation may be.

Auerbach's review of the history of alternative dispute resolution indicates that mediation may be advocated by powerful groups in society when oppressed people start getting favorable court decisions. How can you assess requests to mediate in order to empower both participants rather than contribute to injustice toward one of them? Disputes in business, community, and professional settings may require access to courts in order for mediation to work. However, disputants may not need to share values in order to reach an agreement according to the experience of community dispute resolution programs (Shonholtz, 1984).

Techniques of the Family Mediator

We have described the range of disputes that family mediators may try to resolve. Whether you are learning to mediate or seeking a way to choose the right mediator to help you with your problem, the next question is "How do you mediate?" What knowledge and skills do you need to master? What techniques do successful mediators use?

The certification committee of the California chapter of the Association of Family and Conciliation Courts has recommended a knowledge base and set of skills for court-connected mediators (Baker-Jackson et al., 1983). Family law cases, legislation, and procedures are part of legal knowledge considered to be essential. Knowledge about families generally and the special issues posed by divorce and remarriage is recommended. The child custody mediator knows about stages in the adult life cycle as well as about child development.

Theories of mediation and negotiation, cognition, communication, small groups, and crisis intervention are held to be vital to the development of mediation techniques. We will review how this information leads to practicing skills such as building trust, defusing anger, restating nasty comments, and moving toward an effective child custody agreement.

Knowledge and skills necessary for mediating the financial as well as custody issues facing divorcing couples are more extensive than for court-connected mediators. Koopman and Hunt (1983) developed a checklist of such knowledge that includes property division laws and standards for spousal and child support. They list income tax, real estate, family budgets, employment opportunities, insurance, and investments among the categories of financial information relevant for comprehensive divorce mediation.

Family mediation requires additional legal and psychological information about ongoing families and personal relationships between unmarried people. The family mediator in organizational settings needs still more knowledge relevant to the business, community, or professional issue under dispute. What are the universal approaches? What techniques work best with which kinds of disputes?

What role-play procedures work best in mediating with families? What developments in innovative uses of language in family therapy can be applied to mediation? What are specific procedures for reframing conflicts to help families resolve their disputes? How can a personal computer enhance both the mediation process and the business aspects of a private mediation practice? How might you use videotape as a technique in mediating with families?

Successful family mediators choose techniques that fit the situation; they develop practice principles based on their experience. Good family mediators act alike whether their background is therapy or law. Experienced psychotherapists have been found to be similar despite different paths from psychiatry, psychoanalysis, social work, or psychology (Henry, Sims, and Spray, 1971). Mediating techniques are drawn from law, psychotherapy, and labor and international negotiation. The common goal of these three professions is to reach effective written agreements with disputing people who are trying to structure a continuing relationship.

Exciting work is being done on negotiation techniques applied to personal, professional, and international disputes. We will consider how to adapt these approaches to mediation. Mediators are neutral third parties trying to aid the disputants, while negotiators may have the conflict themselves or be representing one of the disputants.

Family lawyers refine general negotiation theories in representing family members in the context of relevant law. Lawyers who devote a majority of their time to family law range from adversarially oriented representatives to more mediative types. Most divorces in which the parties are represented by family lawyers are successfully negotiated to settlement without a trial and "a full trial is often a result of a negotiating failure" (Smith et al., 1983, p. 254).

In a recent survey of the American Bar Association family law section, about three-fourths of the respondents listed inadequate negotiating skills and lack of communication skills with clients as reasons they had observed for lawyers showing less than adequate care in family law cases. About two-thirds mentioned inadequate drafting of documents as a problem they had observed (Smith et al., 1983, p. 254). Good family lawyers practice and value negotiation, as well as oral and written communication skills. We will see how mediators can adapt their techniques.

Family therapy techniques are used by effective mediators. Building upon insights from individual psychotherapy and behavior therapy, family therapists add knowledge about the way people act in small groups. Communication theories have provided specific techniques that have proven to be effective in reaching mediated agreements.

Family therapists advocate taking time to talk about the ramifications of divorce psychologically. A lot of time. Kressel and Deutsch (1977) report that divorce therapists (not *divorced* therapists, though divorce may lead family therapists and lawyers to become mediators according to Milne's [1983] national survey) spend up to seven years talking with couples about their divorce. Family and child therapists deplore the few sessions available to clients ordered to mandatory mediation by courts in California. They recommend a much longer process of a year or more and say they do in fact mean psychotherapy rather than mediation. They seldom mention addressing financial matters at all.

Do professionals who gravitate toward mediation regardless of their original professions hate conflict so much that they urge "peace at any price, let's make a deal"? Short-term arrangements that assume that the present situation is correct or at least unalterable are potential hazards for mediators. If I worked for a court-based mediation program I would expect that my effectiveness would be measured at least informally by the number of child custody trials avoided. Family court judges have been known to add a little muscle to such mediation by telling disputing parents that the mediator would be making a recommendation to the judge if no agreement was reached, and that recommendation would be made an order of the court.

Even allowing for a generous definition of success, such a procedure may provoke a desperate search for a settlement,

any settlement. Critics of alternatives to the adversary process in settling disputes worry about the possibility that effective negotiators may violate the rights of weaker parties.

Again, most disputes in which a trial is threatened, including divorces, are negotiated by the parties or their attorneys out of court (Smith et al., 1983). So the major danger may
be when a supposedly neutral mediator presses the weaker
party to settle. Requiring each party to hire a skilled negotiator who would tell it to the judge may appear to be the
best way to protect the rights of disputants. However, if the
weaker party does not shape the agreement or learn to negotiate directly, any settlement reached may not work.

Establishing a Mediation Practice

What are the credentials of a family mediator? Should such
mediators be generally recognized as good at helping people
resolve disputes? Don't laugh, they do it that way in Australia.
A mechanic may mediate a divorce after supper. Community
board mediation in this country operates this way, although
usually divorces or conflicts involving lots of money are not
accepted for mediation.

Fledgling fields of practice are uneasy with demonstrated
competence alone. Competence is hard to measure. A profession has a specialized body of knowledge. Few universities offer a specialization in mediation. So, how do you learn to become a mediator?

The Academy of Family Mediators and a number of other
groups require full members to either have at least a master's
degree in a mental health profession or a law degree. Forty
hours of specialized training in mediation is then mandated,
followed by supervision and continuing education requirements. Are these credentials appropriate? Excessive? Too
little?

The unregulated nature of mediation leaves practitioners
without clear guidelines. Just as television was first thought
of as simply radio with pictures, mediation has been called
"just good lawyering" or "what any experienced family therapist does." Labor relations mediators and community board
volunteers have their own views about the definition of media-

tion. Family mediation is interdisciplinary and is distinct from other professions while calling on their techniques.

If you want to mediate only child custody disputes, either as a court-connected employee or as a private practitioner, you may choose a mental health emphasis. If I am successful in persuading you that financial and psychological issues are related in divorce, you will also want to learn relevant law and financial planning information. Maybe a law degree would be an appropriate background. You will still need specialized training and practice in mediation regardless of which preliminary path you choose.

How do you choose the best training for you? How do private mental health mediators avoid the unauthorized practice of law while talking about money matters with clients? How can attorneys comply with their state's version of the American Bar Association's Code of Professional Responsibility?

We will assess recent attempts at ethical standards for mediators by various groups such as the American Bar Association and the Association of Family and Conciliation Courts. Situations where acting as a typical family lawyer or family therapist conflicts with the practice of family mediation will be emphasized.

What are typical fees for family mediation? How can you develop referral sources to build your practice? What are good ways to stay current about changing family law in your state? Why do you need liability insurance specifically covering mediation even if you already have liability insurance for your law or mental health practice? We will go step-by-step through establishing a family mediation practice in the last chapter, which deals with becoming a family mediator.

CHAPTER 2

The Mediation Process: Typical Stages and Techniques

> *". . . The essence of negotiation is creativity. . . ."*
> —Zartman and Berman, 1982, p. 15

Why People May Choose to Negotiate with a Mediator's Help

People negotiate when a relationship is changing. Negotiations sometimes precede a change and nearly always follow a change as a process of adjustment takes place. In daily life, small changes are negotiated almost without notice. However, when major changes are anticipated or are taking place, the accompanying negotiations take on increased seriousness as the consequences of decisions become apparent and more intense emotional responses emerge. It is during these times that mediators can be helpful to people who are trying to negotiate a change.

Family disputes may be appropriate for mediation because of the intimate relationship between the disputants and the possibility of an ongoing relationship. Divorcing parents of minor children are an example. Eisenberg (1976) notes that "the two great tasks of the legal system—the settlement of disputes that have arisen out of past actions, and the establishment of rules to govern future conduct—are also performed daily without resort to that system" (p. 69). The marital settlement agreement of divorcing parents with minor children may reflect both dispute settlement and rule-making without a trial.

Why are most disputed divorces negotiated out of court? There may be pressure from family and friends to negotiate. using power as the sole criterion for setting the rules for the future may cost too much even for the dominant party, for that person may fear that the balance of power may shift in the future, so a process not based only on power may be wise (Eisenberg, 1976).

Eisenberg offers an analysis of the reasons disputants generally prefer private negotiation to a trial. He refers to norms—"standards of conduct with ethical connotations" (p. 71)—as either being person-oriented or act-oriented. Person-oriented norms depend upon the personality of a particular person. "He seems like a good guy, let's do what he wants." Act-oriented norms, such as laws, are not supposed to take into account personal characteristics. "We are a government of laws, not particular people." If several laws collide, one is typically chosen as most applicable to the situation and the other laws are rejected.

Eisenberg (1976) states that jury trials permit lay people acting in secrecy to take into account person-oriented norms and colliding principles. This may lessen an inappropriately rigid act orientation that would result from strict adherence to existing laws.

People seeking mediation have decided that they would be better off if they agree themselves than if they submit their dispute to arbitration or adjudication. Each party can walk away from mediation as if it never happened. Some potential solutions, such as joint custody, require the agreement of both parties in order for it to work. Either parent could veto such a proposal. Even in states where there are laws favoring joint custody, mediation can increase the success of such arrangements.

If an agreement is forced that absolutely ignores what one or both of the parties want, it will not work. Any attempt to create future rules for a continuing relationship must have the needs of both parties in mind.

Mediation may be appropriate for settling family disputes because it is person-oriented rather than act-oriented (Fuller, 1971; Sander, 1983). The complicated personal relationships that may continue—especially if minor children are affected—suggest the need for a solution that allows for the personal characteristics of the disputants.

The need for a continuing personal relationship may lead to a settlement partially to avoid further conflict, without relying solely upon principles (Eisenberg, 1976). However, precedent remains important. How have others solved similar child custody disputes? What have courts ruled in similar circumstances? Eisenberg reminds us that a stranger—the judge—is more likely to invoke act-oriented norms—"Here is the law"—and settle in favor of one such law and disputant as right. In contrast, negotiation by the disputants tends to be intimate and accommodative. "We can work it out."

Much time is spent in a trial explaining to the judge agreed-upon facts as well as allegations under contention. Parties in private mediation may agree on many such facts. The judge seldom can order a person-oriented result. Creative solutions—maximizing tax advantages of a property settlement—or traditional remedies—"Why don't the two of you just shake hands?"—usually are not permitted.

Submitting conflicts to a court may cause humiliation as well as loss of control. Persons in conflict are encouraged to hire an affiliate rather than represent themselves. They do not tailor the agreement themselves. They wait for a judgment by a stranger.

Yet despite all of these factors, attorneys are retained to file suits more often than mediation is attempted. There are a number of reasons that are seldom mentioned by proponents of alternative dispute resolution.

Clients may choose individual representation by a family lawyer rather than seeking a mediator because they are "too timid, unsophisticated, or emotionally unprepared to participate fully in mediation. . . . [S]ome may not want to take responsibility for the result" (Samuels and Shawn, 1983, p. 14) of their own decision making. Others may be seeking revenge rather than an agreement. Many potential mediation clients simply have never heard of such a process applied to divorce or other family disputes. If they first hear about it when under the stress of conflict, they may dismiss it as an overly risky option: "I need a lawyer to protect me."

Most Cases Settle

Although disputants may initially hire lawyers to file their cases in court, in the end negotiation by the parties and their attorneys results in the settlement of about 95% of all civil cases without a full trial. So we should compare mediation with such attorney-directed negotiation prior to court rather than to the few cases that are litigated (Sander, 1983).

An individual engaged in a family dispute may find representation by an attorney useful in conducting constructive negotiations, not just in fighting to win. The attorney may be a better negotiator than the client, and may not be swayed by the need for a continuing relationship with the other disputant to avoid conflict and so overlook an important principle or realistic need. Also, the clients can each blame the attorney for nasty demands so they can remain friendly for the future. "I never wanted to ask for all that, my attorney made me."

Attorneys can give clients information on precedents that may be helpful to them in decision making and negotiation. How have others solved similar child custody disputes? What have courts ruled in similar circumstances?

The threat of being forced into court often produces an incentive to talk about a resolution, rather than waiting for the two attorneys to describe the dispute to the judge and allowing the court to decide. Attorneys may encourage negotiations. Judges often ask before calendaring a hearing if the parties are attempting to settle. Once negotiations start, usually both sides develop an increasing interest in reaching an agreement. If they get to the point of truly deciding to bargain, they begin to exchange information that will weaken their position in court if they do not settle on their own. Now we will consider what often happens if disputants decide to negotiate using a mediator.

Typical Stages of Mediation

Acknowledging the Conflict

Before getting to the usual stages of negotiation, the first question is whether or not both parties think they have a problem that must be resolved. One person may like things the way they are and say there is no problem. The other person may have to escalate in order to get the attention of the person who is happy with the present situation.

GIVING THEM THE BOOT

I am often asked by participants in my mediation training seminar "What if the other person doesn't think there is a problem?" "What if they won't even talk to you?" Here is an example that involves a family service agency rather than a family. The agency was having trouble with tenants from a nearby apartment building parking in the family service lot. There was then no place for agency clients to park. A sign asking people not to park there was defaced. Attempts to ask people not to park there as they were getting in or out of their cars were met with obscene street gestures and suggestions that agency folks relocate in a warmer climate.

The agency people thought there was a problem. The people parking their cars in the lot without permission thought there was no problem, just free parking. What to do? Since the police were reluctant to try to tow cars that were miraculously moved by the time they got to the lot, the Denver Boot seemed the answer. This device clamps on the tire and keeps it from being moved. After the boot is placed on an offending auto, the driver who suddenly is immobile when trying to leave may decide there is indeed a problem with some urgency. Of course, there is always the danger that the driver will simply abandon the vehicle, placing the family service agency in the used car business. The first issue in mediating any dispute is to help each party to realize that if one person thinks there is a problem, then there is a problem.

Selecting an Arena

Whether a divorce or parking is the problem, the disputants have to decide if they are going to settle the matter in the street, in court, or around the bargaining table. In family mediation, once the dispute is clear to both parties, an action may be taken. The next question is "Where do we settle this?" It is at this point that mediation may be chosen or rejected as an alternative.

The First Mediation Session

When the mediator is first contacted by one of the parties it is not a good idea to gather detailed information about the dispute in order to avoid becoming biased or appearing to advocate for that person. All the disputants and the mediator are trying to decide in the first session is whether mediation seems to be be appropriate process for resolving the dispute.

A good general rule is to always communicate with all of the disputants together rather than separately beginning with the first session. They all hear the mediator's information about the process at the same time. They each get to tell their view of the conflict and to hear the other disputants' stories.

The mediator conveys basic information in the first meeting.

> My role is to help you talk with each other so that you can work out an agreement. I think that you know more about what that agreement should consist of than I do, so I'm not going to act like an expert about what you should decide. I am an expert at helping people talk with each other and say what they really need to say. Since I'm not representing either one of you as an advocate, nor am I a psychotherapist for either or both of you, my interest is only in moving along the process of your exploring what this is all about and in seeing if you can solve it together. I believe that if you say what you really mean to each other, you will work out an agreement that suits each of you. You have committed yourselves to the outcome of resolving your conflict simply by coming here.
>
> We are going to focus on the present and the future. I believe that saying what you want works best, so I'm constantly going to ask you tell me and each other what you would like to see happen in a positive way and how you will know when it does happen.
>
> I want you to act as though the other person were someone you were meeting for the first time. You need to reach an agreement with this person in order to accomplish something important to you both. What I am looking for are your best manners. I expect you to be gentle with me and with my furniture. I also hope you will be kind with each other. Since I am a family mediator, I often see people who feel at first that even having a dispute with someone they have had a personal relationship with

is a betrayal by that person. Conflict with people whom you care about and who care about you is bound to happen sometimes. Remember the old saying that love and hate sometimes seem close together, while indifference is their opposite.

If this family dispute is a divorce that involves where minor children will be living, the mediator may want to reassure the parents that although they are divorcing they will remain good parents. Mediation is a way to help them make decisions for their children. Once they decide how they will be taking care of the children in the future, the parents will want to tell them the plan together.

The mediator reminds the disputants that, if they decide to continue, future sessions will be for two hours at a time once a week. The mediator may tell the parties that they will be asked to pay at the end of each session. Each disputant will be asked to pay an equal portion of the hourly rate.

If the first session includes considerable hostility, the next session might be scheduled for two or three weeks later in order to give the disputants a chance to calm down. The mediator says emphatically that it is not clear when, if ever, the parties will reach an agreement. Consequently, it is not possible to predict how many times they will be meeting. If they are willing to consider mediation after the first meeting, the mediator may ask the parties to commit themselves to attending five sessions in order to give the process a chance.

The mediator may want to ask if any of the disputants have consulted an attorney concerning this conflict. If so, they may want to seek legal advice throughout the mediation process and ask their lawyer to review any tentative agreement reached. Parties should usually be advised not to go forward with any court proceedings while mediation is continuing in order to give the process a chance, unless the nature of the conflict, such as potential domestic violence or child snatching, requires immediate action.

The mediator may ask the disputants to sign an agreement stating that the mediator will keep all written and oral communication confidential. This form may also contain a statement that the disputants will not try to subpoena the mediator or any records from the mediation in any future court action. The mediator explains any legal constraints on confidentiality. For instance, suspected child abuse must be reported to social services officials in most states and to police in the remaining states.

Now that they understand the rules, the mediator will ask each disputant to describe the conflict as he or she sees it, without interruption from the other. The mediator may write on a flip chart—a large pad of paper clipped to an easel—those issues the disputants apparently want to address in mediation. This chart serves as the starting point for an agenda.

Speaking a Different Language

You may encounter clients who speak a language that you neither speak nor understand. If family members are politely describing the dispute to you in English but punctuating the session with animated exchanges in this other language, you may want to ask them to translate for you. If when one of the family members tells you what was said the disputant who is not speaking indicates by arched eyebrows, rolling eyes, snickers, deep breaths, or some other cue that the speaker has edited your version, you may want to say so: "I can do a better job of helping you if I understand everything that is being said between you in our sessions. I feel a little lost and I wonder what you are saying when you say things I don't understand. Tell me what you are saying to each other. From that last reaction I seem to be missing the good parts."

Ideally, the mediator should speak the primary language of the disputants. Realistically, in practicing in places like the San Francisco Bay area, many languages are represented and the mediator would not be conversant in most of them even if he or she is multilingual. Further, the distinction between speaking both languages, being bilingual, and having family members in both cultures, being bicultural—with a better chance of truly understanding the nuances of what is being conveyed—is important in addressing interpersonal conflicts.

Rather than attempting to carry on in car cassette Spanish, I prefer to say honestly that I do not understand either the language or the intent of the communication. Then the disputants can explain what they mean, which may actually enhance the process. When they slow down and make it simple for me, they are also educating each other as to what the conflict is really about.

If the disputants speak different languages and have no language in common with each other or the mediator, a translator is essential. The mediator may want to start the session in the nondominant language if one disputant is English-speaking and the other is not or if English is not their primary language (Davis and Salem, 1984).

Using the Same Language Differently

The emotional atmosphere during mediation and the intimate relationship between family members means that messages may be complicated. They may also be in code known only to family members. The mediator who notices the apparently unique meaning of certain terms may want to have them spelled out in order to have some sense of what is really happening. Otherwise, messages will fly back and forth and the mediator will only be dragged in to adjudicate informally by invoking principles previously derived by the parties: "There's a slippage between the word and the experience and there's also a slippage between my corresponding experience for a word and your corresponding experience for the same word" (Bandler and Grinder, 1979, pp. 16–17). Ask disputants for specific meanings of the words they use that seem important to their view of the conflict.

Determining the Impact of Gender

Patterns of language in which men use sports metaphors and action verbs—"Let's hammer out an agreement" or "I'll take my best shot in court"—while women choose the passive voice—"I was told to ask about this"—may reflect the disputants' relative power. However, forceful talk can be bluster, while gentle hints prevail. Speaking in a soothing manner and suggesting ways to settle the conflict, which characterizes more women than men, is typically more effective than taking a hostile bargaining stance. The mediator tries to get the man to listen to the woman in such cases.

Mediators may play against the stereotypes of their gender in order to startle disputants into new potential solutions. Men may speak softly and avoid asking direct questions. Women may challenge attempts to digress or to hide information. At other times, conforming to gender stereotypes may enable the mediator to help the disputants reach an outcome that meets their needs.

Developing Trust in the Mediator and Each Other

People who sell suits and life insurance know that it is important to be liked and trusted first, then the client can be persuaded to buy the product for supposedly rational reasons. Mediation's outcome is less definite than being able to read a life insurance policy or to see in the mirror that the suit does or does not fit. On the other hand, any agreement may be written down and perhaps submitted to a court of law, so that it is more accountable than informal negotiations or psychotherapy. We are still at the first stage where disputants are deciding whether to negotiate or to war on one another and whether or not to engage and stay with the mediator.

Zartman and Berman (1982) have developed guidelines on developing trust from their interviews with international negotiators. What can a family mediator learn from them? They suggest that trust is enhanced when negotiators show they understand the problems of the other side, state their own problems, and work on solving the two as though they were compatible.

Trust is also enhanced by avoiding wild threats or extravagant promises. A considered threat may have its place. Any promise that cannot be carried out damages the credibility of the person who made it.

This is related to having step-by-step agreements so that the parties can see that each side is keeping their commitments. The easiest items are not necessarily taken up first. If major problems are not included early on, one or both disputants may feel that the real issues are being purposely postponed and trust will be damaged. If a divorcing mother and father are so concerned about the temporary custody of their children that they cannot talk about anything else, that issue must be addressed, although not necessarily finally resolved.

Unilateral decisions to trust the other side encourages reciprocity. Agreeing to impose sanctions may also be effective. Putting teeth in an agreement to punish transgressors suggests that the agreement is being taken seriously. Tying together the disputants' futures so that both will prosper or suffer also appears to be effective. An early benefit from having trusted enough to make an agreement reinforces such behavior.

Establishing Limits While Setting the Agenda

There are two aspects to limit-setting at this stage of mediation. The first has to do with the disputants learning to negotiate. Signing an agreement to mediate, as some mediators require before proceeding beyond an initial consultation, may require that the disputants will act civilly to each other and fully disclose all information requested. However, deciding to try mediation or even signing a detailed agreement to mediate is easier than actually beginning to risk by revealing information.

Typically, all disputants will be ambivalent about mediation in the beginning. Do they trust the mediator and each other enough to proceed? Establishing an alliance with all parties and a commitment to the process for at least this session is the goal of the mediator.

The other aspect of establishing limits has to do with setting the agenda for the time being. What is going to be talked about first? What will come later? What is being omitted permanently? Old disputes between the parties that are not relevant to the current issue will not be addressed. If they are divorcing, will mediation consider only child custody disputes, or will financial aspects of the marital dissolution be discussed as well? What is the wish of the parties? What is the stance of the mediator?

The mediator actively builds the trust of the disputants in order to keep them in the process. Items important to either party are allowed on the agenda. The order in which these items are addressed may depend upon the mediator's assessment of their relative importance and other timing issues. One party may announce, "I won't talk about that," "That's already decided," or "We'll let the court settle that." I try to echo the response I gave to adolescents on the verge of running away from the residential institution where I used to work: "You control the outcome of mediation. You don't have to talk about anything you don't want to. You can leave any time. Since we all know that, why don't we see what we can do to write down and try to clarify the issues. You can always go to court or just keep things the way they are now as if we never talked."

The list of assumptions that Saposnek (1983) tells to his clients adds another dimension to the framework for mediation. He staunchly maintains that he will assume throughout the process that both disputants hate each other. He then goes on to assure parents who are seeing him about custody conflicts that they can "hate each other as spouses and still cooperate as parents in making important decisions about their children" (p. 39).

Assessing Personal Relationships

Sir Harold Nicolson (1964) saw nations as predominantly composed of either Shopkeepers or Warriors. Shopkeepers are easy to get along with and want to find a solution that helps the other party as well as themselves. Warriors seek to exploit the other side. This notion has its counterpart in family relationships. Evatt and Feld (1983) describe adults in intimate personal relationships as being either a Giver or a Taker. This idea—derived from Jungian psychological concepts— suggests that these two types of personalities seek one another out and complement each other. What is the role of the mediator trying to help a Giver and a Taker divorce when the Giver says she does not want any spousal support or interest in the pension and the Taker is happy to oblige? What is fair? Should the mediator try to change the way the parties have always related to each other? What if the law says she is entitled to these assets?

Balancing the Power

Davis and Salem (1984) suggested that by its very nature, the mediation process balances the power between disputants:

1. *Respect for human dignity.* Mediation is founded upon a respect for human dignity. Mediators role model respectful behavior. They treat the parties with dignity, listen with care, and project their interest in and concern about what each party says. Their example sets the tone for how the parties can listen to and treat one another.

2. *Open exploration of options.* The mediation process is designed to raise the issues underlying a dispute to the surface and to encourage the open exploration of options. This quality in itself can lead to settlements that transcend solutions which arise out of the sheer use of power.

3. *Recognition of human emotions.* Mediation gives recognition to the human need to express feelings. By providing the parties a safe place to display anger and rage, mediators also give the parties permission to tap into other feelings such as concern, understanding, and empathy. People are better able to see one another's perspective once they have had a chance to express their own.

4. *Recognition of human intelligence.* Mediation assumes that the parties are competent to resolve their own disputes. Often people who have been socialized to feel powerless, rise to the occasion during mediation, especially with the gentle, but insistent reminders of the mediator that they are responsible for designing the agreement.

5. *Impartiality of the process.* Mediation provides an impartial, nonjudgmental forum to air and settle disputes. Throughout the process, the mediator conveys the message that the parties are viewed equally, including the way they are greeted, seated, addressed, listened to, and responded to. This treatment is a strong stimulus for the parties to treat each other as equals.

6. *Confidentiality of the process.* Mediation provides the parties with a private and secure environment in which to explore the underlying causes of a dispute. Confidentiality can act as an effective tool for surfacing the information needed to construct lasting settlements that respond to the needs of all parties.

7. *Voluntariness of reaching a settlement.* Many mediation programs require that entry into mediation be voluntary. This

in itself has an equalizing effect in that it signals each party that neither alone has the power to bring about a settlement. The voluntary nature of mediation encourages the parties to adopt a cooperative frame of mind. On the one hand, no one can tell them how to settle, and on the other, unless they find a mutually agreeable way to settle, they will have to resort to other forms of dispute resolution which may be less voluntary and less satisfactory. (In programs where parties are mandated to try mediation, the mediator is doubly obliged to let them know that they can walk away from the table at any time.)

8. *Openness of the process.* Mediation is stripped of the mystique usually associated with the adjudicative process. Mediators describe the philosophy, the process, and the ground rules and encourage questions. By their openness, mediators convey the message that information is to be shared. [Pp. 18–20]

Davis and Salem also cautioned the mediator against making assumptions early in the process about the balance of power between the disputants.

Everyone has some power. . . . [I]t is equally important to consider how willing they are to use their power and the conditions that might discourage them from using it to the fullest extent. For example, a person might be physically strong and never resort to threats of violence, or a corporation with access to the best legal advice might wish to avoid the bad publicity involved in a lawsuit. [P. 18]

While certain sources of power, such as income or negotiating skills, may be obvious early in mediation, other resources, such as one disputant's choosing not to act when the other one wants a resolution, or the emotional power that one disputant may have over another in an interpersonal conflict, may not become apparent until later in the process.

When to Terminate Mediation

Often, simply labeling my concern about a power imbalance based on the disputants' behavior rectifies the problem. "Recognize the tactic, raise the issue explicitly, and question the tactic's legitimacy and desirability" (Fisher and Ury, 1981,

p. 135). Sometimes, a partial agreement can be reached and mediation can be continued later or the unresolved issues might be settled through another process. Davis and Salem (1984) proposed guidelines for terminating a case when:

1. A party does not fully understand the mediation process.
2. A party is unwilling to honor mediation's basic guidelines.
3. A party lacks the ability to identify and express his/her interests and to weigh the consequences of the terms of the agreement.
4. A party is so seriously deficient in information that any ensuing agreement would not be based upon informed consent.
5. A party is indicating agreement, not out of free will, but out of fear of the other party.
6. One or both parties agree that they want to end the session. [P. 24]

Here is where the role of an active mediator is important. People may never have had this particular problem to solve before. A mediator who has sample custody arrangements, answers to questions about what to do about holidays, or how to value property can provide specific help and keep the parties negotiating.

It is important to balance such information with the need to have the disputants generate their own solutions. Otherwise, they will sit on their hands and ask the mediator to come forward with answers to which they will respond, "Yes, but . . ." or reach an agreement without any real understanding about how to make it work. The family therapy tactic of seeming a little dim-witted and skeptical of any solutions posed either by the mediator or by the parties is a valuable counterpoint to the tendency to give advice.

Mediators can be useful in helping the disputants avoid disaster as they define it. Maybe the mediator knows better than parents, who have never been through a custody battle in court before and therefore do not know what a devastating effect it can have on them as well as their children. Zartman and Berman (1982) refer to both threats and warnings—"The threat referring to a deprivation a party imposes by its own will and the warning referring to a calamity that will take place independent of any human agent" (p. 75). Avoiding a full-blown child custody trial may be one example of justifiable threats by the mediator during divorce. The mediator may also declare an impasse or threaten to do so. This may bring in third parties, such as adversarially oriented attorneys of each disputant as well as the judge. The parties may then decide to return to mediation or go forward with adjudication. We earlier mentioned statistics that show over 90% of such cases settle, often just before the hearing begins. Settling on the courthouse steps is all too common, and that is not the best place to decide where children are going to live for the next fifteen years.

Get disputing parents to at least agree that, if they reel from the courthouse, they will return to mediation and not simply settle hurriedly outside the courtroom. Such a partial agreement may lead to an interim plan that can be emphasized as a normal part of the process.

Listening to Their Stories

Attention to the emotional aspects of each side's view is important to family negotiations. The chance to explain your point of view also forces you to defend it. I have sometimes found folks to be increasingly reasonable and even a bit sheepish as they try to justify a position reached in anger. Pay attention to what each party wants to keep the other from getting as well as what each wants.

Getting Serious About Bargaining

Most stage theories of the negotiation process include what Zartman and Berman (1982) call the Turning Point of Seriousness. At this stage, the parties begin to reveal their real willingness to negotiate. They begin to exchange information that will be damaging if they cannot reach an agreement and have to have a third person decide their dispute.

Settlement may be reached rather rapidly from this point on. Mediators often report that their role lessens during these later stages. They stand back and let the parties work it out. The parties may settle a complex issue in the parking lot after a formal session.

Mediator Strategies to Encourage Serious Bargaining

The mediator's goal is to get the people in conflict to agree on what the nature of their dispute is and on general principles about how to solve it. Mediators are often urged to seek objective criteria or have their clients do so. With experience comes the realization that the question is often "Which objective criteria?" Zartman and Berman (1982) describe five types of justice that disputants may cite while negotiating which formula will be used to settle their conflict. These differing views of fairness involve ethical issues of particular importance to the family mediator.

Five Types of Justice

Let's Use MY Rules

Zartman and Berman (1982) note that all negotiations begin with each party pointing to the particular substantive rules that support his or her interests. If you let me define the situation and agree with my assessment of similar instances, then the result that I want is likely. You have let me choose the formula, with a predictable result. Zartman and Berman label this idea of justice as both substantive and partial, since each disputant can typically find rules that support his or her view of how the conflict should be resolved.

Let's Split the Difference

This idea is ingrained in most of us as justice. It sounds right, is easy to administer, and appeals to our sense of fairness. It is very effective as a persuasion technique. It is also often wrong.

To draw an extreme example from domestic violence, no one would advocate that a spouse or child be beaten just a bit rather than as frequently as before. However, complex and subtle applications of this rule have also had unfair results. Lenore Weitzman has suggested that a 50–50 split of marital property—the presumption by state law in community property states—may be unfair to divorcing women because of their typically lower income after marital dissolution than their ex-husbands. I am careful to examine the particular circumstances whenever a "split the difference" remedy is proposed to resolve any dispute. Zartman and Berman (1982) call this second type of justice *procedural, impartial,* or *numerical.*

Might Makes Right

This type of justice is referred to paradoxically as the justice of inequality. It is also labeled *equitable* by Zartman and Berman (1982). The weaker side gives up more to the stronger party if this idea is applied to the dispute, which often happens in labor-management negotiations.

Another example might be where one person contributed 80% to the purchase of a building and the other person paid 20%. Justice in this instance would be an equitable distribution based on the relative percentage of their shares. In both examples, any agreement reached would favor the party with greater resources if the equitable principle of justice is chosen.

The Meek Shall Inherit the Earth

This "weakest deserves the most" concept is also called *compensatory* justice. If statistics show that men make more money after divorce than their ex-wives, should not women receive more of the property upon divorce than men? This reaches the opposite result of the application of equitable justice if the man owns more property during the marriage.

O.K., Then NEITHER of Us Will Have It

The final type of justice is formally called *subtractive.* It comes up often when people who have been in an intimate relationship are in conflict. Subtractive justice always reminds me of two stories.

The first story is one of those "This really happened to someone I know" sagas that comes around every so often. It goes like this: Someone sees an ad in the newspaper for a brand new BMW—at least here in California it's always a

BMW—for sale for $50. Of course, it must be too good to be true. But when the buyer calls, he is assured that the ad is right. He comes over to buy the car. The car does look to be in great condition, but it just doesn't make sense. "Why are you selling this car for $50?" the amazed beneficiary asks as the deal is completed. "Well, my husband ran off with his secretary. After I hadn't heard from him for two months, he sent me a letter saying, 'Sell my car and send me the money.' So, I am."

The second story has to do with a couple who, during the happy years of their marriage, scrimped and saved to buy land up in the mountains. Every weekend they could they worked together building a little cabin on their land in the mountains. Now they are divorcing. Neither one can stand to think of the other person up in their little cabin in the mountains without them, especially with someone else.

This sort of story is all too familiar to experienced mediators. Maybe the only solution is to sell the cabin rather than distribute it to either party.

The point of these five types of justice is that each reaches a different result. Which one is best? It depends on the situation before you. Zartman and Berman (1982) say that "the most important characteristics of a formula are relevance and comprehensiveness" (p. 109). In the case of divorce mediation, I take this to mean that all four distributional issues—property settlement, spousal support, child support, and child custody—must be considered (Lemmon, 1983). Most importantly, the parties in dispute must agree on the type of justice relied upon if they are each to feel that any agreement reached is fair.

Gathering and Exchanging Information

Now the disputants find out whether issues that are listed on the flip chart are actually going to be settled or if one party is going to balk. This is a very active stage in which the mediator may assist the disputants in implementing the principles for negotiation recommended by Fisher and Ury (1981).

The first is to *separate the people from the problem*. Family members who have a history of an intimate relationship are likely to become emotional during mediation. They may also drag up old problems that are unrelated to the current dispute. Family mediation differs in this way from attempting to settle a conflict between strangers. Family members may be accustomed to expressing their emotions freely.

I have found understating—gently suggesting, "You're not too pleased with that idea, right?"—after someone has cast doubt on the immediate ancestry of another disputant, to be useful in restoring civility. Overstating—"So, you want to tear him limb from limb and mail the parts to his new wife, is that about right?"—may also provoke a smile and produce a return to calmer talk.

Reframing

However, you may say that separating the people from the problem sounds good, but in family mediation the people *are* the problem. Not necessarily. This is where the technique of reframing applied to mediation becomes especially valuable. Reframing is an update of Lincoln's reported statement that we are all about as happy or unhappy as we decide to be.

A goal of mediation is to change a zero-sum—one person's gain is the other's loss—perception of the situation by focusing on the possibilities for a mutually beneficial outcome. We each have a unique view of the world that is based on our previous experience. That view can be revised through persuasion, inducement, or the presentation of alternative perceptions, perspectives, or options for behavior. Bandler and Grinder (1982) published a lively and detailed discussion of how to use reframing with couples, families, and organizations in order to help them reach their goals by matching their behavior with their intentions. They also apply the technique to people who are abusing alcohol and other drugs, a problem that family mediators frequently confront.

According to Bandler and Grinder (1982), the essence of reframing is to distinguish between intention and behavior. Even the most disputatious behavior is working for its originator in some context. If you help them to make the distinction between what they are intending to accomplish and the result, you may help them to change their behavior. You may also show them how to change the way they feel about the behavior of others, which had been causing them to fight or suffer. The best way to reframe is to avoid thinking about what the client's behavior means to you. Instead, focus on sensory experience and respond to it directly. Role-playing is useful in acquiring this skill because the actor is forced to respond immediately, as if the situation were happening in real life.

While reframing is a means of generating new choices for peoples' unconscious minds, Bandler and Grinder (1982) caution that "it is important for some people to have the illusion that their conscious mind controls their behavior. It's a particularly virulent form of insanity among college professors, psychiatrists, and lawyers" (p. 166). Since a number of family mediators come from these and other rationally oriented fields, we need to practice reframing.

Reframing Exercise

There are two kinds of content reframing. One is a meaning reframe. The other is a context reframe (Bandler and Grinder, 1982). If a disputant is doing something that he or someone else feels is negative, you as the mediator might ask yourself, "What else might this behavior mean?" Bandler and Grinder (1982) suggest that meaning reframes are appropriate with a "complaint as a complex equivalence that links a response to a class of events: 'I feel X when Y happens'" (p. 14).

Context reframes work best when the problem is presented as a "complaint as a comparative generalization about yourself or someone else with the context deleted: 'I'm too Z' or 'He's too Q'" (p. 14). Bandler and Grinder (1982) suggest in this situation to try to think about a context in which the undesired behavior would be valuable. "When could this behavior be good for the person?" Here are some sentences for you to reframe. You could also role play these situations with you acting as the mediator and two other people taking the roles of complainer and respondent respectively.

> "He's overprotective of the kids when they're at his house for visitation."
>
> "She always blames me when things don't go well."
>
> "I feel shut out because my partner won't trust me to manage the books of our business."

Bandler and Grinder (1982) suggested a strategy for reframing. First, decide whether the client's problem has been staged as a complex equivalence, so that you will be doing a meaning reframe, or whether the client has stated a comparative generalization, so that you will be doing a context reframe. "He's overprotective of the kids when they're at his house for visitation" sounds like a comparative generalization. Let's illustrate how you might reframe the complaint that the father is overprotective. When might overprotectiveness be a useful behavior? You may need to ask the client for an example. What specifically is she thinking about when she makes this complaint? "Well, he won't let them go over to his neighbor's swimming pool by themselves." Bandler and Grinder (1982) suggested that when you have thought of occasions on which a particular behavior might be useful, you should ask the complainer to repeat his concern. You then restate the behavior in a context in which it might be useful: "You don't have to worry about the kids' safety when they are in his care. If he takes them to a public pool or an isolated beach where they might not be as familiar with the setting, they would also be safe because he always watches them."

Seeking objective criteria may also be useful here. Do the children know how to swim? Is the neighbor's pool supervised by other adults? Is the complainer aware that the second leading cause of child death after car accidents is drowning?

We used a context reframe because the example given was stated as a comparative generalization. We might also consider using a meaning reframe with this couple because implicit in this criticism is that the ex-wife feels annoyed when her ex-husband behaves in this way. Ask her, "What else might this behavior mean?" other than that her ex-husband is too restrictive or infantilizes the children. It might mean that he loves the children very much as well as that she does not have to worry about their safety.

As the problem-solving continues, a combination of these two types of reframing and objective criteria could generate a solution. Perhaps the woman can feel better about her ex-husband's generally supervising the children more closely than she does as simply a difference between the two households, which would be a meaning reframe for her. The ex-husband might work toward a context reframe in which he might not be as protective at the neighbor's pool if the children are carefully supervised by other adults, but continue his personal watchfulness when they go to the beach.

Information gathering may help the mediator find a general outcome that all disputants can agree upon. The mediator may ask the ex-husband, "Bob, what does watching the kids the whole time they are at the neighbor's pool do for you?" He may answer, "I know that they're safe, and they know their father is an important person who can protect them." The mediator could then turn to the ex-wife and ask, "Ellen, what does your demand that he not watch the kids at the neighbor's pool do for you?" She might say, "I want them to know that their mother thinks they're old enough to take care of themselves even when I'm not around, and that I'm a good mother even though I don't supervise them as closely as their father does."

The mediator may now see a common basis for agreement. "Then both of you want to make sure that the children are always safe, and that they know you both can take care of them. Bob, is that right? Ellen, is that what you want?" You want each party to indicate what outcome he is seeking. Later, when the disputants are generating ways of solving the conflict, you can ask them if they begin to criticize one another how such comments help them reach the outcome that they said they wanted.

The mediator can use the information she has gathered to work with the couple toward their common goal. "Ellen, what do you say to Bob when you find out he has been watching the kids over at his neighbor's pool? Tell him now." She may say, "So, you're babying the kids again." Then ask Bob how he feels hearing this. "I feel criticized and belittled." Ask Ellen, "Is that what you intended?" "No, I wanted the kids to think well of me even though I don't supervise them quite so closely and I wanted Bob to think I'm a good mother." Ask her whether she wants to get this message across to Bob. Following Bandler and Grinder's (1982) suggested outline for reframing couples' interactions, the mediator would then ask Ellen, "Have you ever gotten the response that you want? What did you do then?" (p. 148). If she tells you, ask her to do that now.

You would then ask Bob whether Ellen's behavior has elicited the response that she is seeking. If so, she now knows how to say what she means in order to get the outcome she wants. Her intention and her behavior are congruent in terms of reaching this goal. She might have said, "You know, Bob, I don't watch the kids as closely as you do. My parents never watched me that closely and I did fine. But I'm worried that since you do stay with them more that they'll think you care about them more than I do."

Getting agreement on an outcome first allows disputants to rehearse how to change their behavior to reach it. After reaching this goal, the parties may need to gather more information—seeking objective criteria or models of what their desired outcome would look like. The mediator avoids pushing them toward agreement. They may have agreed because they like the mediator or find the mediator to be a powerful person, but if the mediator has not allowed them to reveal the intentions behind the behaviors that brought them into conflict, then any new behaviors may not help the parties achieve their goal.

The mediator may want to continue to use general language that allows the disputants to specify their intentions and then to specify different behaviors that they might use in the future to permit them to get along with each other. The mediator watches the reaction of the listener whenever one disputant is proposing new behaviors to deal with what have been conflicting situations in the past; the listener may be signaling nonverbal agreement in her characteristic manner for doing so. The mediator may have previously identified such a response simply by observing the parties' nonverbal reaction to questions with yes or no answers and no known emotional overtones. ("Were you born in California? Do you drive a car?") Making such casual conversation during the early sessions both establishes rapport and provides the nonverbal information that is valuable during consideration of volatile topics later in the mediation process.

Since the mediator knows both the intention and the proposed outcome, if the proposed behavior does not appear to work, the disputants can be encouraged to continue to generate options until a suggestion receives both verbal and nonverbal affirmation from all the disputants. The mediator may ask the person proposing a behavior, "Is there any aspect of this behavior that part of you might object to or any situation you can think of in which this behavior might not work for you?" If the behavior seems acceptable to the person proposing it, the mediator can turn to each listener and ask, "Is there any part of this behavior that you object to?" It may be helpful at this point to have the disputants think about a time in the future in which they are in a situation similar to the one that has caused them conflict in the past. They can then imagine themselves carrying out these behaviors and observing the result. The mediator may also ask the parties to imagine themselves further in the future after some period of successful interaction. They can then explain to the mediator how they accomplished their goal. The device of imagining future patterns of behavior takes pressure off the disputants and encourages creativity because the mediator both implies that the parties will be successful and allows them to think about how success was achieved based on their own needs, intentions, and possible behaviors.

Since reframing involves changing the internal responses that people have to situations, it empowers disputants. Bandler and Grinder (1982) state that they as helpers work to determine what outcome they are attempting to achieve and what behaviors people seeking their assistance have objections to. They assume that the objections are true and provide information to the person—in our case, the mediator—trying to help them decide what to do next. They suggest asking what else would have to happen before the persons seeking help could do what they say they want to do. One of the goals of mediation may be to build a sequence of behaviors to allow disputants to reach an agreement.

Focusing on Interests

Reframing is essential for implementing another negotiation principle identified by Fisher and Ury (1981), *focusing on interests, not positions.* The mediator may assist the parties to restate demands or positions into what they want to happen. Why do they say that? What basic human need is reflected in their position?

A simple rephrasing by the mediator preserves the need expressed while saving the negotiation from foundering because of an ultimatum. Exchanging and manipulating information in a family dispute may include budgetary data. Manipulation is the right word because the same man who was bragging about his large income at a cocktail party the night before may cry poor on paper when producing an initial budget during divorce mediation. This possibility is not limited to divorce mediation. Judges and lawyers know that a series of financial statements may be required from both parties during a trial, with each statement probably a little more accurate than the previous one.

Searching for Objective Criteria and Mutually Beneficial Options

While Fisher and Ury (1981) recommend that negotiators insist on using *objective criteria*, the five types of justice described earlier suggest that agreement on objective criteria may be difficult to obtain.

One useful technique is for the mediator to treat the disputants' initially disparate views of which objective criteria to rely upon as the beginning of a mutual search for options that will benefit each person in the conflict. Each criteria and its consequences are listed on the flip chart without allowing evaluation by either the person who makes the suggestion or the other disputant. Everyone is encouraged to think of additional criteria and consequences. The mediator emphasizes that no decision will be made yet. The disputants have generated additional options and educated each other about what each considers important for the future.

Which information to exchange as well as verification of its truthfulness may be aided by criteria that can be accepted by all disputing parties. This is more complicated than it looks at first. Income tax returns for the past three years may reflect some of the best examples of recent fiction written in the United States. Court schedules offered as guidelines for child and spousal support may not be precise enough to reflect actual housing costs and other factors.

Still, if the parties can agree on certain rules, they can then go forward and continue to exchange information and attempt to mediate their dispute. The fact that a longtime mortgage payment is relatively low compared to the present cost of buying a house can be taken into account when parents are working out living arrangements with their children in mind.

Modifying Positions

Although the mediator may be attempting to follow Fisher and Ury's (1981) recommendation to keep the parties from stating positions, the disputants usually see their interests in that way. Positions may be modified in two ways. We typically think about each side making concessions. Zartman and Berman (1982) say that concession-making may take two forms, the initial statement of need and the rate at which concessions are made.

They recommend "a high opener, few concessions until a final one for agreement, and the inducement of trust by other means" (p. 171). Although a number of strategies recommended for negotiators and mediators involve reaching a number of agreements early, the more concessions that are made, the more that are expected.

Also, in family mediation, a number of factors are linked together psychologically and financially. As any professional negotiator or parent knows, once you offer a desired item, even if it is contingent upon certain behavior by the listeners, they tend to hear only the concession and expect that to be the minimum for future bargaining even if they do not agree to the conditions.

Another possibility during the modifying positions phase is that one or both sides will not change their position at all. This seems to be ethically straightforward. "My first offer is my final offer because it's what I really need and believe in."

However, a first and final offer ignores the pressure most of us feel to make concessions as a sign of bargaining in good faith. Such rigid positions are probably the reason for the need to mediate to begin with. If neither party moves, the dispute will continue.

This is where the mediator's ability to reframe the needs of the parties so that they can see themselves as staying with their original positions in principle while changing behaviors in such a way that agreement can be reached is vital. "I will never give her custody of our child!" can be restated as "You need to have a significant role in your child's life." Perhaps then options the parents in this example do not know much about, such as sharing custody, can be suggested by the mediator. The mediator may want to explore such options reluctantly, making the parents persuade the mediator that they could cooperate in this way.

The third possibility during the modification of positions is that one or more sides will begin to escalate demands. Whether their initial positions are rejected or accepted, they increase what they say is essential for reaching an agreement. Why would they do that?

Perhaps they have no intention of agreeing at all. Perhaps they view concessions as unilateral and a sign of weakness, and hope to induce further concessions. Here, assessment by the mediator is important. Should the mediator declare an impasse? What are the parties' real interests? Why are they in mediation if they do not appear to want to move toward agreement? Are they fearful of trusting the mediator and the other side, so that just now their real needs are being made known? Is there a power imbalance that escaped the mediator until now? There may be a hidden agenda, such as the wish by one divorcing spouse to reconcile.

Narrowing Differences

Here the mediator attempts to identify or introduce what Haynes (1983) calls overlapping or mutual self-interest. Assessing from each disputant's statements what he or she thinks is really needed can aid the mediator in leading them toward creative solutions. Again, this stage presumes that each party is making concessions. If one or both of them escalates demands, bargaining may end here.

Homework may be crucial to the process. Valuing of assets that are under dispute may be important. The opinions of outside experts about other issues in conflict should be folded in at this time. Reliance upon objective criteria previously agreed upon by the parties will help in sorting out the information. Attention to which types of justice appear to be relied upon cues the mediator to the sort of settlement that may be emerging.

Creating and Reacting to Deadlines

"If it does not matter when you agree, it does not matter whether you agree" (Cross, 1969, p. 28). Deadlines sometimes compel agreements. A comparison to the psychotherapy process is useful here.

People in mediation over a family or business dispute may face a court deadline. In a number of psychotherapeutic approaches, there is no external deadline. However, a number of these apparent differences fall away when we look at what people actually do.

In some of the new approaches to psychotherapy, the client and therapist agree on a set number of sessions, often relatively few, such as eight to ten. The client may also impose a deadline, such as "I will decide about whether or not to leave my husband by the first of the year."

The emotional aspects of deadline behavior are well known to psychotherapists. I call it the "door closer." The session is nearly over. The client seemed to be preoccupied and did not talk about anything important. Just as she starts to go through the door, she turns, closes the door, and wants to come back in and tell you what is bothering her.

In mediation one of the parties may announce a deadline. "If you don't agree to what I need for the kids, I'm taking them back to Iowa to live with my parents at the end of this month." Zartman and Berman (1982) say that deadlines are usually analyzed for how reasonable they are and how serious they are. If threatening to take the children out of state on short notice appears to be an act of vengeance rather than an economic necessity, it would probably produce both panic and anger in the other parent.

The other question is how serious the threat to move really is. Let us return here to motivation, capacity, and opportunity, those old standbys for assessing seriousness in suicide and crimes against others as well as the problem-centered approaches to psychotherapy. Does she really appear to want to leave with the children? Does she have the money to make the trip? Finally, does she have the opportunity? Is a temporary custody order in place from the court that would prevent her from legally taking the children out of state pending court permission?

"Deadlines tend to facilitate agreement, lower expectations, call bluffs, and produce final proposals, but also lead negotiators to adopt a tough position if—and therefore when—negotiations fail" (Zartman and Berman, 1982, p. 195). In mediating intimate family relationships that need to continue in some way, deadlines may be viewed in a different fashion. The present deadline may be seen as only interim. Even court hearings can be postponed.

Conscious use of deadlines as a part of a continuing process works particularly well for family mediators. A number of therapists who help families work out custody arrangements at the time of divorce mention the need to work out interim plans. This fits with the "first do nothing" response to crisis that is often recommended. Families may be absolutely at their worst in terms of coping day-to-day. Asking them to work out rules for the future of their children for the next ten to fifteen years during the first year after separation and divorce is difficult, although required in order to reach a legally enforceable agreement.

So, a good family mediator may combine attention to deadlines in order to get the parties moving or to reach a particular result with the idea that, where children are concerned, both with regard to their custody and financial support, the issue is never finally settled as long as they are under age eighteen. Therefore, attention to what works now is a priority. The children's needs as well as those of both parents will indicate the necessity for changes in the future.

The imposition of deadlines can force people to negotiate in a marathon session without regard for the clock. Federal and state legislatures often resort to this tactic when passing annual budgets. This manipulation of reality is effective because all involved affirm the imminence and finality of the deadline. As with a filibuster or an all-night poker game, the participants are not allowed to leave the scene so that the limitations of fatigue as well as the "rules of the game" put pressure on the disputants. Family mediators may stop the clock and hold an extended session, but disputants are seldom able to stop the clock in real life.

The second response to a deadline may be what Zartman and Berman (1982) refer to as stepped sanctions—gradually imposing penalties on the initiating party. "I'm going to start charging you interest on the money you own me." A third possible reaction to a deadline is a reverse deadline—going ahead with a threat and bargaining about its removal. "I'll drop my sole custody suit if we reach an agreement."

Serious Bargaining

If mediation has progressed this far, draft agreements may be exchanged. Comprehensive documents that attempt to address every concern are appropriate at this point. The parties may feel that they are facing either a self-imposed or an externally created deadline—"I'm tired of all this. Let's settle once and for all or let the court take over." Here Fisher and Ury's (1981) principle of negotiation that each party should know his or her best alternative to a negotiated agreement (BATNA) becomes vital to reaching a workable settlement. Fisher (1984) has said that a better way for disputants to think of this issue is for each to know his best self-help option. Can one or all disputants obtain a good outcome to their dilemma without negotiating an agreement?

Add-ons that have been carried to this late date begin to fall away. "I don't really mind if you have the children every weekend. I just want to make sure I receive enough child support."

As agreement appears imminent, the mediator will avoid peace at any price. The mediator may have objections about certain child care arrangements or other ethical concerns that might get lost in the rush to have the parties sign off on what has been a process that all three participants have invested considerable time in and have become eager to resolve.

"Concessions are made to convey a message, but they are justified by principle" (Zartman and Berman, 1982, p. 202). It has been noted in studies of court decisions that justices appear to make their decision and then seek precedent to justify it. Most of us make important decisions in somewhat the same way. Reaching a successful agreement may really hinge on the messages being conveyed to one another as they exchange and manipulate information during the working out of details in the final phases of negotiation.

After the disputants decide to negotiate seriously, the final stages are often considered to be swift and successful. However, this is where tentative agreements may unravel. One or both of the parties may not have been bargaining in good faith. Only at the point when the deadline either imposed by the court or decided by the parties makes it necessary to sign a document does it become clear that the person had no intention of doing so. Perhaps they were not clear about the implications. Details that seem unimportant to a disinterested mediator may evoke regression or a general inability to act by one or both of the parties. Division of such highly symbolic personal property as baby pictures of their children is an example.

Several techniques are useful. Keep focused on the agreement in principle and see where that leads in sorting out the details. Do not let the parties move backward easily, keep reminding them that they have already agreed on those principles or even on certain details. Emphasize the positive aspects of a partial agreement. Allowing the parties to agree not to agree on some details may salvage an agreement that is workable.

By too much attention to detail, the mediator who is stitching the agreement together may not notice that some of the specifics are incompatible. My recommendation to avoid this problem is to ask each party to rehearse a "day in the life, week in the life, month in the life, year in the life" scenario so that it is clear that the parties have walked through in their own minds what they are agreeing to and may be able to bring up potential problems and solve them as we draft the agreement.

Reaching a Mediated Agreement

In writing down the details of the agreement, if they have not been committed to paper as mediation progressed, the mediator's skill in using appropriate language is valuable. Compare

"Bill and Susan Jones will share responsibility for their children [in the following way]" with the typical language in marital settlement agreements: "Custody shall *reside* with the childrens' mother, with reasonable visitation to the father." The latter lacks the specificity and *mutuality* that most parents need in order to care best for their children after divorce.

Some disputants find themselves uncomfortable with particular provisions when they see them in writing. For this reason I recommend a modification of Fisher and Ury's (1981) one-text procedure. They suggest that the mediator listen to each disputant's position and ask them why they feel that way. The mediator then develops a draft of the needs of each disputant and asks them to criticize it. Subsequent drafts incorporate these criticisms until the mediator believes that the proposed agreement cannot be improved further. The final draft is recommended for the disputants' acceptance.

Bumbling Drafts Throughout

Writing down my understanding of what the parties have agreed to at the end of each session and sending them each a copy prevents the sort of shock that may occur when they see a virtually final document at the end of mediation. It can be typed and mailed to the parties after each session. Each such draft might best be accompanied by a statement of disclaimer to give the parties room to maneuver if they have second thoughts. They can blame the mediator as a bad recorder rather than each other for reneging.

This procedure can be set up by the mediator with an introduction that "to help me, I'm going to try to write down where we are each time, especially points of major interest as well as tentative agreements. I'm not very good at this, so you'll have to help me and correct the errors that appear in the drafts each time. I sometimes have trouble understanding the ideas that people are talking about, so help me keep at it until we get it all written down right."

Such ongoing drafts are useful if one or both parties are seeking legal advice from attorneys who are their individual representatives during the mediation process. Rather than taking a chance that significant omissions during such sessions with their lawyers might lead to some surprises when the draft of the final document is reviewed, their counsel can review the record prepared by the mediator and offer legal advice as needed. Agreements are less likely to unravel at the final stages because the parties and their attorneys have contributed to the final document. This can be particularly important for disputes such as divorce where the final mediation agreement may need to be drafted as a legal document and filed with the court. Again echoing Eisenberg (1976), most agreements both resolve the present dispute and list rules for the future conduct of the parties.

Conclusion

The techniques described in this chapter enable the mediator to enhance communication among the disputants so that they can successfully negotiate an agreement. These techniques work well whatever the nature of the conflict.

The mediator is not an expert who proposes solutions to the disputants. The mediator listens to help the disputants themselves identify what each is trying to accomplish with present behavior so that, once all participants in the mediation process are aware of what *outcomes* are being sought, they can work toward creating new behaviors that will accomplish their goals.

Since these techniques are intended to help the mediator direct the process, rather than to propose specific remedies, you may want more details. *Family Mediation Practice* describes what happens during a successful mediation and what the mediator does to influence the process. While later chapters focus on specific subjects such as divorce and family-owned businesses and the particular knowledge that may be useful for mediating any disputes involving them, the techniques described in this chapter and in the next one apply to all mediations.

CHAPTER 3

Mastering the Mediation Method: Art and Technology

Now THAT YOU KNOW the typical stages of mediation, essential techniques, and how to influence the process, we can focus on specific aspects of practice and advanced techniques. Mediation is a skill and an art. Skills can be taught. The art involves blending your personality—what works for you—with skills. The way to do this is to practice.

Empathy and the ability to demonstrate it to the disputants is vital. One of my most relied-upon techniques is to ask, "Why would they say that?" and "Why would I say that?" I want to create a working relationship between myself and each participant, and I want to help them improve their relationship. Then the specific issues are easier to resolve.

Making Participants Feel Comfortable

Patience is essential for mediators. I remember the opening aspects of group process whether I am beginning a mediation, a workshop, or a university seminar. Since people typically start by wondering why they are there and whether I know what I am talking about, and eyeing the door, this is not the time for flashy techniques. People can be offered coffee, tea, or mineral water, and given a chance to decide where they are going to sit and if they are going to give the process a chance.

Family mediators need to be self-confident. If you expect clients to reveal their worst view of themselves and their income tax returns for the past three years, you had better demonstrate that you know how to help them. Both surroundings and personal manner help convey a sense of self-assurance. An attractive location for your office and a secretary to answer your phone create a better mood for your clients before you even see them than their arriving at a run-down building after having been cut off by an answering machine with a thirty-second limit for messages. Dressing the way business people in your community usually dress also enhances your image.

Telling clients about your training and experience helps them assess you. Personal experience with the problem they are having also may reassure clients. Nevertheless, avoid the temptation to imply that you know just what they mean; you have not been in exactly the same situation and you do not know their views.

It can be difficult to preserve self-assurance in the face of client antagonism. What do you say when a client asks, in the first session, "What do you know about this anyway? How can you help us?" You might respond with mock self-deprecation; other mediators simply restate the allegation. Calmly repeating the insult often reassures the client that the mediator is competent and in control.

Directing the Mediation Process

Mediators balance toughness and softness, deciding when to stand firm and when to be flexible. Mediators may warn the parties that they are considering declaring an impasse. They may also point out when a written agreement will be legally binding or when the failure to reach an agreement will result in the case being turned over to a court.

But while a mediator firmly discusses issues and seeks agreement, she does not commit herself to one position—her own or that of one of the disputants. Encourage disputants to think of themselves as the mediator. What would they think if they were asked as an impartial third party to settle a conflict like the one they are now confronting? "The best negotiator is not an advocate. The best negotiator ... could perform the role of mediator in the negotiations if he were called upon to perform that role. ... [W]hile he may have to engage in advocacy to reach a common ground, he should never be overly persuaded by his own advocacy. Advocacy should be a tactic and not an end in negotiations" (Arthur Goldberg, quoted in Zartman and Berman, 1982, p. 115).

Stamina is an important asset in mediation. Family mediation often takes place in the evening in a two-hour session. Some mediators are calmer at that time of day; others are tired and irritable. The physical and mental strength to remain patient may be crucial in helping clients move toward an agreement. When scheduling mediation sessions, ask yourself, "Am I an early-morning type or do I function more effectively at night? Do I get grouchy if I haven't had my regular meal or a cup of tea?"

Accuracy is another valuable asset in mediation. Although disputants may exaggerate, the mediator must keep the issues clearly in focus. This generally means keeping the discussion simple, writing down relevant points, and not talking too much. Constantly direct clients' attention to the task they are working on and point to the flip chart.

Reacting to Anger

Clients may get angry and lash out at you and each other. Recent behavioral studies have suggested that the expression of anger increases its intensity (Tavris, 1982). There is an escalating rather than cathartic effect when anger is expressed. Directing people to place their faces in what are considered to be representative expressions of certain emotions will produce those emotions in their autonomic nervous system (Ekman, Levenson, and Friesen, 1983). Making a happy face may actually make you feel happy. The mediator usually discourages the expression of negative emotions by clients; he or she restates the issue underlying a vicious comment to highlight the positive preference implied. In addition, the mediator models positive behavior and uses unexpected humor or other unanticipated behavior, such as leaving the room, to shock clients into behaving civilly when the situation becomes particularly tense.

Using Humor

Laughter is good for people because it raises blood circulation rates, as in aerobic exercise; afterward, blood pressure drops, so that the person feels relaxed. In addition, the muscles vibrate, providing an internal massage that breaks up tension, and endorphins are released, promoting a feeling of well-being (Elias, 1983). These sensations are beneficial for both the mediator and the disputants. Laughter not only can improve the parties' mood and foster rapport, but it can also help control a social situation, which is what the mediator is trying to do. There are similarities between making a joke—putting two things together that are usually seen as quite different—and creativity. Generating creative solutions is a part of the role of the mediator.

Humor may be used to diffuse tension, create rapport, and convey unpleasant information in an acceptable way. Kiechel (1983) mentions that people remember the main ideas of presentations best if they are stated humorously or tied to a joke.

I am not proposing *The Mediator's Jokebook*. I am suggesting that part of the art of mediation is integrating techniques with your personality. Humor may reduce conflict. Self-deprecating humor that I mentioned earlier may preempt attempts by the parties to characterize the mediator as the self-important expert as well as relax them so that mediation can proceed.

If comments are spontaneous and appropriate to the situation they can promote a "we're all in this together" feeling that encourages trust. Be yourself. Do not rely on the formula approach of any flavor of mediation.

Tailoring the Technique to the Outcome Sought

Good therapists, executives, and salespeople have three things in common (Bandler and Grinder, 1982). First, they know what outcome they are seeking. Second, they try many different ways to achieve their goal. Third, they observe the reactions they are eliciting so they can tell when they have attained their objective. By paying close attention to listeners' responses, rather than assuming that everyone reacts in similar ways, the mediator is likely to reach his objective —helping the parties work out an agreement. This has been called the Platinum Rule: "Deal with people the way they—not you—would like to be treated" ("Consultant's Consultant," 1982, p. 4).

According to the theory of coordinated management of meaning, ambiguity enhances communication: "How a listener interprets a speaker's remarks, and acts upon the interpretation, is more important than whether the two understand each other" (Barden, 1982, p. 9). Leaving comments open to different interpretations may increase the chance that the listeners will choose a meaning that causes them to act the way the mediator would like.

People usually are more motivated by potential negative consequences than by positive consequences. We are much more worried about losing things that are important to us than about gaining what we want but lack. Reframers know that clients are also much more likely to accept a negative outcome if they can think of it as a cost rather than a loss—"Increased child support is a cost of seeing your beloved daughter" rather than "You lost your attempt to avoid paying more child support."

Role-Playing: Psychodramatic Techniques

Effective role-playing in mediation requires the mediator to use specific techniques in directing the action to achieve certain goals. An active mediator directing the role-play can help the parties decide what they really want and rehearse their possible reaction to a particular event or behavior. Role-play is not synonymous with catharsis. On the contrary, most mediators attempt to minimize the parties' emotional reactions throughout mediation.

Classic psychodrama has three stages (Yablonsky, 1976). In the warm up, participants are asked to react to a theme, such as the loss of a loved one. Someone who has a problem related to that subject and who wants to talk about it is chosen as the protagonist; this person, the "star," will then become the focus of the session.

The star is asked to make an introduction that includes a brief description of the problem. Then she may choose auxiliary egos. These are other people in the group who remind the star of significant persons related to the problem that the protagonist is going to role-play.

The next stage is the main work of the role-play. The director controls the action and makes sure that whether the event depicted is in the past, present, or future, the action takes place in the here-and-now. "This is the way I felt when I was separating from my spouse" is restated by the director, "You are separating from your spouse. How do you feel?"

Immediately after the role-play, the other participants and observers are asked to express what the role-play means in their own lives—"I feel that way, too, when I confront my boss." Only after emotional reactions have been shared are more analytic comments permitted—"You seem to relate better to women than to men."

Mediators can use a number of role-play techniques suggested by Yablonsky (1976); however, the setting is different because the participants typically are family members or close associates, rather than strangers. The purpose is more focused in mediation: resolution of the dispute, leading to a mediated agreement, is the goal, not increased emotional self-awareness. Finally, there is no intention to evoke a cathartic reaction in mediation.

Future Projection

Role-play helps people rehearse potentially stressful situations. Family mediation involves assisting people to resolve disputes and to create new rules for future conduct. When I ask family members to rehearse a day, week, month, and year under the proposed agreement, it is sometimes useful to role-play key behaviors.

Suppose a couple has come to you two years after their divorce. The problem is that they fight when exchanging the children for visitation. Attempts to deal with this conflict by having each parent pick up and return the children at school have reduced the number of contacts and, therefore, spats. However, there are times when the parents must meet. Other issues could also be better handled if the parents were able to talk freely with each other.

Initially, the mediation focuses on the specific problem of bickering while exchanging the children. Susan sees this more as a problem than Bill does. The mediator asks her to role-play a typical visitation scene. She chooses to role-play picking up the children from Bill. She and Bill agree to play themselves.

Soliloquy

The mediator asks Susan to say aloud what she is thinking as she drives up the street toward Bill's house. "I hope he has them ready. I'll bet he didn't feed them any breakfast except a granola bar. They've probably been watching cartoons all morning while he sleeps in. I hope *she* doesn't come to the door."

Susan rings the doorbell. Bill answers.

B: Hello, how are you?
S: Fine.
B: Just a minute, I'll get the kids' coats.
S: Are you going to invite me in or do I have stand out here?
B: Um, uh, sure, come on in.
S: That's all right. If you don't want me to, it doesn't matter.
B: I thought we were going to try to get along.

Doubling

At this point, the mediator goes over to sit by Susan, assumes her posture and tone of voice, and says what might be on Susan's mind: "Why can't you ever be nice to me anymore? Where is *that woman*? Look at this place, it's a mess." Susan may either say nothing; admit "Yes, that's it. That's exactly the way I feel"; add her own statement of what she's thinking; or say "No, that's not it at all." The mediator watches for cues from both parties as to whether the doubling comment seems to fit.

Role Reversal

Now the mediator may ask Susan and Bill to exchange identities and role-play each other. Yablonsky (1976) identified four possible benefits of role reversal. The first is two-way empathy. Susan and Bill learn what it is like to deal with one another. The second is the possibility of seeing a mirror image of the way the parties appear to others—"Is that the way he sees me?" The third potential advantage is to shift one or more parties out of their usual way of coping. If playing the person he has the dispute with, the role-player must come up with a new way of reacting. She cannot play herself. Her usual behavior is typically not appropriate to the other person's role. Finally, role reversal may help someone in the mediation who is playing an auxiliary ego—an absent person who is important to the focus of the role-play—to understand the way that person is viewed.

Time Shifting

Time shifting is a technique used to reduce conflict during mediation (Saposnek, 1983). Let's return to Susan and Bill's dispute over exchanging their children for visitation. The mediator can combine future projection with role reversal and ask them while playing each other to talk about how their children are doing at several points in the future—five, ten, and fifteen years from now.

Without a script or further guidelines, Bill and Susan are going to have to decide whether they have both continued to see the children throughout the years. Are the children doing well in school? Do they still visit both sets of grandparents and other relatives? What do the children think of each parent?

If Susan and Bill create a scenario that one or especially both of them are unhappy with, the mediator can point out that, since this was a role-play of the future, now is the time for change. The mediator may need to be active here, combining techniques such as doubling for one and then the other disputant in a soliloquy.

Role-play is useful in the process of reaching a written mediation agreement because the disputants must come to trust each other enough to rely on the creation of future rules. Altering their perceptions of one another and giving them a chance to rehearse their new roles through role-play is an intervention that helps them to verify whether they really can do what they are agreeing to do. They may also see how the dispute started and learn how to prevent future conflicts by asking themselves, "Why is *he* doing that? Why would I do that?"

Innovative Use of Language

Successful mediators are sensitive to the nuances of language. They choose words that take into account the responses of the parties. There are inflammatory words to avoid and terms that are particularly appropriate for certain types of conflicts. The optimum use of language, however, involves much more than simply choosing correct terms. Several mental health professionals have developed strategies for using words and narrative as means to achieve a particular therapeutic result, which can be adapted to the mediation process.

Fairy Tales

Fairy tales help children master the developmental tasks of growing up. Fairy tales teach the child that "a struggle against severe difficulties in life is unavoidable, is an intrinsic part of human existence—but that if one does not shy away but steadfastly meets unexpected and often unjust hardships one masters all obstacles and at the end emerges victorious" (Bettelheim, 1976, p. 8). According to Bettelheim, since fewer children today take part in an extended family or a close-knit community, it is especially important to provide them with stories of people who succeed on their own. Most of the major developmental tasks of childhood are represented by classic fairy tales. Participants are either heroes or villains. The structure is predictable. The action took place a long time ago. The telling of stories to children helps them accept and cope with childhood anxieties and foster the development of certain behavioral goals and cultural values.

Milton Erickson used stories very effectively in psychotherapy. His goals were simple, but his methods were inspired. "First you model the patient's world. Then you role model the patient's world" (Rosen, 1982, p. 35). Most of us like to be told stories. Instead of focusing on whatever the problem is in mediation, the disputants can sit back and wait to be entertained. First, the mediator can show disputants that he or she understands the way they see things. Then the mediator shows them how the situation could be viewed in a way that would help them solve their conflict.

Stories need not be threatening. They can be about another person a long time ago someplace else. The listener is trying to make sense out of the story and decide what it means for him or her. Ideas can be presented metaphorically or embedded in commands. Since they are not presented directly, the listeners cannot refute them.

The listeners suspect, however that the story must have something to do with the present dispute. Just as Erickson used other techniques at the same time as he told his stories, we will consider how to integrate useful anecdotes with other mediation strategies.

Erickson's stories have been grouped by Rosen (1982) into a number of categories. Two that are most appropriate for mediation are reframing and future orientation. If you have read some of Erickson's stories you may say, "They are brilliant, right to the point. But because they are tailored to the particular problem he was trying to solve, if I tell the same story to disputants I'm facing, it just won't work. Even if at a very general level they are all the same: somebody has a problem and struggles with it—that's not specific enough to help my clients." The answer to this concern is that, according to Gordon (1978), a metaphor is a story in which one idea is described in terms of another idea, with the intent to have the listener experience things in a new way and to behave differently. Gordon offers a precise model for building metaphors to achieve a successful outcome that we can adapt to mediation.

Gather information about the client's situation. Who are the significant people? How do they relate to one another? What events are identified with the problem? How does the problem unfold? What changes do the clients want to make to solve their conflict? What outcome are you seeking? Is it obtainable? How will you know when you have reached it? It is also important to identify how the clients have already tried to cope with the problem and what might be preventing them from making the changes allegedly sought.

Building the metaphor. What is the context or setting going to be for your story? How are you going to make sure that the metaphor fits with the information you have gathered? How are you going to move the clients from the way they usually and unsuccessfully cope with the problem to the outcome you are seeking? How do you plan to reframe the problem?

Telling the story. People who are good at telling jokes or anecdotes remember the order of the information, yet know how to change the context or characters slightly to tailor it to the audience. Therapeutic metaphors differ from other anecdotes. While they probably should first be good stories, certain syntactic rules set them apart from other anecdotes. Their general purpose is to allow the clients to fit themselves into the story. The way this is done is to avoid being specific so that the listeners can project themselves into the action.

This is different from other kinds of storytelling. Good fiction may be noted for featuring specific descriptions. Writers note details of people and places so they can evoke them for the reader. When the writer gets it right by describing precisely rather than telling us what happened, we have that shock of recognition that delights us. "I've seen, heard, or felt that, too." Maybe the description is so detailed that we feel as though we have returned to a place where we have never been.

However, if the purpose of your story is to help people to change, you want to avoid making the stories so specific that it could only have happened to the characters and does not allow the listeners to put themselves into the action. You do this by avoiding including too many specifics about the people in your story and what they're doing. You say, "A *couple* is getting a divorce," rather than "Bill and Susan Jones are divorcing in Orange County this month." Therapeutic metaphors use "unspecified verbs"—"a couple *having a dispute* about how to end their marriage" is more likely to be identified with by your audience than "Bill and Susan Jones are fighting about who will own the beach house after they divorce." Another technique is "nominalization," turning verbs such as "I think" into "I *have a thought*." This seemingly fuzzy way of communicating forces the listeners to try to figure out "have a thought about what?" They try to determine in terms of their own experience what you mean.

Finally, therapeutic anecdotes use "embedded commands." This technique allows the mediator to tell the listeners what to do through the dialogue of the metaphor. You say the clients' names or "you" followed by an imperative. If I am talking to a fighting couple, I might say, "That reminds me of when my mother used to come out to see what my brother and I were having a dispute about. She would say, 'You two get along!'" This comment is usually marked by some action to emphasize the command—I pause slightly and lower my voice. You also could touch the listeners or make any other sort of motion that you have been trying to have the disputants associate with cooperating. This technique is examined in detail later in this chapter.

Satir's Communication Categories

Satir (1972) described the characteristic style that many people use to communicate. Her categories can help you analyze the way your clients typically communicate. You can then make the people in your story communicate the same way. If, for example, the husband usually blames and the wife usually placates, let your characters do the same. You can begin the story with the people acting the way your clients usually do and then have the characters switch communication styles to achieve a successful outcome, modeling change for the disputants that way.

Placater. Placaters usually want everyone to get along. They lack self-confidence, are happy just to be invited, and feel responsible for whatever is not going well.

Blamer. Every placater needs a blamer. Such persons point their fingers at others. Whatever goes wrong is somebody else's fault: It is the other parties' fault that there is a dispute and it is your fault that you are such an incompetent mediator that you cannot settle the dispute.

Computer. These people are infinitely reasonable. They stay calm no matter what. While they may seem less troublesome than the blamer, they may not know what they really want. This makes helping them to achieve a satisfactory outcome difficult.

Distracter. This category, which Satir says is least common, is maddening because the persons who fit it keep changing the focus of their attention. What they say does not seem to fit what is going on in the mediation.

Representational Systems

People experience what is going on around them by seeing, hearing, feeling, smelling, and tasting. Bandler and Grinder (1979) described how to assess this process:

> The visual accessing cues, eye scanning patterns, will tell you literally the whole sequence of accessing, which we call a strategy. What we call the "lead system" is the system you use to go after some information. The "representational system" is what's in consciousness, indicated by predicates. The "reference system" is how you decide whether what you now know— having already accessed it and knowing it in consciousness—is true or not. [P. 28]

According to Bandler and Grinder (1979), each person favors a certain way of consciously describing the world to him or herself. People either "see what you mean," "hear what you're saying," or "feel that I'm in touch with you." The way to establish clients' trust is to match the way they characteristically experience the world with your own comments. Listen to the verbs clients use and choose verbs from the same category. Eye movements are also indicative of clients' typical way of experiencing and describing the world. While individuals differ, most people exhibit characteristic eye movements when they are visualizing, recalling spoken messages, and so forth.

Once you understand your clients' representational systems, you can incorporate this information in the therapeutic
metaphor. If the husband of the divorcing couple uses visual
verbs and the wife uses kinesthetic verbs, start your story
with each corresponding character doing the same. You can
then switch these verbs to suggest different behavioral or
emotional consequences for your clients. You role model how
they might act in ways that will help them agree with each
other in the future.

Anchors

Anchors are present experiences that remind us of past experiences, though we may not be conscious of the connection
and the fact that the earlier experience is affecting our response to a current one. Recounting a past experience can often lead to teller to re-experience those emotions as he thinks
about it. Since you know this, when you ask them to talk
about the experience, you introduce at that time a cue of your
own that they will associate with this memory.

You could do this by touching their shoulder. Bandler and
Grinder (1979) recommend that you start with touch anchors
when you are learning this technique because clients might
look away or not hear when you try visual or auditory anchors. Also, when you lean forward to touch someone you are
changing the way you look to them and the sound of your
voice, so you are really anchoring in all three major representational systems. However, I recommend that mediators master this technique in supervision and then rely on visual or auditory anchors with clients. So you might look out the window
when the disputant is experiencing feelings of rage or frustra-
tion—which you detect as rapid breaths, raspy speech, and a
rigid posture—related to the conflict that you are mediating
with them. You want to be able to elicit those negative feelings so you can see if a proposed behavior to solve the conflict
diminishes or increases them. You will also ask each disputant to think of some positive experiences of how they dealt
with situations like the present conflict. You might lower
your voice when they think about that experience and smile to
themselves, take a deep breath, and drop their shoulders.

You can use anchors to help construct an effective metaphor. At the points where you have your characters change the way you want the listeners to change, you simultaneously make the cues—"fire the anchors"—that they associate with negative and positive feelings. Since they can't experience both emotions at the same time, they must integrate their reactions. If your strategy worked they will no longer have the negative feeling when you just look out the window or the positive feeling when you lower your voice, which is what you do to verify your result.

Triggers. Triggers are events that elicit behaviors from the disputant. Picking up the daughter from the house where both parents once lived may trigger unpleasant emotions and behaviors. Gordon suggests that you reframe such a trigger as a future cue for the changes you have made through anchoring. In the future, when the parent walks up the sidewalk to the house, they remember how much they care about their daughter and smile. The actual setting has become an anchor that means something more positive to that parent.

Quotes. Quotes are particularly useful for giving advice within the context of a story. You are making statements, but they do not seem to be directed to the listener because they are in quotes. I gave an example earlier about my brother and I quarreling and our mother saying "You two get along." Since her comment is in quotes and seemingly directed at us, it does not appear to apply to the listeners. However, the word "you" refers to them and the message commands them to do something. When you combine quotes with analogue marking by touching someone's shoulder or dropping the tone of your voice, you have two powerful techniques to influence the mediation process.

Flexible Use of Communication Techniques

The techniques described above for storytelling also work by themselves without going into a long metaphor. Quotes are a great example. If someone is using quotes on you, you have the feeling that they are affecting you, but you can't figure out how they are doing it. They say to you, "Someone came right up to me today and said, 'Go to hell!' I thought, 'Why would someone tell me "Go to hell"?'" The embedded command is to the listener, but because it is in quotes it may not be noticed consciously. Since the behavior is attributed to someone else, the speaker feels free to say things that otherwise would never be said. Bandler and Grinder (1979) noted that families often use quotes when they start talking to each other. However, since the reaction is almost as strong as if they had said it directly, they stop quoting and start fighting.

Family mediators who understand when a quote contains an embedded command that negatively influences the process may choose to point out what is happening. "I feel cursed at, even though you say your comment is intended for someone else. Maybe that's why your wife responded as if you were angry at her just now."

Giving Positive Instructions

Tell people what you want them to do. This is much more powerful than saying "Don't feel angry." First, they have to think about what it felt like to be angry and experience that. Only then can they tell themselves not to feel that way. Asking a disputant to "Please face me and talk to me" works better than saying "Stop shouting!"

Telling people clearly what you want and watching to see what reaction you get is the key to most communication. Bandler and Grinder (1979) say that "The meaning of your communication is the response you get. If you can notice that you are not getting what you want, change what you're doing" (p. 61). They point out that no matter how great your metaphors are, if you cannot figure out the reaction you are getting, you will not be able to change people with them.

If a technique like an elaborate story based on all the ideas discussed above does not work, do not conclude that "these folks aren't good listeners." Instead, watch what they do, learn from it, and try a different technique.

Nonverbal Communication

The interpretation of nonverbal cues, like eye movements, can influence the course of negotiations. Bandler and Grinder (1979) give an example of negotiation in a corporate setting in which, after one person presents a certain amount of information, the other person may avert their eyes. If you agree with Bandler and Grinder's idea of what that means, you stop talking and let the listener think about what you just said.

However, if you interpret looking away as boredom or avoidance, you might talk louder and faster. This will irritate the listener and the result may be an impasse. Bandler and Grinder talk about trying to sort out how people represent experience and then overlapping them. They say that if they are good at this, they can get one of the parties to act in just the way that the other party would love to get them to act, and vice versa.

Such modeling helps disputants cooperate enough to solve their present conflict and provides guidelines about how they might act to resolve future problems themselves.

Pacing and Mirroring

Therapists often stress the importance of establishing rapport. We are going to explore two ways to match the clients' behavior to achieve that trust with them.

The first approach is to match your speech to theirs. We have already talked about noting the kind of verbs they use and attempting to choose the same category when we start a session with them. When they say "I see," you say "I see what you mean." In addition, there are several kinds of nonverbal matching.

Direct Mirroring

Here you attempt to assume the same body posture as the other person, breathe the way he does—do exactly what he is doing. A second way, which Bandler and Grinder call crossover mirroring, is to "substitute one nonverbal channel for another" (p. 79). You can cross over in the same channel, for example, moving your hand in time with the breathing of the person. The other kind of cross-over mirroring is switching channels—you might match your voice to their breath rate. You have changed representational systems.

The idea here is that once you have paced them, you have established a powerful rapport with them. You can then begin to lead them into the sort of behavior that will result in the desired outcome.

Avoiding Burnout

Bandler and Grinder have a recommendation with implications for mediators who want to avoid going home feeling like the dumping ground for all the angry feelings of the disputants they have seen all day. Cross-over mirroring prevents the change agent—in our case, the mediator—from feeling what the client is feeling. So, choose a representational system different from the one chosen when matching the client. For example, if they breathe fast, you can speak at the same rate.

Out of the Corner of My Eye . . .

Bandler and Grinder recommend trusting your peripheral vision. You can see what you need to know without looking directly at the person you are interested in. They also suggest that, when there are a number of people in the room—which applies to the typical mediation—do not look at the person who is talking. Watch the listeners to observe their response for cues to what you should do next. Bandler and Grinder work to associate new emotions with various visual, auditory, and kinesthetic cues. They condition positively by adding options rather than trying to go back and get rid of the other behaviors. They give an example of an attorney whose nonverbal cues caused clients to mistrust him. He learned to tell people when he first consulted with them that it was important that they trust him. He asked them to think of someone they trusted, and when they thought of that person, he anchored that feeling. He then asked them how they decided to trust that person. After they described what that trust looked, sounded, and felt like, he simply told them to experience those same ways of representing trust while he cued them with the anchor.

Videotaping as a Mediation Technique

Mediation sessions can be recorded as they occur or re-created in order to produce a videotape that illustrates the process. Such tapes are popular in training and can be useful in supervision. They also educate the public when television stations include them in broadcasts on mediation.

Videotaping mediation sessions may have powerful immediate benefits. The first benefit is to the mediator. Whatever the impact on the disputants, videotaping will probably cause the mediator to lose weight and dress more formally. In addition, the mediator has the opportunity to see how he or she looks and sounds while mediating. Do you literally lean more toward men than toward women? What other body messages do you send? Videotaping also permits the mediator to review how certain techniques work in disputes and to assess the value of alternative methods.

Second, the disputants may resolve their conflict more quickly if they see themselves acting in an uncivil manner on videotape. One of Satir's (1972) classic blamers may become a little sheepish while watching the replay of typical finger pointing during attempts to solve a problem. Five or six statements in a row that "the problem is that your parents are interfering with our trying to share custody of our kids. You don't know how to manage money or you wouldn't need so much child support. You just don't know how to make kids mind" may lead this contestant to take a more conciliatory tone.

When would the disputants watch the replay of the videotape? One possibility is to set up a monitor so that the parties can see themselves and receive instant feedback on their behavior. Another possibility is to play the tape when the mediator thinks it will help the process and not to do so if sessions are proceeding smoothly or uneventfully. A third option is to routinely play back the portions of the session at the end as a kind of winding down and summary. A fourth variation is to start each session with an edited videotape of the important points of agreement and dispute from the previous session.

There are a number of books on using videotape in family therapy. Berger's book *Videotape Techniques in Psychiatric Training and Treatment* is an excellent source. Mediators who come from the mental health professions may be more familiar with the use of videotape as part of the process than attorneys or labor negotiators who are mediating.

There are limitations to having one camera set up with a wide enough shot to include all the participants. More sophisticated techniques—for example, the use of several cameras, split screen, and even just zooming in to focus on the face of each person speaking or the reactions of others—are not possible with such a rudimentary rig. Still, there is no need for a camera operator. Videotape may act to calm disputants; seeing themselves red-faced and screaming obscenities may be a revelation even though they have been doing it for years in family arguments.

Videotape archives would be valuable for research on the mediation process. Written permission could be obtained from disputants as part of the agreement to mediate; however, if there were concern about confidentiality—a valid issue given the lack of clear guidelines for mediators—videotapes could be erased after each session or upon closing the case.

Personal Computers and the Mediation Process

Personal computers can enhance the mediation process in various ways. Chapter 9 explores the use of computers in establishing a mediation practice. This section considers the computer as a tool to assist in the mediation sessions.

Drafting Agreements

The ability of a computer to be used as a smart typewriter becomes important when drafting mediation agreements. This application depends upon the technique of the particular mediator. I have suggested that giving the disputants a written copy of a summary of each session, including any issues that have been placed on the agenda or taken off the table, as well as any tentative or more permanent agreement, would be useful.

Certainly, the ease with which drafts can be typed in and corrected on a computer with word processing software can encourage ongoing drafts. Also, as the various points change, revisions can be limited to those changes because the document is stored on a diskette. The advantage here is primarily to the solo practitioner using part-time secretarial services who may do some of their own correspondence and whose style fits with giving the disputants drafts at the end of each session.

These drafts can be mailed to the disputants within a day or so for review before the next session. Having such a written summary may help people to avoid misunderstandings. They may also see more clearly what they have agreed to in case they want to reconsider. The power of the printed word suggests to the parties the binding nature of what they are about to agree to.

Financial Planning

Another reason to use a computer in your work and learn to operate it yourself is that you can use it to help clients rehearse financial options during mediation sessions. Current software for personal computers allows the user to generate "what if" statements. Berg (1983), a family mediator, matrimonial attorney, and financial planner, described the advantages of allowing a couple to quickly see how much money is available for, and the consequences of setting up, a trust fund for the children's college education. You may also want to project the tax consequences of characterizing support as child support or as spousal support.

Financial analysis may be particularly helpful in business mediations. For example, a statement of the probable cost of moving forward with litigation, as well as of the chance of success, may be prepared with the help of a computer (Wilkins, 1984). Software programs that assist in financial planning are invaluable to the family mediator seeking an accurate and affordable source of such information.

Legal Research

One way to stay current about legal information useful to your family mediation practice is to include a modem with your computer system so that you can subscribe to a legal research service. Both computerized legal research systems— Westlaw and Lexis—are accessible through personal computers at an hourly rate. The solo practitioner or a member of a small office who says, "How am I going to keep track of legal developments that affect my work?" may find the instant access to the most recent case decisions valuable. The American Bar Association is currently developing Ambar, which includes secondary sources published by the ABA. And, of course, the modem necessary to access legal databases enables you to access other databases. You can also develop a network of family mediators with computers and talk to each other via your terminals.

The Computer as Mediator?

A new computer program called "The Negotiation Edge" was written by a former IBM computer salesman who is also a clinical psychologist. The program user is asked a number of questions about his personality characteristics and typical negotiation behavior, as well as about the personality and negotiation behavior of a particular opponent. In about half an hour, the computer offers a step-by-step strategy composed of opening bids, counteroffers, strategies for working with the other person, methods of countering objections, and techniques for closing a deal (Eckhouse, 1983, p. B-2). Mental health professionals are also using computers by asking clients to answer questions directly into the machine. Proponents report that this technique saves money and clients are more honest with the computer than they are with the psychotherapist (Lewyn, 1984).

    With programs available for negotiation and psychotherapy, will we soon see the Family Mediation Program? Law researchers are developing a national databank that will draw upon standard forms as an attorney answers a number of questions from the computer. A new document will be created and printed out. "Eventually the computer could track current law and change the forms appropriately on its own. . . . [This is] the point where computer technology begins to impinge on the aspect of legal practice that lawyers so jealously guard" (Wilkins, 1984, p. 299). However, the strength of family mediation is that it avoids such a prescriptive approach, creating a climate in which disputants can pay attention to what is *not* being said and tailor any agreement to meet their unique needs, which may not be easily quantifiable.

    We will consider other uses of the computer in the mediator's office in the final chapter of this book. Selection of equipment for such applications as client files and billing, as well as word processing and financial planning, will be discussed.

Techniques Found in Other Chapters

I describe a number of techniques as we consider mediation of a specific type of problem in the following chapters. Some of these techniques are used by other people with whom the disputants may be in contact during mediation. These strategies may not be mediative in themselves, but can be taken into account by the mediator to enhance chances of settlement. Typical advocacy techniques of family lawyers can move the mediation process along as well as hinder it, although the latter is more often described in the mediation literature.

Other techniques are appropriate because of the status of the participants. Radical psychiatry's procedures described in the chapter on personal relationships depend in part on shared values, including political views, of the disputants. Telling participants that, as part of the agenda for mediation, each session will end with "strokes" (Jenkins and Steiner, 1980) might lead representatives of two major corporations to anticipate either a flogging or a visit to a massage parlor. Both possibilities may be more stimulating than the verbal compliments that end many humanistic psychology gatherings. Still, hugs all around may not travel well to the corporate boardroom. Certain behaviors are appropriate to the corporate culture and will be discussed in the chapter on business and professional applications of mediation.

A community dispute on a block where everyone has known everyone else for a long time may require different techniques than a referral from a criminal court to a diversion program in a neighborhood justice center. So, read the chapter that contains the type of conflict you are most interested in as well as this chapter on general techniques and the previous chapter on typical stages.

Do I Have to Be an Expert on the Problem?

Should you be a certified family law specialist in order to mediate divorces? Do you have to be an expert on computer hardware in order to mediate a dispute between two high-tech companies over a patent? A number of leading mediators would say, "No, but. . . ."

Gary Friedman, a pioneer in training lawyers to mediate, says that laws as well as lawyers can oppress people trying to settle their conflict. He feels that law is not irrelevant, but should serve as a background for guiding the parties toward reaching their own sense of fairness in settling their dispute.

Phillips and Piazza (1983) discuss integrating mediation into a civil litigation law practice. They suggest that knowledge of the substantive issues in the conflict is not essential and can be harmful. The parties may look to the mediator for advice or a decision rather than generating their own solution. A mediator who has good interpersonal skills and is practiced in mediation techniques can listen to the parties educate the mediator as to the nature of their particular dispute. This may produce a better agreement than simply seeking a mediator who has the most expertise on what seems to be the substantive problem. In fact, being educated by the parties forced them to make their points clear and may move them toward a more reasonable description as they try to explain to the ignorant stranger, the mediator, exactly what the issues are.

On the other hand, the law does provide a context for the settlement of disputes. In complex areas, such as divorce involving minor children or considerable property, knowledge of relevant law may be useful to the mediator in behaving ethically as well as suggesting creative solutions based on other people's resolution of their problem.

Mnookin and Kornhauser's (1979) description of bargaining in the shadow of the law, by parents attempting to privately decide the order of distributional issues to be settled as they divorce, is an excellent example of the legal implications for negotiation. The law is too blunt an instrument to reach the tailored result the parties could if they trust one another enough to take into account their own private history and sense of fairness.

However, an agreement that completely disregards relevant law might not be fair and probably could be successfully challenged by either of the parties later if they are unhappy with the result. Formal discovery may not be as important to a "barking dog" community dispute or a conflict involving child custody as it might be to valuing a business as part of a property settlement.

A Case Example

Here is an illustration of how some of the techniques described in this chapter are used in the mediation process:

The psychiatrist who practices in the building across from your office calls to say that he and his wife, who is a clinical psychologist, would like you to mediate their divorce. He starts to describe their situation, and you tell him "That's all right, we can cover that when we meet. Ask your wife to call me just so I know that she wants to come in as well."

The wife calls your answering service after office hours, leaving a message that she will be in next Thursday evening with her husband. On Thursday you greet them at the door because the session is scheduled from seven to nine in the evening and your secretary has gone home. You take their coats and show them directly into the room where you mediate, inviting them both to sit on the couch. Your chair is against the far wall, with two small tables that can be drawn close to the couch if the clients need to do some writing. A flip chart stands to your right; both of them can see it from where they are sitting.

You sit down and say that you are glad that they came to mediate. Now is a good time for each of them to tell what they want to accomplish in mediation. Since the husband called you, you ask the wife to start. She, however, defers to him and says, "No, you go first."

He says, "We chose you because you're not a lawyer." You ask him what he means. He continues, "We can settle this quickly without having to go to court and without having to pay attention to what the law says. Saves us a little money, too. How many sessions will it take?" You say that you do not know when they will reach an agreement or whether they ever will. You are not a lawyer. While they may not feel bound by what the courts might do, you are concerned with the legal context of their divorce. Precedents may provide standards of fairness. They may need legal advice, as well as legal information, and you advise each of them to hire an attorney who specializes in family law to review any draft agreement reached in mediation.

She looks up quickly first at you and then at him when you say this. He looks away, saying, "Well, I read in a professional journal that mediation is not always such a good idea." You respond, "Believe me, I have days when I would agree. There *are* a couple of issues that we can address here that the court will not consider. Since you have two adult children and a fifteen-year-old daughter still living at home, you'll probably want to do some financial planning for them. We can also minimize adverse tax consequences, using my computer over there."

He brightens when you mention saving money on taxes. You turn to her. she seems more willing to talk now, perhaps sensing that he cannot bulldoze you. She says, "We're here because he wants it. He's afraid a messy divorce will harm his practice. I'm only worried about embarrassment to the family." You ask what she wants to accomplish in mediation. She says, "A divorce, I guess." You write the word "divorce" on the flip chart under the heading "agenda." She winces when you point to the word and say, "Is this what you want?" she says, "Well, he wants it, so I have no choice." Yo ask her, "Do you want to be here?" and she replies, "Yes, I do."

You ask what else she wants placed on the agenda. She says she wants to make sure the children's interests are protected. He wants to work out the financial arrangements. You write these issues on the flip chart. You tell them, "this was a good session. You both say what you mean. [You hope that this embedded command will produce results in later meetings.] Here are some forms to help each of you prepare a budget for living apart. Since you're still living together, you may want to help each other with the categories you each know best. We'll talk about money needs for each of you next week."

In the next session, he shows you a detailed budget. She has completed about half of the form. When they tried to work together on their budgets they began to fight and stopped collaborating. After you put the budgets on the flip chart, you ask each of them to talk about their financial plans. You are trying to assess what principles of justice they are each assuming in discussing division of their assets.

He appears to be working on an equity model. He makes more money in private practice than she does working for local government. He feels that since he has made a greater financial contribution, the division should reflect the difference. As we consider what to do about the family home, he wants to buy out what he estimates to be her 20% share in the home. She apparently prefers the subtractive type of justice. "Neither of us will live there. I couldn't stand to hear my daughter talk about him in there with that woman!" This is the first you have heard about "that woman." She goes on to say, "Oh, yes, that's why he's rushing me along. He wants to remarry."

Now you know he has a deadline. That is why he has been focused on money issues and moving the process forward, while she has been reluctant in describing emotional concerns.

The work he has done in preparing his financial information shows signs of consultation with an attorney. When you ask him about this, he says, "Yes, I did talk with a lawyer just in case things don't work out here." You ask her what she thinks about consulting an attorney. "Perhaps an attorney who has only *your* interests in mind might provide you with the same sort of access to information that your husband has." She decides that she will see a family lawyer and mentions the name of a specialist who supports mediation, although her own practice is limited to representation.

You say that you would like to call both attorneys and tell the couple that, since from now on you will be writing a summary of tentative decisions in each session, the lawyers might want to review these interim drafts. He likes the idea of having a written record of progress in each session. She thinks having her own attorney balances their power.

You notice as you work with this couple that he uses verbs like I "see," while she "hears" what "sounds" like a good idea. So you use visual *verbs* when talking to him and auditory *predicates* when addressing her.

When they begin to argue, you sometimes look puzzled and ask, "How is this relevant to valuing your condo at Lake Tahoe?" You periodically lower your voice, slow down your speech, and say, "You are moving along well." You have the feeling that she is still not committed to divorcing, so you build in some interim steps that she has agreed to, such as exploring the costs of another place to live, as you move toward the detail phase.

The most important step is that she has said she will move out of the house prior to their selling it. However, when the date comes, she does not move out. She now states her hidden agenda. She wants to reconcile with her husband.

You ask them to reverse roles and state their needs and fears. She gradually accepts that she cannot stop him from getting a divorce. She also finds some comfort in future projection; you help her reframe what is happening by rehearsing through role-play a year from now, when she imagines herself as happy. What she had at first viewed only negatively may represent an opportunity for growing and for pursuing interests that she has neglected because of family commitments.

Since both of these people are mental health professionals, you thought they would recognize the usefulness of videotaping sessions and all sessions have been recorded. Showing them an excerpt from the last session each time you meet slows his tendency to dominate the conversation because he is embarrassed by his quickness to blame her. She has said that she hates hearing herself say, "Yes, dear, whatever you say." She is beginning to ask for what she wants.

When parenting responsibilities for their fifteen-year-old daughter are discussed, serious bargaining begins and they talk mostly to each other. She has more to say about this than about any previous topic. You are less active than in the earlier stages, limiting yourself to the flip chart as the couple refers to the budgets and financial information they have prepared. You do suggest some shared parenting schedules that have worked well for people with time commitments similar to those of this couple. They adapt one to meet their own needs.

They move quickly toward a 50–50 division of the family home. She will stay in the house and he will not seek to sell it to divide the equity until their fifteen-year-old daughter reaches eighteen. He is happy about reaching a settlement so that he can remarry. She likes remaining in a familiar setting during this difficult time.

Her attorney has made a valuable suggestion about how to divide the pension that he will eventually begin to collect. You have the feeling that since both attorneys are free to review the weekly session summaries that the comprehensive draft agreement the couple is moving toward will be recommended by these representatives to each of their clients.

When the parties do reach an agreement, you label it a draft and give each spouse a copy without asking them to sign it. You remind them to take it to their respective attorneys for final review and incorporation into a formal marital settlement agreement to be filed with the court.

You realize when thinking about this mediation that the couple used fewer generalizations and mentioned fewer "rules" or "shoulds" than do clients who are not mental health professionals. On the other hand, their pain reminds you that having read the books on stages of divorce does not make the experience hurt any less.

You compliment them on their hard work in mediation and their willingness to risk by saying what they really wanted. She has tears in her eyes. He shakes your hand firmly and clasps your left shoulder with his other hand. They go out the door for the last time.

The process took seven two-hour sessions over the course of three months. You have their permission to review the videotapes of the sessions in your supervision group in order to determine which techniques work best at which stages in family mediation.

Conclusion

This chapter on the art and technology of mediation has described advanced techniques. These strategies also apply to all of the conflicts that you might address as a family mediator. However, they are optional. You can learn to tell a therapeutic metaphor or direct a psychodramatic role-play after you have mastered the fundamental techniques of mediation and experienced helping a number of disputants through the process. Some of these advanced techniques may fit better with the way you mediate than others. Using a personal computer requires an investment of money and time to learn to use it, which you may want to defer until your practice is thriving.

Experienced mediators choose many of the techniques you read about. They no longer distinguish between their rudimentary and advanced strategies. They may combine techniques based on their experience. You will develop an individual style of mediating that works for you.

CHAPTER 4

Divorce Mediation

REGINALD AND SANDRA SMITH have been married for ten years. They have two children—Jason, seven, and Jennifer, five. They also informally share custody of thirteen-year-old Reginald, Jr., with Reginald's first wife. You receive a call from Sandra saying that she and her husband would like to schedule an interview with you to discuss divorce mediation.

You learn in the first session that Reginald is a dentist and that Sandra taught grade school to help put Reginald through dental school. She has not worked outside the home since Jason was born. Her parents contributed money for a down payment on a house six months before Jason's birth. The Smiths are disputing the following issues.

Custody and visitation. Reginald has heard about joint custody and wants to explore this option. He does not have a specific plan but would like to spend a significant amount of time with the children. Sandra is worried that under such an arrangement she would have to allow him to drop in anytime at her home. She is also uncertain about the effect of joint custody on child support. At this point, she prefers sole custody. She also wants to stay in touch with Reginald, Jr.

Child support. Neither client has a clear idea of the size of typical awards. Sandra wants to make sure that support payments would enable her to maintain the family's current standard of living and would cover the children's college and graduate educations. Reginald is interested in the tax implications of child support.

Spousal support. Reginald sees no need for spousal support. He plans to provide adequate child support and Sandra is a college graduate trained and experienced in a profession. She has heard of a court case that awarded the wife of a professional a portion of his future earnings. She wants to know whether that was spousal support and wonders how much support is typical in circumstances like hers.

Property settlement. Sandra challenges Reginald's financial statement, saying that he certainly makes more money. She suspects him of hiding assets from his dental practice, as well as from a real estate partnership that their tax attorney manages. Although title to the house is in both their names, she says that since her parents gave them the money for the down payment he should not receive a half interest. Reginald says that he has made all the mortgage payments and paid the expenses of taxes and improvements, so Sandra should feel lucky to get half.

We will follow the Smith family in this chapter to see what divorce mediators do. The trend toward no-fault divorce has not put an end to disputes about spousal and child support, property settlement, and child custody and visitation. Mediation offers families an alternative to fighting over these issues in court or to feeling coerced into signing an agreement. It promotes communication, which can assist ex-spouses in establishing the trust and working relationship necessary for sharing custody of the children.

Public or Private Mediation

Divorcing parents have to choose a way to settle any dispute about the children or money. Each can employ an adversarially oriented attorney, but they will both be compelled to attend court-based mediation sessions in states with a mandatory mediation law if they cannot agree on child custody and visitation. Alternatively, they can employ a private mental health professional or an attorney as a mediator. The advantages of private mediation over the use of court-based services include choice of the mediator; freedom from coercion, as the usual court procedures are available to both parties if the private mediation fails; no limit on the number of sessions; and freedom to negotiate all the issues to be decided without pressure to separate them. A leading family law specialist recommended that courts in a state with mandatory mediation develop a list of qualified private mediators that can be offered to parties as an alternative to court-based services (Adams, 1982). If the private mediation fails to result in an agreement, court-based mediation will not be required, which would reduce the cost to the public of the mandatory program.

Court-based mediation is usually limited to custody and visitation issues. Yet there are three other elements to every marital settlement agreement that involves children: property settlement, spousal support, and child support. Applications of theories of dispute resolution to divorce suggest that all four elements are inextricably linked, and that they are negotiated simultaneously by the parents, despite the efforts of court-based mediators and judges to separate them. To further complicate the decisionmaking process, the process of reaching a legally enforceable contract without arbitration by the court is influenced by knowledge and estimates of the judge's probable decision in the event that both parties cannot agree.

A mandatory mediation law limited to child custody does not always create adequate incentive for reaching agreement. Bifurcation, which presumes that financial issues—such as property settlement, spousal support, and child support—can be negotiated without reference to child custody and visitation, fails to take into account the interdependence of these issues as reflected in current federal and state law.

A major study of court-related mediation programs in Los Angeles, Minneapolis, and Connecticut found that while none of the mediators addressed the financial aspects of the divorce, half of the clients they were working with regarding child custody and visitation conflicts reported that they had financial disputes concerning the marital dissolution (Pearson and Thoennes, 1984). So the issues that Reginald and Sandra are disputing are typical.

The relationship between child custody and property settlement is one example of how issues concerning money and children are inextricably intertwined. A leading California case (*In re Marriage of Duke* [1980] 101 Cal. App. 3d 152) holds that the court may defer sale of property until a later time, often the age of majority of the youngest child, where it would be economically, emotionally, and socially detrimental to the children and the custodial parent to move out of the family home. This means, in effect, that the family residence is awarded to the custodial parent without a present buyout of the other spouse's interest. Indeed, the property settlement can be deferred for as many as eighteen years before the outspouse receives the equity in what is typically the largest and often the only major item to be divided in the property settlement. This can mean that, unbeknownst to both parties, the property settlement is decided when the child-custody issue is decided, despite the absence of a legal relationship between the two issues.

Therefore, mediators who say that they are only concerned with child custody and visitation matters and who see these issues as unrelated to other aspects of the marital settlement agreement can find that drafts of such agreements unravel when the financial implications become clear to the parties. At the least, mediators who draft agreements that fail to take into account the legal norms in their state for property settlement and child and spousal support as well as for child custody and visitation, may be missing opportunities to help couples reach solutions to their problems.

Bargaining Theory in Divorce Mediation

The fact that the court stands ready to decide any issues unresolved by the divorcing couple has been referred to as "bargaining in the shadow of the law" by Mnookin and Kornhauser (1979). They suggest (p. 964) that five factors are relevant to divorce bargaining: "(1) the preferences of the divorcing parents [concerning money and custody of any children]; (2) the bargaining endowments created by legal rules that indicate the particular allocation a court will impose if the parties fail to reach agreement; (3) the degree of uncertainty concerning the legal outcome if the parties go to court, which is linked to the parties' attitudes toward risk; (4) transaction costs and the parties' respective abilities to bear them;

and (5) 'strategic behavior.'" If these authors are right, all issues under dispute must be addressed by a mediator who has
considerable knowledge of family law and procedure. How
does that proposal compare to the norm? What happens if we
cannot agree? How much will court cost? How long will it
take? What have judges ruled in similar circumstances? The
mediator will be expected to answer these questions as the
parties seek to determine whether they would rather settle in
private or take their chances in court.

As discussed earlier, any successful mediation requires
the application of legal and psychological knowledge. In the
case of divorce mediation, both kinds of knowledge must be
applied to all four basic issues: custody and visitation, child
support, spousal support, and property settlement.

The Elements of Divorce Mediation

One early approach to divorce mediation defined the process
as one of using a mediator and agreed-upon procedural rules
and guidelines to decide the property division, terminate mutual dependence, and determine the future nature of the ongoing interaction initiated by the spouses, such as child custody
and visitation (Coogler, 1978).

Another author described the tasks facing the divorcing
parties in mediation as these: reducing emotional reactions
sufficiently to permit rational negotiation concerning the dissolution and its aftermath; making both short-term and long-
range financial plans; beginning life reconstruction efforts,
possibly necessitating new employment, as well as new intimate relationships; and understanding the legal ramifications
of property settlement, spousal support, child support, and
child custody and visitation while reaching a binding agreement (Taylor, 1981).

Still another description of the mediation process indicates that the parties develop current and future income information, develop budgets, inventory marriage assets, begin
to define short- and long-term goals for each party, define general areas of agreement, define substantive areas of agreement, identify symbolic and emotional issues, work through
visitation rights and responsibilities, negotiate financial dif-

ferences, develop an agreement, and take the agreement to an attorney (Haynes, 1981).

Reginald comes into the second mediation session and says that when he told an attorney friend he was getting divorced, the friend said, "Make sure you don't get *Duked*" (referring to the *Duke* case described earlier). When Reginald explains that he is worried about having to take a note deferring payment for his share of the house if Sandra remains in it, Sandra says, "I knew it! All this talk about joint custody was just to save you precious money. You don't care about the kids."

As the mediator, you say, "You both have said that you want to do what's best for your children. Let's talk about them first and then the house. You may want to go together to get legal information from an attorney, or you may each decide to seek legal advice from your own lawyers. You remember, you did agree that you would have your own attorneys review any tentative agreement we might reach here. We will consider every concern each of you has about the financial aspects of your divorce. Right now, though, let's focus on your children. What schools are Jason and Jennifer going to now? What about Reginald, Jr.? You may reassure each other when you each tell the other what your plans are for caring for your children. Reginald, why don't you start. I'll try to write it down here on the flip chart."

Increasing Emotional Acceptance of the Divorce

The narrow definition of successful divorce mediation is a signed marital settlement agreement. Success is measured both by resolution of the current dispute and by creation of rules to govern future conduct between the parties (Eisenberg, 1976).

To what extent does the mediation process make the current situation psychologically acceptable? The intimate relationship between the negotiators and, if they are parents of minor children, the possibility that they may have considerable interaction for one or two decades after the divorce make a psychological adjustment particularly germane to divorce mediation. Willingness to agree to rules concerning child custody and visitation is related to psychological acceptance of the divorce. Wallerstein and Kelly (1980) found that parents who received brief divorce counseling had fewer disputes regarding adherence to the marriage settlement agreement, including payment of child support, which often becomes a problem. In the absence of personal resolution of the divorce, the disputing parties can use laws as weapons; their attorneys are unable to satisfy them, although they do as bidden—at great cost to the spouses, children, and taxpayers. Mediators also can assist spouses going through the emotional process of divorce by such therapeutic techniques as summarizing to the clients the current situation as they describe it and providing an accepting atmosphere that allows the spouses to reveal his or her awful self and worst fears as well as their hopes for the future. The mediator who makes specific problem-solving behavior the primary focus of divorce mediation, future-oriented as it is, can help clients rehearse the reality of facing life tasks apart.

Arrangements concerning child custody and visitation can be an accurate barometer of successful mediation, for both the amount of consultation and the amount of interaction to be determined by rules made by the couple are greater for some arrangements than they are for others. Joint legal custody, joint physical custody, or both can be considered a positive outcome of mediation, and joint custody is preferred by state law in California. Are couples who undertake mediation successfully more apt to provide in the marriage settlement agreement for shared decisionmaking, shared physical care of their children, or both? Research indicates that such decisions often result from unsuccessful as well as successful mediation (Pearson and Thoennes, 1982).

Legal and Financial Knowledge

Knowledge of current tax laws can enable one family member to pay another more money in support than otherwise would be possible because such payments are deductible, a considerable benefit even to low-income families (Howard, 1982). Since one of the realities that the mediator and both parties often face is income inadequate to support separate households, information about how to increase the amount of money available to the family in transition can be one of the most important contributions the mediator can make. Yet neither the mental health professional nor the lawyer in general practice may have learned the tax implications of family law in their formal training.

Deciding in mediation who will claim the children as dependents can avoid conflict between divorced parents each year when they submit income tax returns. Such a provision can also avoid the audit that might be triggered if both make the same claims. Noncustodial parents may have a particular vulnerability to being audited if they are claiming dependency exemptions for children who do not spend a majority of time in their household. Attaching the agreement on claiming the dependency exemption to the income tax returns each year may prevent an audit. Appendix A contains portions of Public Law 98–369, which substantially changed federal tax requirements concerning support payments and dependency exemptions (effective January 1, 1985) and property transfers (effective July 18, 1984) related to divorce. Structuring any property transfers to minimize increased taxes prevents unpleasant surprises later. Federal and state tax laws may change each year, so mediators should review new provisions and refer disputants to tax specialists to generate informed options.

Like the tax consequences of support, the financial implications of being the custodial or the noncustodial parent may be considered in mediation. If the mediator and the disputing parties are aware that they are simultaneously negotiating property settlement, child support, spousal support, and child custody and visitation, then a number of solutions are possible. The amount of child support can be reduced if the noncustodial parent defers his or her share of the property settlement. One judge recommends adjusting the amount of child support by one-half of the difference between the support that would have been awarded under court guidelines and the fair rental value of the house (Adams and Sevitch, 1982). If the parents are considering joint physical custody, they may see the advantages of both having a home adequate to house the children, in which case they may wish either to sell the existing family residence or to reach an arrangement whereby the children remain in the home and the parents take turns caring for them there, with each parent maintaining a second residence. These are possibilities to explore with Reginald and Sandra as what they really want for themselves and their children becomes clearer during mediation.

Court Guidelines

The role of the divorce mediator includes providing the parties with information about what child and spousal support the court will award if the parties cannot agree (Coogler, 1978; Haynes, 1981). A number of jurisdictions have well-established and even published guidelines, which can help couples make realistic comparisons between their expectations and the court's probable decision.

California is developing statewide child support guidelines to minimize differences among jurisdictions. Such guidelines may not be precise enough to reflect particular needs. The cost of buying a house may vary considerably depending on the neighborhood. However, the schools in the part of town with cheaper houses may be inferior, so that parents feel they need to pay for private education. One city may have rent control that limits the amount of any increase for apartments each year while another city does not. Court guidelines are only a starting point, even for the judge. Parents know best the priorities for themselves and their children.

Your goal in working with Sandra and Reginald is to remind them that since they thought of each other as good parents before the decision to divorce, they probably still think so. You can help them focus on parenting rather than on their own pain in deciding not to live together anymore. You may ask them what they had been planning for their children's education and other aspects of their future. There will be less money now, but they can cooperate in setting specific goals for their children and assessing the costs. This approach works better than arguing over how much monthly child support payments should be, which inevitably leads to the potential recipient wanting the amount to be as high as possible, while the person who will be paying seeks to keep the sum low.

Support Insurance

If persons who are to receive child or spousal support are worried that they will not continue to get checks each month, the payers might consider buying insurance that would cover a default (Saitow, 1983). Like all other issues involving custodial arrangements, this is a highly charged topic and may elicit emotional outbursts from either or both parties. The payer may feel his integrity is being questioned.

> F: I read that most men stop paying support after a while.
>
> M: Don't worry, *I'll* always send you your money. Don't you trust me?
>
> F: Look, don't you have insurance on the contractor for your new office building in case he can't finish the job?

The mediator encourages the couple to make the financial aspects of their agreement as businesslike as possible.

In deciding whether to recommend support insurance, the mediator keeps in mind that a divorced couple could collude to defraud their insurance companies and collect money illegally. The mediator considers the personalities and financial situation of the clients before making such recommendations. Still, nonpayment is a major problem and insurance can be a solution. The Family Support Systems company recommends increasing spousal support by the amount of the premium, which may make it deductible by the paying spouse (Saitow, 1983).

The family residence is typically the largest asset in a divorce. A mediator attempting to aid a couple in reaching a marital settlement agreement that includes a property settlement should know the statutes and influential cases. In California, a community property state, there is a presumption that all property acquired by either spouse during the marriage is to be divided equally on divorce. This presumption can be refuted but may hold. In a leading California case (*In re Marriage of Lucas* [1980] 27 Cal. 3d 808), the principal family residence was purchased during the marriage and the title was held in joint tenancy, although the initial payment was from the wife's separate property trust funds and she claimed, on divorce, that she had a greater than 50% interest in the house as a result. The California Supreme Court ruled that her payment was to be considered a gift in the absence of agreement or understanding to the contrary.

Community and Separate Property

The California legislature attempted to rectify the *Lucas* problem by passing a statute providing that all property—not just the family residence—that spouses acquire as joint tenants while they are married is presumed to be community property. If they intend for it to be separate property the deed or title or some other written agreement must say so (Civil Code Section 4800.1).

Reimbursement is now required of traceable separate property contributions to community property, unless the contributor has waived such reimbursement in writing. This could include down payments. However, no adjustment is to be made for interest, appreciation, or inflation (Civil Code Section 4800.2).

This is just one example of one aspect of one distributional issue in one state—and a community property state with a 50–50 presumption at that. Most states have equitable distribution of marital property which, given the long list of factors considered, creates much less predictability as to how the judge might rule in a particular case.

A Model Law

The National Conference of Commissioners on Uniform State Laws drafted model legislation to help states define marital property. The model act defines marital property as:

> (1) earnings during marriage; (2) property and enhanced value attributable to personal effort during marriage; (3) income from individual property of either spouse received during marriage; (4) an interest in deferred employment benefits attributable to the earnings or personal effort of a spouse or to employer contributions during marriage; (5) a gift or disposition at death from a third party to both spouses during marriage; and (6) compensation for loss of earnings and expenses incurred during marriage which result from a personal injury to a spouse not caused by the other spouse. [P. 3]

This draft does not recommend how to distribute marital property when spouses divorce, although it assumes a half interest in all marital property for each. They do suggest clauses permitting binding arbitration to settle any property disputes. Mediation might better serve the purpose of unclogging the courts as a step before any arbitration.

Putting a Spouse Through School

Should future earnings of a professional ever be considered marital property? In the following case the wife worked while her husband finished school. They separated just before he started his practice. The trial court (*In re Marriage of Sullivan* [1982] 134 Cal. App. 3d 634) agreed with the husband that his education, degree, and license were his separate property as they cannot be transferred.

The appellate court first held that the wife should be reimbursed because the couple had separated before she could get any economic benefit from helping him to become a physician. Then, they reheard the case and decided that his professional education, degree, and license were not property (127 Cal. App. 3d 656, 1982).

This is the sort of situation where the couple may know best the contributions of each and their intentions at the time. Dr. Doris Jonas Freed has said, "Courts generally agree that contributions of a working spouse to the career potential of the other spouse are to be taken into consideration. What they disagree about is how to do it and how much" (Dullea, 1982, p. 44).

Some courts take this contribution into account in setting spousal support. Others reimburse it as part of the property settlement. However, a number of courts have held that spouses made these contributions without expecting that they would be reimbursed. The later failure of the marriage does not change that fact. Compare the legislation in California requiring reimbursement of separate property contributions (Civil Code Section 4800.2 described above). California law now provides for reimbursing to the community property any education or training during the marriage that substantially increased one spouse's earning ability. The judge is required to take into consideration the contributions one spouse made to the other's education or training when awarding spousal support.

Sandra Smith is asking for more than half of the house's value because her parents supplied the down payment. She also feels that she is entitled to some of Reginald's future earnings since she supported him while he went to dental school and his practice is just now beginning to pay well. Mediation can help the Smiths reach a financial settlement that both parties are comfortable with. If they were to go to court, they would have to abide by the property distribution scheme imposed by state law.

Mediators also develop a sense of when consultation with a specialist is essential in order to obtain objective criteria and aid the parties in negotiation accordingly (Fisher and Ury, 1981). Valuation of a business interest may be beyond the scope of a general practitioner, especially if there is a dispute as to its true worth and as to the means of assessment.

You will want to recommend to Reginald and Sandra that his dental practice and real estate partnership be assessed by a financial specialist. An accountant can determine what Reginald's pension is worth; both accountants and investment bankers may be consulted to determine the value of tax shelters such as a real estate partnership.

It is relatively common today for couples to live together without getting married. One of the issues that mediators can confront is assisting in the dissolution of such an arrangement, as we shall see later in this book. It is useful for mediators to know when a property claim under such circumstances might be held valid by a court under the precedent set by California law (*Marvin v. Marvin* [1976] 18 Cal. 3d 660). The length of the relationship, joint tax returns, children born of the relationship, and evidence of express written, oral, or implied agreements to pool property without consideration for sexual services are relevant factors (Adams and Sevitch, 1982). The same problem can occur for divorcing couples when one party wants to count, for the purposes of claiming marital property, the years in which the couple lived together without getting married.

Do judges refuse to accept mediated settlements and instead impose uniform spousal or child support schedules or visitation guidelines? Do they intercede if atypical property settlements are proposed? Anecdotal evidence suggests that, when the parties agree, the judge seldom exercises the independent power of the state to intercede unless proposed child support payments are so low that the custodial parent is likely to require Aid to Families with Dependent Children or other public assistance. Divorcing couples who choose to tailor their own agreement with the help of a mediator are empowering themselves.

Court-related mediation of custody and visitation disputes is available in an increasing number of states. The 1980 White House Conference on Families recommended that all states establish court-related mediation. Public auspices allow mental health professionals employed and supervised by a judge to offer as many as six sessions focused on custody and visitation issues to the spouses without cost; the judge decides financial matters related to property settlement, spousal support, and child support if these matters are not negotiated by the parties or their attorneys. Mediation is therefore limited to one of the four distributional issues to be decided in the marital settlement agreement—custody and visitation—while the other three issues—property settlement, spousal support, and child support—are left for adjudication. This hinders private resolution both because disputants cannot separate these matters when they negotiate a divorce and because they are forced to negotiate in the shadow of the law. Nevertheless, a number of judges here and abroad favor such an approach.

Confidentiality

Court-based mediation has been both lauded for reducing the number of child custody disputes that come to trial and criticized for using coercion under the guise of mediation. A California appellate court held that court mediators making a recommendation to the judge after their attempts to mediate a child custody dispute had failed were subject to cross-examination by the attorney of the parent not preferred unless both parties had specifically waived such a right (*McLaughlin v. Superior Court* [1983] 140 Cal. App. 3d 473); this case reproduced in Appendix B. I recommend that you read the entire *McLaughlin* decision. It considers the essential elements of mediation, compared to arbitration or a blurring of a process freely chosen and "muscle mediation." It is also the only major family mediation case so far.

This case illustrates the discretion of trial courts, whether through written local rules, informal rules conveyed orally, or simply through their interpretation of state and federal legislation, cases, and regulations having the force of law. *McLaughlin* also addresses questions of constitutional law concerning the due process right to cross-examination. Finally, look at the footnotes. They contain information about "how it's really done" in court.

Family mediators may note that the argument against cross-examination because only "temporary" child custody or visitation was being determined ignores the need for children to have predictability in their daily lives; children should not have their living situation changed later because of a more rigorous legal procedure. At the same time, the judge will probably make the mediator's recommendation an order of the court. Given the amount of time before a trial, any such temporary order is likely to be found to be in the interests of the children by a child custody evaluator. It is also true that child custody and visitation are always temporary in the sense that they remain changeable until the child reaches age eighteen.

The tactic of seeking a waiver before courts in light of *McLaughlin* makes the process closer to arbitration, which is why other courts have a local ruling against any recommendation by the mediator. A separate staff conducts child custody investigations. Chapter 8 discusses at length the subject of confidentiality in mediation. See also the *Macaluso* case in Appendix C. That based the privilege of a federal mediation and conciliation service mediator not to testify on the need for that agency's perceived as well as actual impartiality in future labor mediation.

One advantage of court-based mediation is that, under a judge's supervision, the mediator is not likely to misinterpret the law, nor is the mediator apt to interpret the law exten-

sively to clients. Whatever the reason, no court-based mediator has been charged with ethical violation by a state bar association (Silberman, 1981).

Credentials

Court-Based Mediators

In California, the legislation that mandates mediation specifies the credentials of court employees providing this service.
A master's degree in psychology; social work; marriage, family, and child counseling; or other behavioral science is required, plus a minimum of two years' counseling experience,
preferably family court–related among the ethnic or cultural
population to be served. Knowledge of the state court system
and of procedures followed in family law cases is mandated,
as is knowledge of community resources, adult psychopatho-
logy, and the pathology of families. Knowledge of child development and pathology and of the effects of divorce on children, as well as sufficient familiarity with the research on
child custody to assess the mental health needs of children, is
also required.

In Michigan, both attorneys and mental health professionals provide divorce mediation as court employees or privately under contract to the court. Members of both professions are required to complete a training program in divorce
mediation. Maine has passed a law providing for the mediation of financial as well as child custody and visitation disputes.

Judges who contract with private mental health mediators trained to address financial matters or with attorneys
can be expected to see the benefit of this approach early on,
even if the initial referral is only to resolve conflict over child
custody issues. Experienced mediators who are not barred
from doing so by law or by constraints of time or money consider all issues revealed during the process to be relevant to
reaching a lasting agreement. The cost of training court employees or of paying the fees of mental health professionals or
attorneys in private practice to mediate all relevant issues
may be offset by saving taxpayers the expense of litigation.

Grandparent and Stepparent Visitation

Court-connected mediators in California must mediate between divorcing parents and grandparents or stepparents seeking visitation rights unless both parents oppose such contact. This law reflects recognition of the importance of grandparents to children whose parents divorce (Kornhaber, 1984; Manuel, 1983). Although forty-two states now have grandparent visitation laws, the financial and emotional cost of a court battle dissuades grandparents from seeking visitation. Mediation may provide a forum for realizing the goal of such legislation.

Under California law, stepparents who have become psychological parents by taking care of their stepchildren regularly have an opportunity to remain in touch with those children if this subsequent marriage breaks up. Remember our opening vignette?

What if Reginald doesn't want his oldest son by his first wife to visit Sandra after the divorce because he fears she might "turn him against his father." She might then say, "I've raised that boy more than you have for the last ten years—since he was three years old—and now you don't want me to even see him? Well, in that case, I certainly don't want your pushy parents to see *my* children anymore!"

De facto stepparents—Marvinizers who are not married—have no right to petition the court under this law. Grandparents denied access to their grandchildren although the parents are not divorced have been asking to use the services of the Los Angeles court-based mediators. Both groups have legitimate interests that indicate a need for family rather than simply divorce mediation.

How to Avoid the Unauthorized Practice of Law

Since the decisions entailed by divorce agreements usually involve complicated schedules as well as volatile emotions, it is natural to put the agreements into writing. At this point, the other three distributional issues—child support, spousal support, and property settlement—can be brought up by the clients. Since the last three distributional issues are all financial matters, the psychotherapist can choose to tell each client to discuss them with a family lawyer.

However, with experience and with increasing awareness of state law and procedure, the mental health mediator may begin to address money matters, making clear to clients that independent counsel should give legal advice on any tentative agreement that is reached. Expansion into all relevant issues is hastened if a number of the carefully crafted custody agreements previously drafted have been aborted when the parties discovered their financial implications.

Chapter 9 discusses generally the problem of providing mediation clients with information on legal matters without at the same time actually giving them legal advice. Divorce mediation creates unique issues in this area. Mediators may find it difficult at first to resist giving advice when divorcing spouses express painful emotions. The negative impact that fighting has on children may cause mediators to suggest parenting alternatives that have worked for other divorcing couples. Such options sometimes have legal consequences both in terms of finances and future planning regarding the children.

Private mediation of divorces by mental health professionals became an indentifiable option in the mid 1970s. Coogler (1978), an attorney who became a licensed marriage and family counselor, published detailed rules that called for a couple seeking a divorce to meet with a private mediator who had a master's degree in a human service profession, three years of counseling experience, and training regarding law, finances, and mediation techniques. The agreement reached would then be drafted as a legal document and filed with the court by an impartial advisory attorney.

Haynes (1978) presented a model that incorporated techniques from his experience in the resolution of labor disputes and addressed the psychological ambivalence that sometimes prompts dishonest or confusing communication or reconciliation by the couple during this stressful period. Haynes (1981) recommended that both parties should take the agreement reached with the aid of mediation to their own attorneys so that each attorney could scrutinize the draft for individual interests. Examples of lawyer-therapist teams began to appear in the literature (Black and Joffee, 1978).

But Canon 3 of the American Bar Association Code of Professional Responsibility bars a lawyer from practicing law in association with nonlawyers as well as from splitting fees with such persons. The Oregon Bar Committee recommended that the mental health counselor and the attorney should each bill separately for their time to avoid the appearance of fee splitting. The prohibition against lay association could be avoided if mediation was offered by a corporation composed solely of attorneys, who would then utilize the independent services of a mental health counselor when needed (Silberman, 1981).

Even Coogler's (1978) model, which employs an impartial attorney to draft the final agreement, has attracted charges of the possible unauthorized practice of law by the mediator before that point is reached. Certainly, a mediator who meets with divorcing spouses to discuss property settlement, spousal and child support, and child custody and visitation is apt to apply or interpret the law to their particular situation, which is a traditional definition of the unauthorized practice of law. However, mental health professionals have often served in roles where knowledge of the law was considered essential to the endeavor but not the primary service being provided. Relationship difficulties and divorce counseling are among the leading reasons given by clients for seeking the services of a mental health professional, and often such counseling includes help in transition during a divorce.

Even preparation of the marital settlement agreement as the exclusive function of lawyers can be questioned. Although only licensed attorneys are to prepare legal documents, exceptions have been created for other occupations. Real estate agents, accountants, bankers, and tax counselors prepare legal documents associated with their work. The typical practice of these professions has not been attacked by bar associations as the unauthorized practice of law. Mental health professionals trained in social learning theory and behavior therapy approaches have used written agreements as a major part of their work with families since the 1960s (Patterson, 1971; Fatis and Konewko, 1983). Caseworkers at family service agencies have long provided financial planning that resulted in written budgets.

The point at issue appears to be the degree to which legal knowledge is employed or whether the private practitioner charges a fee. Fees are an important aspect of the controversy. Lawyers who practice mediation have to expect that their fee will be lower if the mediation is successful than it will be if the controversy escalates into a prolonged court battle. Also, a number of lawyer-therapist teams charge less per hour than the typical lawyer does. Finally, while lawyers who also mediate may bill fewer hours than they do for a typical divorce case, they must fear censure by the state bar association for playing this ill-defined role.

In contrast, the mental health professional with a master's degree may find that divorce mediation can command a fee greater than that for the typical service offered. Further, such mediation has met with little censure from either mental health or law associations. Indeed, divorce mediation can be viewed as a logical extension of clinical practice in which the laws are relatively unimportant boilerplate applied after the behaviors have been addressed. Folberg (1981), professor of law at Lewis and Clark Law School in Portland, Oregon, and president of the Association of Family Conciliation Courts, predicted that mediation will increase as an alternative to litigation because of the "recognition that divorce is as much an emotional process as legal and that feelings may be as important as facts" (p. 4). He sees an increased reliance on the private sector in the provision of divorce mediation. However, the professional liability insurance carrier for both the National Association of Social Workers and the American Psychological Associaton did not extend coverage to divorce mediation or even to divorce counseling until recently, since it viewed both roles as outside the practice of social workers and psychologists. The president of that company now states that the mediation of mental health issues is covered, but not the giving of legal or financial advice ("Malpractice Insurance," 1983). The Association of Family and Conciliation Courts and the Academy of Family Mediators both offer coverage specifically for mediators. Mediators should read such policies carefully in order to determine both the scope of protection and the credentials required.

Obstacles to Successful Mediation

Emotional Ambivalence

Divorce causes painful emotional reactions in one or both parties. One prominent theme in such reactions is the ambivalence created by persistence of attachment to the spouse after affection has eroded (Weiss, 1975). Ambivalence of this nature, combined with other reactions such as loneliness, anger, anxiety, tension, insomnia, loss of appetite, increased use of alcohol and other drugs, inability to concentrate, and feelings of depression—can influence the motivation and ability of the spouses to negotiate the legal terms of a divorce.

Couples who take separate residences may move back in together, although many subsequently divorce. Viewed from either a psychological or a negotiation perspective, threatening divorce, consulting a lawyer or a therapist, filing for divorce, or even jointly seeking divorce mediation can be a ploy. Theorists of the psychological aspects of divorce note that whether a legal divorce occurs at a given point in time depends in part on the stage each spouse has reached in the emotional process (Federico, 1979).

Stages of Divorce

Smart (1977) compared marital dissolution to impending death and the other life cycle crises identified by Kübler-Ross (1969) and Erikson (1950, 1980) respectively. Denial of loss, depression, anger, and ambivalence are typical initial responses; once the party begins to re-experience feelings of trust, identity, and intimacy, he or she can accept the divorce. The divorce adjustment process has also been characterized developmentally as deliberation, litigation, transition, and redirection (Federico, 1979).

Kressel and Deutsch (1977) described three stages of psychic divorce. The predivorce decision period, marked by increasing unhappiness and tension, is often felt more by one spouse than by the other. This period often sees attempts to reconcile, a decline in marital intimacy, and knowledge by others that the marriage is in difficulty. The decision period includes a clear move by one partner; anxiety about living alone; the possibility of renewed intimacy, followed by renewed fighting, with the pattern often repeating itself; and recognition that divorce will occur. In this stage, the couple fights over the legal terms of the marital settlement agreement. A period of mourning, which is complicated by the possibility of reconciliation, follows. Acceptance of a divorce and a period of re-establishing equilibrium complete the process of psychic divorce. The stage of psychic divorce that each spouse has reached influences the course of dispute resolution. The ability to make decisions and to plan rationally is impaired during this period. It is frequently possible to obtain a legal divorce without achieving an emotional divorce; in this event, subsequent legal battles are likely.

Legal Advice

While experienced family lawyers will readily recognize the behavior just described, their training and traditional practice do not provide them with the techniques taught to family therapists to aid their clients in making decisions during such transitions. Adversarially oriented attorneys who tell their clients not to talk to the spouse and to leave the bargaining to the lawyer can impede the mediation process. Spouses who are told by their attorneys not to talk to or trust one another and who are advised to conceal assets or otherwise to behave in a way that allegedly gives them an advantage in negotiations are not likely either to trust each other enough to mediate or to feel motivated about participating.

Family lawyers who routinely offer "empty the safety deposit box before he does" advice should probably not be involved before and during mediation. Matrimonial lawyers may maintain that their negotiating expertise is very similar to mediation. However, the process they are preparing for is adversarial, as illustrated by the articles in an issue of *Family Advocate*, the journal of the family law section of the American Bar Association, devoted to trial techniques. Titles included: "Boxing in the Hostile Witness" (Bugdanowitz, 1983) and "Preserving Your Witness's Stellar Testimony" (Momjian, 1983). Lawyers may not permit their clients to settle directly with their spouse (Adams and Sevitch, 1984).

We'll Take Care of Everything

Family lawyers retained to represent a divorcing spouse are trained to assume responsibility for the case. They may tell the client, "Let us worry for you." Clients often do come in looking for someone to take over. "The divorce lawyer as amateur shrink" (Dullea, 1983) refers to the fact that some clients may see lawyers as authority figures who remind them of their parents.

There are several problems with this all too natural response by both clients and attorneys. Clients may not provide sufficient information or actively participate in reaching a marital settlement agreement that they are going to have to carry out. Clients may become upset when they realize that their lawyers did not really make it all better, which may account for the subsequent bad mouthing of attorneys: "My lawyer told me to do this. I never intended to ask for so much money. I didn't want to fight in court." The lawyer did not seek out the client. The client came in and acted bewildered. The attorney took over and thoroughly prepared for the possibility of a trial while negotiating for a settlement.

These techniques by traditional attorneys tend to leave the clients uninvolved both in resolving their present dispute and in creating rules for the future, although they know best what they can carry out. Mediators also must guard against a tendency to make decisions for a couple rather than helping them to reach what is the best agreement for them. The standards of practice for mediators that we discussed in Chapter 2 encourage direct communication between the divorcing spouses, while rules of conduct for attorneys typically assume an adversarial process in which the lawyer represents one of the combatants. Unlike the lawyer, the mediator strives to find a solution which is satisfying to both parties, both financially and emotionally.

With increasing sophistication about the emotional aspects of divorce—which can lead clients to reconcile, seek revenge, and vacillate about wanting custody of their children within a single week—attorneys may begin to value insight into psychological issues as much as they already value knowledge of the law. Such awareness can lead from negotiation on behalf of a single client to consideration of situations where mediation might produce the best marital settlement agreement in terms of both finances and custody of the children.

Divorce Mediation and Labor Mediation Compared

In many ways, divorce mediation is similar to mediation of other kinds of disputes. For instance, the purpose of both labor and divorce mediation is to reach an agreement. Both are often oriented toward money issues. Both are legally regulated, so that neither disputant can simply refuse to negotiate with no further recourse by the other. Both may involve a continuing relationship between the disputants if the divorcing spouses have minor children.

The differences between divorce mediation and labor mediation, however, are significant (Markowitz and Engram, 1983). There may be a greater duty for the divorce mediator to assess the fairness of the agreement, particularly because the spouses are negotiating for themselves without much experience. Typically, they are much more emotional and the consequences are much more personal than in labor negotiation. Divorce is a crisis second only to death of a spouse, according to a number of stress rankings.

Therefore, the divorce mediator may use more specific techniques and a more structured approach than the labor mediator does and ask participants not to go forward with adversary proceedings. The mediator may recommend specific plans that she believes are best for the children. She may refer one or both spouses to a legal or financial specialist in order to balance power between them. Disputants are asked to disclose a great deal of information. Finally, more time may be spent dealing with extreme positions because, unlike labor disputants, divorcing spouses may be more emotionally motivated and honestly believe that what they are demanding is the only solution.

Hostile or Involuntary Clients

While beginning private divorce mediators may have trouble finding enough cases for a full-time practice, the clients they do get are often easier to work with than those referred to court-connected mediators. The latter often report feeling burned out from seeing all too many angry parents and trying to help them make major decisions about their children in a limited amount of time. Mandatory mediation does not mean disputants are forced to reach an agreement, but they are forced to attend. Involuntary clients may not value the process as much as those who consult and pay a private mediator. People who seek a mediator voluntarily are more likely than court clients to be upper-middle-class, and they are often on their best behavior—at least early in the process. Experienced court-connected mediators report that a significant number of their clients are "hostility junkies," violent, narcissistic, or just not particularly concerned with their children. They are not happy about mediating. Yet these are parents whose children may need the mediation process most.

Waldron et al. (1984) developed a model for resolving child custody disputes between parents in mandatory mediation. At the first meeting, the male and female mediator team describes the mediation process and signs an agreement to mediate with the parents. Then each parent is asked to take time to tell the story of the relationship from when the couple first met up to the decision to divorce. Next, the mediators hold a separate session with each parent to elicit additional information.

In subsequent sessions, each parent is asked to talk about the children in terms of how he has taken care of them in the past and what he hopes for their future. Caucuses may be held at this point if the mediators think they will be useful.

Finally, the children are brought into the mediation sessions with their parents. Children over the age of three are also seen individually. The mediators tell the parents how the children appear to be coping. Only then is there an attempt to develop specific goals for sharing the rights and responsibilities for taking care of the children. Caucuses are once again sometimes used.

Any agreement reached is written down and signed by the parents and the mediators. The court is notified whether or not an agreement has been reached. The agreement is then taken to the parents' separate attorneys for review and translation into a formal marital dissolution decree to be filed with the court.

Despite the fact that all of the couples seen by Waldron

and her colleagues felt that they were required to attend, most of the participants in this study liked the mediation process (Waldron et al., 1984). This study is especially important because the social class and ethnic background of the clients was more varied than in private mediation.

The parents who were not able to work out an agreement were described as rigid and concrete: "According to them there was only one right way to do things. . . . These parents saw little good in the other parent and no other solution but their own (Waldron et al., 1984, p. 17). Agreement also was unlikely between parents who denied that they were really divorcing or were so angry about the divorce that they could not communicate with the other parent.

One reason for the success of this therapeutic mediation model may be its involvement of the children in the sessions. Pearson and Thoennes (1984) found in their large sample of court-based mediation programs that most parents approved of the mediator's seeing their children. They wanted their children to have some say in the divorce process and valued the mediator's opinion about how the children were faring during the crisis. The 10% of the parents who did not want the mediator to meet with their children were worried that the children would be frightened by this experience. The most important aspect of including the children in mediation is to make clear to the parents and to the children that the children are not going to decide custody arrangements. While many public as well as private mediators choose not to see the children in a typical custody or visitation mediation, knowing something about each child might help the mediator to focus the parents more specifically on their children's needs.

Custody Options

One of the major responsibilities of divorce mediators is to help parents structure custody and visitation provisions of marital settlement agreements. Custody is an unfortunate term that evokes images of prison. Still, that's the term in most state statutes. Some newer laws refer to access of children to their parents or the rights and responsibilities of parents regarding their children. Custody is an emotionally charged word that mediators may try to avoid as they help parents to work out living arrangements for children. Eventually, however, when the mediated agreement is incorporated into legal documents to be filed with the court, the word "custody" is typically used because it is the legal term for sharing parental rights and responsibilities.

Sole Legal Custody

The traditional and still most common provision for minor children is to give one parent, typically the mother, the legal right to make major decisions concerning the child. In the past, this usually meant that the child also lived with and was supervised by that parent, while the other parent visited, which is called sole physical custody.

Split Custody

If divorcing parents have more than one child, one parent may have sole custody of some of the children, while the other parent is sole custodian of the other children. It is also possible for parents to alternate custody of a particular child, which is also called divided custody. For example, if Reginald, Jr., is to live with his mother during the school year, she will make major decisions concerning him then; his father will make decisions when his son is with him during the summer. This plan can cause Reginald, Jr., trouble if his parents disagree about whether he should continue cello lessons or play football, or whether he should go to Mass or to temple.

Joint Custody

Joint legal custody means the parents make major decisions about the child together. Joint physical custody means that each of the parents has frequent contact with the child. This arrangement has several advantages over the preceding plans, as subsequent discussion will make clear.

What do the children want? There is no specific age in state law at which children may be consulted about their custody. But if they appear to the court to be old enough and smart enough to state an informed preference, the judge may take their wishes into consideration.

An important provision of California's joint custody law is that the judge must specify the types of decisions that require the consent of both parents. Changing the child's religion or school might be examples. If the issue is not named, either parent may make the decision. If the judge orders joint physical custody, the rights of each parent to spend time with the child must be specified in enough detail so that instances of child snatching or kidnapping are clear enough to trigger a legal response.

Mediators soon learn that most judges will approve any arrangement that parents can agree to. I have found that a "day, week, month, and year in the life" rehearsal by the parents is more important than the particular label attached to the custody arrangement in predicting its workability. Education is needed because the parents simply have not had experience sharing rights and responsibilities of their children between two different households.

Joint custody is relatively new and the mediator should take time to explain how parents can share child rearing. The benefits to parents and child depend on proper implementation of this option. For instance, parents may not understand the strain to which they expose their children by attempting to share custody with mathematical precision. Huntington (1983) pointed out that divorced parents who work outside the home while sharing custody may put very young children in two different day care centers. This experience, combined with living in two homes, is overwhelming to most small children.

There is concern that if child support is based on the percentage of time that each parent spends with the child, then sharing custody would penalize the mother, who may already be risking the feminization of poverty in getting divorced. Men typically increase their disposable income after divorce, while women's income drops.

A proportion of income "one-pot" approach that sets child support based on each parent's income without regard to time spent with the child is being tried in a few courts. Will the parent with the greater income opt out of spending time with their child in this case, especially if they are looking for a new mate or have remarried and had other children?

ADVANTAGES

Joint custody increases the likelihood that children will have a meaningful and continuing relationship with each parent and their extended families. Children do not have to choose one parent over another, thus preventing feelings of loss following separation from the noncustodial parent. Research indicates that the most important factor in helping children adjust well after divorce is a dependable and affectionate relationship with both parents who relate fairly well to each other (Wallerstein and Kelly, 1980). Fathers have said that they do not visit not because they do not care but because they care so much that they cannot bear to witness the change in their role from custodial parent to occasional visitor (Greif, 1979). Continuing an equal parental role enables fathers to be directly aware of their children's needs.

Joint custody provides an alternative to a dispute in court so that neither parent must lose or attempt to prove that the other is at fault. Review of 414 consecutive custody cases in one court over two years determined that parents who were granted joint custody were relitigating custody only half as often as those couples in which one parent was awarded sole custody (Ilfeld et al., 1982). Shared custody assures each parent of the opportunity to shape the socialization of their children. Both may legally consult with teachers, health care professionals, and other persons involved with the children. They are expected to make future decisions concerning the children and are more apt to do so if they have an equal voice and a feeling of responsibility. In instances of joint physical custody, neither adult has to be a full-time parent, insuring time for a career, as well as other relationships and interests.

Joint custody is a social policy that benefits society. Courts are permitted more flexibility in determining the best interest of children and may legally recognize the importance of both parents. This may reduce child snatching and forum shopping. The public expense of attempting to collect defaulted child support payments or of having single parent families subsidized by governmental programs could also be diminished.

In 1983, a bill to amend title IV of the Social Security Act to require, as a condition of receipt of funds by a state under the Aid to Families with Dependent Children (AFDC) program, that the courts of the state consider joint custody as the first option in child custody cases was introduced in the House of Representatives. This bill did not define joint custody. However, the best practice is to make the court order concerning a particular family as specific as possible rather than trying to anticipate every contingency in the state law (Shear, 1983).

In addition to meeting the psychological needs of family members, joint custody offers a child care resource that may prevent poverty and reliance upon governmental support programs. Mothers may find even relatively low paying jobs cost effective if they have free child care available, at least part-time, from fathers. Moreover, the physical and mental health of all family members might be improved, decreasing future costs to society. The psychological as well as financial resources for the children who have both parents caring for them may lower the incidence of abuse, neglect, children in need of supervision, and juvenile delinquency, benefiting society as well as the families affected. A cooperative response to marital dissolution provides a workable solution to this increasingly frequent crisis in family life. If joint custody is such a positive response to family dissolution, why are such awards not more common?

PROBLEMS

Legal and personal obstacles to successful joint custody abound. First, parents may not know about this option or their attorneys may discourage them from pursuing it. Second, judges may refuse to issue a joint custody decree unless the parents have been cooperating in this fashion for some time or the court document is very specific about the custody plan. Third, a few states prohibit this type of custody or permit its consideration only if the mother is judged to be less fit than the father.

When parents disagree about joint custody, the court will probably order sole custody, most often to the mother, although it has been argued that custody should be awarded to the parent advocating joint custody if both are suitable. Under California's law, frequent and continuing contact with children and both parents is preferred.

Expecting two people who are unable to continue living together to agree to share custody at a time that is typically stressful and marked by strong emotions can be unrealistic. Possibly one or both of the spouses simply do not want further contact with the children or each other. Perhaps one of the spouses has a negative effect on the children and should not be permitted to share either decisionmaking or physical custody. However, even if an agreement is reached, subsequent problems may jeopardize the arrangement. Joint legal custody gives both parents an equal voice in structuring their children's lives. Continued feuding by parents may place children in considerable conflict. As families separate, each parent has to assume certain fixed costs such as housing, food, etc., which were formerly shared. This may reduce the purchasing power of each to less than half of what it had been. In the case of joint physical custody, the need for one parent to obtain a second home large enough to accommodate children and equip it for their care may be financially impossible.

Even if all family members thrive on joint physical custody, logistical problems remain. The popular notion of joint custody as consisting of each parent caring for the children a part of each week does not allow for such financial and psychological issues as how child care centers, schools, and other resources must be within the geographical range of both parents. One parent may choose to move away, precluding frequent sharing of physical custody. Despite his or her loss of a child care resource and the children's loss of frequent contact with the other parent, an opportunity such as a new job or remarriage may prevail.

Individuals who live with either parent in the future may object to sharing their lives with the children of an earlier marriage. Those persons might also have children from a previous relationship, resulting in a blended family. These parents may decide to have children of their own, and the potential problems of a household consisting of his, hers, and mutual children, some of whom are only living with the family part-time, are considerable. While guidelines for such families have been recommended, help is not widely available.

Reginald and Sandra have been laboring under certain incorrect assumptions about custody and joint custody. As each of them describes in detail his or her plans for caring for the children, it becomes clear that Reginald has not given much thought to how he actually is going to take care of Jason and Jennifer full time and Reginald, Jr., part-time.

The emotional aspects of working toward an agreement are complicated by the revelation that Sandra has a lover whom she intends to marry. Reginald has been critical of her throughout the sessions and she finally retorts, "I know someone across town who likes me just fine." Now you begin to wonder whether Reginald's refusal to be specific about how he plans to care for the children, combined with his reluctance to confront financial issues, is motivated by a desire to remain married to Sandra.

Sandra's lack of experience with managing money continues to be a disadvantage for her. You recommend that she read Rogers' *Women, Divorce and Money* and consult a financial planner to help her complete a tax organizer. This lengthy form is designed to help people trying to organize their finances; it is more detailed than the budgetary form you usually provide clients after the first mediation session.

You are concerned about the Smiths' children, particularly Reginald, Jr. You know from Judith Wallerstein's research that children who have the most trouble coping are those whose custodial parents' subsequent marriages end in divorce. Sandra's apparent inclination to remarry while still negotiating the terms of her divorce from Reginald threatens further disruption in the children's lives.

After thinking about what both Reginald and Sandra seem to be attempting to accomplish for themselves and their children, you meet with Jason, Jennifer, and Reginald, Jr. The children know that their parents are divorcing. They are frightened that they will have to choose between them. Reginald, Jr., is afraid that he will not see Sandra anymore.

Since you saw the children without their parents, you share with the parents what you have learned. Reginald has been attending a men's support group at your suggestion and he is beginning to accept Sandra's decision. He is also realizing that his attempting to hold Sandra by professing more interest in caring for the children than he is really prepared to fulfill, as well as being difficult about financial matters, is not going to get him what he wants, and it may even harm his children. You suggest that the children attend a group for children whose parents are divorced, which is held once a week at their school. Reginald and Sandra both begin to be more realistic about making a plan for sharing their responsibilities of raising their children after the divorce. They would like to try joint physical custody, with Sandra spending about 60% of the time with the children—mostly during the week—and Reginald caring for them the remaining time, when he will be available to be with them.

You write up a tentative schedule for custody and give them each a copy. You point out that this will not be exactly the schedule that works best, so they will want to talk with one another about making necessary changes.

Using both the information from outside experts about the value of Reginald's dental practice and real estate partnership and the financial plan Sandra has worked out with a financial planner, they arrive at a lump sum that Reginald will pay Sandra instead of monthly spousal support or a percentage of his future earnings. This agreement meets her needs for a minimal future financial dependence on Reginald and offers him a definite amount to pay rather than an unspecified continuing obligation.

Now that the custody schedule and the financial aspects of the divorce have been resolved, Reginald and Sandra decide that it would be best for the children to remain in the family home when they are with their mother. Reginald will find a place to live that is in the same school district. Finally, they decide that each owns a half interest in the house; Sandra acknowledges that preserving a legal right to the amount of the down payment her parents contributed is not as important to her as the lump sum property settlement and the ability to remain in the home while the children stay in touch with Reginald. Reginald defers his share of the house until Jennifer is eighteen, when it will be sold or Sandra will buy his share.

They are all happy that they will stay in each other's lives as parents and children.

Visitation cannot be compelled. Laws do not force spouses to live together, and did not even when legal divorce was difficult to obtain. Laws cannot force the creation or continuation of relationships. In a leading case in California, a member of a prominent Los Angeles law firm at first acknowledged fathering a little girl and paid support for her for a year after she was born in 1976 (Blake, 1981). When he stopped paying, the mother, also an attorney, sued and successfully established paternity. The father made the payments ordered by the court, but refused to visit the girl.

Her mother sued again, this time asking the court to order him to visit his daughter. The trial court refused to do so, and an appellate court agreed, saying that, under the Uniform Parentage Act, visitation by an unwed father is a right, not a responsibility (*Louden v. Olpin* [1981] Cal. App. 3d 565). One of the appellate justices talked about the problems of granting such a request: "Is the sheriff going to go out and handcuff papa, drag him to mama's house and say, 'Sit there for two hours and I'll let you go home.' Suppose he goes every two weeks, says hello, sits down for two hours and doesn't say another word?" (Blake, 1981).

The attorney for the father argued that, not only was there no legal authority for such an order, but it would be a violation of the Thirteenth Amendment to the United States Constitution, which prohibits involuntary servitude. The point here is that, while the court can prohibit people from seeing each other under restraining orders, they cannot force them to contact each other to maintain a personal relationship or determine the quality of any such contact. Mediation may allow people to work out how they would like their relationship to continue.

Joint Custody of the Cockapoo

On the other hand, some divorcing couples both want their pets or other possessions so much that they are willing to fight it out in court. After a year of wrangling, one judge used the state child custody law to award joint custody of the dog to a couple ("Joint Custody . . .," 1983). The husband had offered his wife $20,000 to buy out her share of Runaway, who favored lobster and was generally well treated by the childless couple.

The judge ordered them to alternate months caring for Runaway. Neither can take the dog out of state without the written permission of the other. Now, keep those cards and letters. I happen to be the proud owner of Ben, the smartest and best-trained golden retriever around. I would miss him and so would my son, Michael, if our "sock mouth retriever" were gone.

Pets and other possessions are especially important during the losses experienced by divorcing couples. Mediation can help them get what they need by talking directly with one another rather than petitioning the court about such personal matters.

Blades (1984) described mediation of a conflict over a dog:

> John and Kate both want to keep the dog. Kate argues that she should have the dog, because it protects the house and because their son, Dave, is fond of it. John says that he should have the dog, because he trained it and because he is going to have Dave 40% of the time so Dave will still see the dog in either case.

When it became apparent that John and Kate would bicker about the dog if given the chance, the mediator directed their attention to a blackboard, explained how to brainstorm, and suggested that they spend two minutes brainstorming solutions that they could both live with. These were the resulting suggestions: John gets the dog and Kate takes the dog on weekends. Kate gets the dog and John takes the dog on weekends. John buys Kate a new dog and helps her to train it; their present dog stays with Kate until she feels safe with the new dog. Kate buys John a new dog. They switch custody of the dog when they switch custody of Dave. The dog spends one week with John and one week with Kate. [P. 76]

People moving because of a divorce may consider getting rid of their pet. However, pets provide a routine and feelings of being needed and can lower the blood pressure of their owner, which may be especially useful to divorcing persons. It is important to listen to what such a possession means to a particular disputant.

The Bird's Nest: A Therapeutic Metaphor

A few years ago, a couple of rare birds—California condors—were nesting with the only egg known to have been laid that year. Scientists watched while the huge momma bird and daddy bird began pushing each other off the nest. They even fought in the air for hours, leaving no one to incubate the egg. Finally, while they were again pushing each other off the nest, the egg fell to the rocks below, smashed, and was eaten by ravens.

While this true story might seem like a good cautionary tale to tell parents heading toward a custody battle, I change it into a therapeutic metaphor by giving the listeners positive commands and demonstrating change in their usual ways of coping rather than simply telling them a horror story.

My version usually goes something like this: "A momma bird and daddy bird built a nest. Soon there was an egg in the nest. There was only one egg. Both momma bird and daddy bird thought about how precious and special it was to them. They thought about what it would be like once the egg hatched into a baby bird. What would its life be like once it flew away?

"Momma bird and daddy bird couldn't get along. Daddy bird blamed any troubles on momma bird, and she always agreed that it was her fault. They bickered over who was better at sitting on the nest. Sometimes they would argue so much that no one was sitting on the nest, which wasn't good for the egg.

"Finally, one day, while they were trying to push each other off the nest, they jostled the egg. The egg rolled to the very edge of the cliff on which the nest was built. Together, they just caught it in time. For once the momma bird fiercely said, 'We should be working together,' and the daddy bird was so scared he agreed instead of blaming. They looked at each other and said, 'We will take care of it together.' They felt thankful that they had a chance to save what was most important to them. From then on they shared sitting on the egg and taking care of the healthy baby bird that hatched from it."

I am describing the change I want the listeners to make in sight, hearing, and feeling. I also slow down and lower my voice when I say, "We will take care of it together." (See the new techniques chapter for more on therapeutic metaphors.)

Custody and visitation of children may be the most emotionally draining aspect of divorce mediation. In addition to the techniques described in earlier chapters, there are ethical issues particular to divorce considered in the last chapter of this book. How can you avoid having a classic Giver sign off on a skewed marital settlement agreement? How can you protect the children?

Power Balancing

The mediator, worried about our Giver, may refer her to outside experts for more information. If she does not take the hint, the mediator may provide information directly. A more intrusive option would be for the mediator to say, "I don't think the way this is shaping up is fair." Finally, the mediator may threaten to stop the mediation or attach a note to any agreement the parties reach saying that the mediator does not think the settlement is fair.

Galbraith (1983) says there are three kinds of power. The potential to inflict punishment sufficient to command submission is what he calls condign power—"You try that and I'll never see the children again." Compensatory power offers enough reward for the wielders to get their way—"I will pay you more spousal support if you let me have the sheepdog." Conditioned power changes what people think by persuasion or education or appealing to "what's right" or "the decent thing to do."—Look, that pension is mine. It's connected to my job and I won't even draw it for another twenty years." Mediators trying to balance the power between divorcing spouses may find it useful to analyze just what sort of power is involved.

We mediators may like to think that we mainly educate, such as pointing out the possible advantages of sharing the care of the children. However, we may also be tempted at times to threaten what the court will do if the couple does not decide between themselves about their children. We are also offering rewards when we expand the pie or even praise spouses for cooperating during mediation. Mediators may also benefit by analyzing the kind of power they are flexing as part of any attempt at power balancing.

When Sandra suspected Reginald of hiding assets, an accountant who specialized in valuing professional practices and an investment banker familiar with real estate partnerships provided the information. If Sandra had been bullied in mediation or between sessions by Reginald because he felt maligned, a brisk note from her attorney suggesting to his attorney how the case might be handled in court could have balanced the power, allowing mediation to proceed (Haynes, 1981).

Planning for Future Negotiation

Peoples' lives change, and even the most specific mediated agreement is not going to continue to meet the needs of everyone involved if parents of young children maintain contact until the youngest child reaches eighteen. People move quite often today, sometimes as part of their jobs.

Suppose a couple has successfully shared custody of their children according to the arrangement reflected in the marital settlement agreement filed with the court. There is a constitutional right to travel, but would it be better for the children if they stayed with the parent who is not moving? In 1981, New York's highest court prevented a mother from taking her eleven-year-old son to a western state because the father's visitation practices, which he had been maintaining since their divorce in 1975, would have been impaired (*Weiss v. Weiss*, 436 NYS 2d 862, 1981).

As the children grow up, they will have new needs and they may begin to state their own preferences. One or both of the parents may remarry, changing the financial and emotional resources available to the children. While the participants do not have to be told that they need ongoing mediation, it is a good practice to normalize the need for future negotiations. They may work these changes out themselves, using the skills they learned in mediation, or they may need to seek help from a third party for the tougher issues.

Returning for the final time to Reginald and Sandra, you know from talking with their children that Reginald, Jr., Jason, and Jennifer are articulate and know what works well for them. You have encouraged them to tell their parents about what they need. You know that any future mates of the parents or emotional changes, as well as the developmental needs of the children, may suggest changes in the current sharing of them. You have the feeling that this family in transition has learned in mediation to say what they really mean and listen to each other. You feel good about their negotiating with each other in the future and you tell them so.

Conclusion

Child custody and visitation, spousal support, and property settlement are legally and psychologically linked. How can the knowledge required for a comprehensive approach to divorce mediation be obtained? Specialized training programs are available. Practitioners often enroll in my graduate seminar on family mediation through the university's continuing education program. The standards for membership in the Academy of Family Mediators call for comprehensive introductory training, followed by fifteen hours a year of continuing education in the area in which the mediator feels the greatest need for further study. Mediators from both the mental health and the law professions will recall that referral to someone more expert in a subspecialty is recommended practice in their discipline. If attorneys and mental health mediators are considered to stand at opposite ends of a continuum defined by the typical concerns of each group, then mental health mediators can begin with a practice limited to child custody and visitation disputes and move toward drafting written agreements incorporating financial matters. Lawyers who choose to mediate divorces can become comfortable with the psychological stages that parties are going through and decrease their use of the adversarial approach.

Both mental health and lawyer mediators may consider the recommendation of the American Bar Association that the mediator should advise and encourage both parties to seek separate legal representation throughout the mediation process (Bishop, 1984). Mental health mediators must be aware that a generic training program will not provide them with even the rudiments of the unique family law of their state. Attorneys with a general practice may have noted the rise of family law specialists recognized by the bar in a number of states. There is much for each of us to learn if we are to mediate all the issues that divorcing families must face.

CHAPTER 5

Mediation Throughout the Family Life Cycle

MOST PEOPLE SEEK permanent intimate relationships. The baby boom generation appears to be overwhelmingly in favor of marriage. Accordingly, the high divorce rate may indicate the need for a companionship marriage or other high hopes for relationships. Most divorced people remarry, suggesting that people become disenchanted with spouses, not with the institution of marriage. Reflecting on this fact, Collins (1983) noted that couples need to learn how to negotiate marital conflicts. Conflicts arise in families at critical developmental times and not only concern the marital couple but frequently involve the grandparent or offspring generations as well.

There has been increasing awareness of the influence that all three generations of a family have on one another. A text that recommends using the family life cycle as a framework for family therapy suggests that it is useful to look at stages in the family life cycle (Carter and McGoldrick, 1980). They consider unattached young adults who then marry, have young children who grow into adolescents, and then leave and begin their own families. We will look at some developmental tasks that families encounter throughout the life cycle, as well as at some unexpected crises that mediation might address.

Mediation Before Marriage

Premarriage contracts, or prenuptial agreements, as they are often called, are increasing in popularity. Such contracts were once used mostly by middle-aged and older couples remarrying after their children had grown up. They wanted to set their children's minds to rest about inheritance so that the new marriage would not be sabotaged. Now, more and more couples entering a first marriage are looking realistically at the divorce rate and at problems that their married friends have encountered. The contract attempts to clarify the couple's expectations; the issues involved are both legal and psychological, a natural application for mediation.

The legal implications of prenuptial agreements are so complicated that in 1984 an entire issue of *Family Advocate* examined this topic. Some states recognize premarital agreements solely as they regulate property distribution. Agreements on support rights are not enforceable. Any indication of lack of full disclosure of the property interest waived or lack of opportunity to seek legal advice may render the prenuptial agreement unenforceable as well (Freed, 1984).

Attorneys consulted to draft a prenuptial agreement tend to focus on monetary issues, the only legally enforceable element of such agreements. Prospective spouses who feel the need to tailor a written agreement going into a marriage may be signaling a number of psychological concerns as well that can be addressed in mediation.

AND THE SOUP KITCHEN GOT THE CAKE

Wayne calls to tell you that he and Anne got engaged, set the wedding date, and sent out the invitations. On the wedding day, Anne said she could not go through with the ceremony. This astonished Wayne. Some of the guests were notified in time; others were not. The hall and the orchestra had to be paid for and the cake was donated to the local soup kitchen. Wayne and Anne decided to fly to Aruba for a couple of days to talk things over. The only hint he had of Anne's hesitation was his refusal to sign a prenuptial agreement drafted at the insistence of Anne's wealthy family. Did her family assume he was a gold digger and that the marriage would not last? Otherwise, Wayne was certain that everything was fine between Anne and him.

When Anne comes into the first mediation session, she is very embarrassed. Wayne takes the lead and describes the problem in more detail; repeating the view he had expressed earlier. Ann is quieter, volunteering little, but in setting the agenda for mediation it becomes clear that she would like a chance to talk about some of the psychological aspects of marriage. Wayne had pursued her, surprising her with an engagement ring, and had talked with her mother about setting a date for a wedding sooner than she would have liked. She says she feels rushed. Her father died about a year ago, and she says she has been feeling numb since then.

Wayne's agenda is to do whatever is necessary to persuade Anne to marry him as soon as possible. She wants to talk about where they might live and how many children they might have. Could they live in her family's community? Would she and Wayne join the family for the annual summer vacation on Martha's Vineyard? She and Wayne are of different religions; what religion would any children be brought up in? Wayne says that people work these things out as they come up after they get married. As the mediator, you may suggest that if Anne thinks it's an issue then perhaps it is an issue, and that it wouldn't hurt to talk about it a bit now. You also remind them that although such personal matters are not enforceable by the courts, it is important to give each other a chance to think about what each would really like and what their expectations are for one another.

A discussion of any prenuptial agreement that focused only on money issues would miss what is the most important dispute between this couple. What Anne learned during mediation was that she did not want to get married right now. That was a valuable result of the mediation process. Roger Fisher of the Harvard Negotiation Project notes that a successful negotiation has a good outcome, not necessarily an agreement (Fisher, 1984). Anne learned that she had the option to discuss what was important to her rather than to be bulldozed into marriage or to simply fade. Wayne learned to listen to Anne. If they do marry later, they will have a better chance of resolving future issues that come up between them as a result of mediating over whether or not to get married.

One researcher says that a questionnaire that has been administered to over 30,000 engaged couples across the United

States can predict with 80% accuracy which couples will divorce, separate, or have serious problems and which ones, will do well during the first three years of marriage ("Premarital Test . . . ," 1984). David Olsen of the University of Minnesota says that his premarital inventory, called Prepare, has four factors that seem to be the best predictors of how well a couple will get along:

> *Personality Issues.* Are one or both spouses worried about the other one's drinking or smoking, of being too messy, being jealous, not doing what they say they are going to do, or being too dependent?
>
> *Communication.* Can they share their feelings with their potential spouse? Are they overly sensitive to criticism? Is there too much carping and complaining?
>
> *Conflict Resolution.* Are one or both of them so afraid of conflict that nothing gets resolved? Do they argue too much over minor issues?
>
> *Realistic Expectations.* Do they understand that most couples have issues that have to be resolved during marriage? Do they realize that their future partner can't meet all of their needs?

Agreement on religious values was also effective in predicting whether or not people did well in marriage according to Olsen. His Preparer is a computerized inventory that clergy from a wide variety of denominations had administered to engaged couples. Some religions have either formal or informal prenuptial counseling, sometimes up to forty-five hours ("Marital Caution," 1984). Mediators who are aware of the general areas that predict difficulty in marriage may explore them as part of the agenda with couples in mediation for prenuptial agreement, especially if they appear to be part of a hidden agenda.

Domestic Violence

David and Delia have been sharing custody of seven-year-old Jane since their separation and divorce three years ago. David has been living with Myra for the last two years, and Delia married Norman a year ago. Norman has called you to set up an appointment for mediation at the suggestion of the police officer who asked him to leave the home after three calls by Delia for police assistance. She was frightened when she and Norman exchanged blows while arguing. Delia filed a restraining order keeping Norman from seeing her, returning to their house, or even calling her. Norman called Child Protective Services and said that Delia was neglecting little Jane, leaving her alone for long periods of time and making her stay in her room much of the time whenever her mother was home. Delia is receptive to mediation because she wants Norman to stop threatening her.

In the first session you learn that Norman's agenda is to keep the marriage together; Delia's agenda is to end the marriage with no further contact with Norman. You learn that there have been previous instances of domestic violence in which the police were called. Child Protective Services have had reports filed by Norman before; they have viewed them as spiteful rather than having merit. This time, however, they have investigated more thoroughly in the wake of the repeated witnessing of violence in the home by Jane, and they have filed a neglect petition in juvenile court. In wading through this blizzard of paper you learn that there have been previous restraining orders, and that Delia filed for divorce several months ago and then withdrew her petition. She reports that David, Jane's biological father, had filed for sole custody in the past, but they were able to reach an agreement without going to court after she assured him that she was divorcing Norman and the violence would stop. Delia is worried that she will be designated an unfit mother and her ex-husband will receive custody of Jane.

It is obvious in the first few sessions that both parties are not going to feel like they won in this negotiation. Norman continues to want to remain married no matter what. He is heavily invested in his relationship with Delia. Norman is extremely frustrated and, while he says he does not want to go to jail, continues to contact Delia in violation of the restraining order. Delia has realized from previous restraining orders how little protection they provide. She has changed the locks on the doors of the house and changed her phone number, and is considering moving. However, Norman knows where she works and where Jane goes to school, so it would mean those changes as well if she were to have to avoid him. She is very interested in mediating the breakup of the relationship so she can avoid what she sees as further harassment.

How would you proceed with Delia and Norman? What is best for little Jane? What should be done about the restraining orders and the neglect petition? Should court personnel or Child Protective Services be included in mediation? Can you prevent further violence? Is there a chance Norman might kidnap little Jane from school? If things calm down, should you encourage a continuing contact between Norman and Jane even if the divorce goes forward, and after the divorce?

This hypothetical case illustrates how the police, public social services, and previous family members may all become drawn into a family dispute. There are legal as well as psychological consequences to the various options that might be explored during mediation. Is reconciliation likely? What are the chances that Norman would continue to see little Jane once he was not longer married to her mother? Are the allegations of neglect bogus or real? Neither the police nor the investigator from Child Protective Services is likely to have the time or training to give both Delia and Norman time to tell their stories and to do some specific problem-solving and planning for the future. However, if they can't stop fighting, first the police and then the courts may take action.

Each of the parties has different interests. Delia wants to get Norman out of her life. Norman wants to keep Delia and Jane in his life no matter what. The mediator wants to prevent any future violence. Once again, the goal is a successful outcome rather than necessarily a completed agreement between the parties. If each can learn that they can't control the other but only themselves, that may be educational. If they can see the impact on Jane of screaming and beating upon one another in front of her that may be helpful in preventing it in the future. Norman will learn that he can't make someone live with him. The law does not compel the maintenance of relationships. Delia may learn that simply refusing to talk about ending the relationship, followed by verbal taunting, is infuriating to Norman and evokes the sort of violent reaction that she dreads. By giving Norman a chance to tell his story uninterrupted and asking Delia to talk about what attracted her to Norman, his self-respect may be restored so that he can accept the end of the relationship. In mediation they can each stop calling on the authority of strangers—the police and social service workers—to try to influence the other. Instead they can talk directly to each other and make a plan.

Delia and Norman's written agreement should specify what each of them plans to do to prevent further violence. Focusing on what is best for Jane may give them a common goal. While a leading child psychiatrist has cautioned that no child should ever be deprived of a beloved person (Kornhaber, 1984), this remark was made in the context of advocating the right of grandparents to see their grandchildren. Another prominent child psychiatrist has stated that in his experience stepparents seldom continue contact with the child once that marriage breaks up (Gardner, 1982). Nevertheless, if Delia agrees, Norman might make a commitment to continue seeing Jane. If he comes to realize that such contact is not leading to reconciliation with Delia, he may break off contact with Jane. A plan that provides for access may permit a gradual transition in the disputants' relationship with less chance that Norman will file spurious charges of child neglect in the future or harass Delia. He is also less likely to contact Jane at unauthorized places, such as on the school grounds.

Family violence in the form of wife battering may begin even before marriage and escalate with increasing financial and emotional responsibilities. We will look at spouse abuse, child abuse, and elder abuse. These three areas of family violence are of such concern that a task force has been formed by the Justice Department to study solutions to this problem ("New Task Force . . .," 1983). A number of groups are critical of an attempt to mediate family violence. However, programs have reported success in stopping wife battering. Judith Jackson, director of the Citizens Dispute Settlement Program in the Minneapolis City Attorney's office, says that most of these victims don't want to bring charges against their spouse, they just want the battering to stop. The mediation done in her program has been successful (Profile: Judith Jackson, 1983).

The first objective in the mediation of any conflict involving physical violence is to stop the violence. This is a prerequisite for the initiation of any negotiating and should not be tied to any concession by the abused party. Guidelines for determining the feasibility of mediation appropriate for work with either male or female battered spouses have been suggested by Rodbell (1983). In evaluating such cases three questions need to be answered: "1. How recent, often, and substantial was the violence?" He obviously differentiates between continuing, life-threatening beatings and occasional verbal threats. "2. How accepting is the abuser of the impropriety of the abuse?" If the abuser sees nothing wrong with what has been done or when the abuse is dangerous, mediation would not be indicated. "3. What support is there of both the abuser and the abused outside mediation?" Rodbell might recommend legal advice for the victim, as well as individual counseling for both parties.

Lerman (1982) has suggested that "a good mediator can do more for battered women than a bad prosecutor" (p. 430). She notes that since many courts either refuse to prosecute domestic violence cases or do little once they reach court, law enforcement does not help victims much. She offers the following guidelines:

1. Mediation involving physical abuse should focus primarily on preventing any subsequent abuse.
2. There should be an attempt to balance power between the parties. She suggests that this might be done partly by requiring each spouse to go to individual counseling several weeks before beginning mediation. She then suggests an initial individual meeting with each party. Then, finally, for power balancing, she suggests perhaps there might be an advocate for each party. The battered woman may not be powerful enough and the abuser may be too embarrassed to move toward any problem solving.
3. She suggests that any time couples come in for mediation of any sort, there should be an assessment as to whether abuse has occurred and it should be addressed in mediation even if they haven't brought it up.
4. She suggests that mediation should focus on opportunities for enforcement of negative consequences if there is any future battering, and encourage the victim to move forward with a more formal remedy while mediation is going on, and the mediation should focus on the victim's future safety. She also suggests that the mediator should stay aware of what to do if the agreement is not reached and to identify to the parties, in the event of any agreement, what aspects might be most likely to break down and to build in what is going to happen if there is noncompliance.

Bethel and Singer (1982) suggest that domestic violence cases are as suitable for mediation as other interpersonal disputes. In the mediation program they describe, no case with domestic violence allegations will be mediated if there has been serious harm to the victim, a gun was used, the battering is long-standing repetitive behavior, or the parties seem to be too unequal in power. They also note that the mediation should be timely, directly address any coercive aspects of consequences, and include at least one private caucusing session between the mediator and each party. They find that most of the mediated agreements were being honored at least two months after hearings. Other means for evaluating any domestic violence program would be (1) that there is less chance of any future violence, (2) both parties think the process is fair, and (3) it doesn't cost any more or take any longer than any other remedy available (Bethel and Singer, 1982).

There may be other implications, depending upon whether or not it is a court-based program, a neighborhood justice center offering mediation, or a mediator in private practice. Certainly, the question as to who is the client arises, depending upon the auspices under which mediation is offered. The question that we often return to concerning the ethical dilemma in caucusing emerges here. Mediators may be lay persons with brief training, who may have difficulty understanding and intervening in a family situation that is legally and psychologically complex. There is general recognition that domestic violence sometimes occurs for the first time when a relationship is ending. It is important to recognize and communicate to clients that mediation in such instances is not an attempt to reconcile couples (Orenstein, 1982) but an opportunity to make new plans and goals that will affect their future.

The American Bar Association's Special Committee on Alternative Means of Dispute Resolution assessed 180 programs and found that there was a 60%–70% chance that both parties would show up for mediation in a court or prosecutor-related program and if they did show up there was a 70%–90% chance of an agreement being reached, and that most such agreements contained an agreement to stay away from each other or to end the relationship. Disputants tended to like the process and thought they had a chance to tell their story and most of the cases were handled within one month (Ray, 1982).

Police as Mediators: Social Workers After Six

Is is often pointed out that mediation is supposed to be a voluntary process and that mediation, therefore, may not be indicated for domestic violence. However, one of the common and most dangerous calls police respond to is a family dispute. Kohlberg (1982) reviews statistics that show domestic violence calls are a leading cause of police death. They constitute a large percentage of complaints, especially on night shift. Most of these calls are filed by women.

Palenski (1984) reports on the use of mediation by police in New York and New Jersey. He suggests that ideally this would be an additional problem-solving technique for police who often have to return several times to a disputing family's home to react to what are essentially personal concerns. Palenski points out that the reality is that officers seldom use mediation methods or refer disputants to a mediation program. Such programs are usually not integrated with the police organization. A number of officers were never told what happened after mediation. At least if they file a petition with the court, it is a matter of record and they know they've done their jobs, doing good police work rather than being accused of acting like a counselor or traveling shrink. Traditional notions that police should stay out of family disputes and maintain respect and authority inhibit officers from taking a mediative stance. The one goal of most officers if they do actively intervene is to ask the man to leave the house. This may stop the violence at the time, but seldom solves the ongoing problem.

Palenski suggests that the police must be involved in the early stages of planning mediation programs as well as carrying them out. Whether police refer couples to mediation or do the mediation themselves, their experience with domestic violence situations could be crucial to the success of mediation programs. Police are more aware than most critics of mediation that simply filing a restraining order offers little protection to a victim of domestic violence. In fact, if the alleged perpetrator files a cross-complaint, the police may view the situation as a stand-off and hesitate to intervene.

What do these cases look like? Sometimes the husband

batters whenever he's been drinking and claims later that he doesn't remember or didn't mean to and will never do it again. Sometimes it becomes clear to the mediator that what is going on is the Billy Budd Syndrome—perhaps the wife is more articulate and verbally aggressive and the husband can't respond in kind and so escalates with the advantage of upper body strength. Abuse may occur in a cyclical fashion with instances of abuse and remorse followed by a fairly consistent period of time in which tensions build to the breaking point again. Batterers in this case might benefit from a referral to stress management training. While it is certainly true that most victims do not want to be battered, Evatt and Feld (1983) make the point, in their book about Givers and Takers, that sometimes when Givers serve as a punching bag, they feel needed. Both batterers and victims may find groups composed of and focusing on the issues of each of these roles particularly helpful for long-term behavioral change. Mediation is not the proper place to sort out any such complicated dynamics of an intimate relationship. The physical violence must stop; the verbal violence must stop as well. Court action can be initiated and put on hold as a backup in the event that any agreement reached by the parties is not kept.

Impact on the Children: Screaming Hurts Too

One benefit of involving a mediator may be educating the parents to realize that, although the child may not be the direct victim of the violence and they may seem to be getting along fine, we know that these children have a number of psychological problems, such as depression, separation anxiety, difficulty with handling aggression, and aggressive impulses ("New Study Highlights Needs of Child Witnesses . . .," 1983). These children tend to parent their parents, which robs them of important childhood play and exploration. As adults they may be afraid to grapple with conflicts. They may also grow up to abuse their own children.

Even infants are disturbed by verbal violence (Elias, 1984). Little kids may cry, while older children may try to make it all better. A mediator can help parents who may not be aware how much pain they are causing their children whenever they appear to be out of control while arguing.

Child Abuse and Neglect

The birth of the first child produces the greatest strain on a marriage, adversely affecting marital satisfaction according to a number of studies. The family needs more money. They may not have enough sleep. Physical abuse of children is most frequently done to infants under one year of age, according to national statistics. One pilot program uses attorneys working for little or no pay to mediate between parents and social service agencies to either place foster children back into their homes with protections or to move them forward to live with other permanent guardians (Rios, 1983).

Mayer (1984) reported that "the thrust of national policies and standards about termination of parental rights is to insist that serious parenting deficiencies be decisively proved and at the same time permanency decisions be made in a timely manner so as to insure that children not remain endlessly in temporary homes. These two purposes are often in contradiction with each other" (p. 9). According to Mayer, the Denver Department of Social Services estimated that 80% of claims brought before the court alleging child abuse or neglect could benefit from mediation. He recommended using a trained mediator who is not an employee of either social services or the court. The mediator can be paid by the social services department as a third-party vendor or, perhaps more appropriately, the cost could be shared by the social services agency and the parents.

Mayer also noted that while the techniques used by the mediator would be similar to those applied in other settings, the disputants would include the family, the child protective services worker, and any guardian appointed for the child during litigation or other interested parties. "Not having to evaluate the family, testify in court proceedings, make substantive recommendations, or enforce outcomes" (p. 7) gives the mediator advantages over the usual process of negotiation between the family and the protective services worker. Successful mediation could "forestall court battles and could change the court's focus in many cases from making treatment decisions to reviewing them to insure they comply with legal guidelines" (p. 7). Mayer cautioned that whether or not a child is being abused or neglected is never negotiable, nor is whether the child should be removed from the family home for protection; however, parental involvement is negotiable.

If the mediator can persuade the family to agree to making behavioral changes that would remove concerns about abuse or neglect, they are more likely to carry out the mediated plan. Moreover, child protective service workers would not be confronted with the dilemma of whether to send the child back into a home in which the parents' behavior was problematic or involuntarily to terminate parental rights, an irrevocable step.

Adoption

Sometimes termination of parental rights is the best plan. Mayer (1984) suggested that mediation might help parents to voluntarily terminate their legal relationship with their children and perhaps continue some contact so that they might support the new home that the social services agency finds for their child. The ideal new relationship for such children is often adoption. Mayer has found that birth parents may be helped through mediation to endorse the adoption of their children by a new family.

Adoption consists of two legal steps. First the legal relationship between the birth parents and the child is terminated by court order. Then a new legal relationship is created by the court between the adoptive parents and the child. It may be appropriate under any of the following circumstances to involve an outside mediator in the process of terminating parental rights:

1. The birth parents or potential adoptive parents request it.
2. The birth parents have indicated some awareness that they are unwilling or unable to parent but are uncomfortable with relinquishment.

3. The prospective adoptive parents are open to some contacts with birth parents but are uncomfortable about giving up what they see to be their parental prerogatives.
4. The potential for substantive agreement exists but the level of emotionality or distress between the parties involved is great.
5. An alternative other than adoption (e.g., permanent guardianship) is still under active consideration.
6. A set of adoptive parents have been identified and involved with the child prior to relinquishment procedures. [Mayer, 1984, pp. 14–15]

Mediators can help families and social service workers develop a plan to improve the home situation while the child remains there. They may also help in drafting an agreement on conditions for returning the child to the parents if the child has been removed because of abuse or neglect. Finally, they can assist in the termination of parental rights when adoption is the best plan for the child. Mayer described several cases in which mediators had helped birth parents and social service workers to decide on voluntary termination of parental rights, avoiding the court battle that had been shaping up. The mediator met separately with each party until relatively late in the negotiations. Only after agreement in principle had been reached did the parties meet to work out the details. The mediator also talked with attorneys, guardians *ad litem*, social workers, other family members, and judges.

Parent-Child Disputes

A more normal, or typical, negotiation occurs constantly between parents and children ranging from "Can I stay up just another five minutes?" to "Can I have the car Friday night?" The ongoing family experiencing difficulty in successfully negotiating conflicts is more likely to think of the family therapist than the family mediator now. That may change, however. Active family therapists often work toward specific behavioral contracts between family members and use techniques similar to those used by mediators. Now, however, mediation is most likely to be sought after involvement with problems with school or contact with juvenile or family court.

The Juvenile Court Continuum

All fifty states have juvenile courts. The purpose of the juvenile court is to consider allegations that children under the age of eighteen are dependent, neglected, abused, status offenders in need of supervision, or delinquent. These legal labels form a continuum from the need for outside care, through no fault of either the child or the parents, to allegations of fault of either the parents or some other adult, to assumptions that the child is at fault.

> *Dependent.* A dependent child is not being taken care of well enough, possibly through no fault of the parents. The mother and father may have become physically or mentally ill or do not have enough money.
>
> *Neglected.* Neglect implies that the parents are not doing a good job and it is their fault. They are failing to feed, clothe, or educate the child.
>
> *Abused.* Physical abuse is an act of commission rather than the omission implied under neglect. As we mentioned before, the category of one-year-old is most frequent and almost half of all abuse occurs to children under three years of age. Sexual abuse also occurs among young children, but, of course, occurs among older children as well. The fault lies with the perpetrator of the abuse.
>
> *Status Offender.* Some of those children have been referred to the few parent-child mediation programs around the country. They are generally beyond the control of their parents or guardians, habitually truant, are in violation of a lawful court order, or perhaps using drugs. What makes them status offenders is that if they were older, being beyond the control of their parents or guardians or skipping school would not be a problem. There is a constant battle over whether to treat these children as in need of social services or whether to define them as in violation of law. However, since they are doing things that would not be a problem if they were an adult, they may be considered appropriate for a parent-child mediation.
>
> *Delinquent.* These young people have committed an act that would be a crime were they adults; they violated

a lawful ordinance of some government. They most clearly are blamed for their behavior.

The problem is that professionals who work with young people know that any one child may fit a number of these categories at different ages. It has been suggested that one way to stop family violence is to make available to children who witness such violence proper conflict resolution in the schools. A number of programs run by community boards around the country do have mediation in elementary schools. Status offenders and delinquents are often referred to the court. Davidson (1982) reviews Mahoney's discussion of why status offenders are referred to the court by parents: "Either a signal of (a) an unresolved crisis in the parent-child relationship; (b) an attempt to bring real coercive authority (and the threat of a limitation of freedom) on the child; (c) a device to 'dump' the child (and parental responsibilities) off on the court; or (d) a genuine call for help (based on a misconception of the court's power or resources)" (p. 489). Mahoney interprets research on children in need of supervision as indicating that the court actually causes further difficulties for the family.

While the court may be able to fulfill the first part of the process, adjudication (determining if the allegations in the petition are true and which legal label to affix of the categories we just considered), they have fewer resources to tailor disposition (what, if any, intervention should be ordered and what services are available). So, the child may be given a negative label and either returned to the family with no other change or the family feels powerless because the court orders social services to take over planning for the care of the child wholly or in part.

What is needed is a procedure to help parents and children talk with each other to explore how they might work out their differences to improve the situation and continue to live with one another if possible.

"At the court intake, the child is assigned a lawyer, and, in some cases, so is the parent. Parents may be required to testify against their child" (Children's Aid Society Suggests . . .," 1984). Margaret Shaw, who founded a pioneering mediation project for status offenders, has drafted legislation to mandate mediation for such cases throughout the state of New York.

The Children's Hearings Project

A widely cited model program mediates family issues between parents and children usually involving the various juvenile court categories that we have discussed: abuse, neglect, and being beyond the control of the parents (Wixted, 1982). This Cambridge, Massachusetts, project borrows the Scottish procedure of using trained community volunteers who reflect the community's makeup. Caucuses are held. Another feature is that a panel of two or three trained community volunteers conducts the mediation. A final point is that any agreement reached is written and signed by all parties. Each disputant receives a copy and one is sent to the court if a petition had been filed. Mediators find the private caucus particularly useful in getting teenagers to talk about what's really on their minds. These tend to be one-shot, two- to five-hour mediations; occasionally a second hearing is held.

The use of a case coordinator to prepare the family for mediation and the use of follow-up may blur the distinction between mediation and case management in social services. Certainly, the issues addressed appear to cover most of the concerns of families, ranging from psychological issues to specific concerns about what time children might be expected to be home on the weekend. A case coordinator may subsequently broker the family's use of services, which is different from other forms of mediation. Wixted also reports some benefit to mediation even if the family members don't reach an agreement. The family seems to learn from the process. The abuse, neglect, and status offender cases have all involved children over twelve years old. It may be too difficult to mediate complicated problems with children who have not reached a stage of abstract thought. Another unusual feature of the Children's Hearing Project mediation is that they ask other people who are involved with the family, such as other family members or therapists or teachers, to participate. At times, their process sounds similar to case coordination involving delivery of social services or network therapy.

Another mediation project involving status offenders and their parents found that it was important to have more than one session (Shaw, 1982). One session was needed just to get communication going. Subsequent sessions reached the more difficult problems. These cases were referred from Manhattan Bronx family courts. One pattern that emerged with this program was that Hispanic females were disproportionately referred. This was explained as a cultural tradition that women should be protected, and that if things weren't going well Hispanic parents were more likely to seek the authority of the courts to control their daughters. This brings up again the importance of awareness of the cultural and class context of mediation.

Assessing Cultural Context in Family Mediation

An excellent book entitled *Ethnicity in Family Therapy* by McGoldrick, Pearce, and Giordano assesses how important it is to be aware of the traditions of a particular family.

1. What do they define as a problem?
2. What do they see as a solution to their problem?
3. To whom do they usually turn for help?
4. How have they responded to immigration?
5. What are the typical family patterns of the group?
6. How do they handle life cycle transitions?
7. What may be the difficulties for a therapist [or mediator] of the same background or for a therapist [mediator] of a different background? [P. xv]

It is important to learn to what extent ethnicity is an issue in mediating the particular family before you. Are you missing information because you don't understand this family's values? Are they using "cultural camouflage"—"That's just the way [our people] are"—to avoid working on their particular problem (A Major Challenge: Therapy and Ethnicity [II], 1984)?

Solomon's (1983) work on oppressed minorities of color is useful in developing practice principles for mediating families. While oppressed groups may not share the values of the dominant culture, family members belonging to such groups should not be assumed to believe in the values attributed to that group. The importance of membership in an oppressed group or other ethnic designation should be assessed for each family member.

Both the preferable problem-solving approach and the mediator's expectations may be different for racial minority families than for those from the dominant culture. These families may have unique attitudes about family harmony and consensus, expression of emotion, religion, and human nature. When a family member discusses such attitudes or if I am wondering whether they are relevant to the dispute being mediated, I say, "You know, my family is mostly Irish. I don't know much about your people. Can you explain to me how the point you just made affects our reaching an agreement here?" If I suspect cultural camouflage after they respond I may simply repeat their contention. "You mean *all* women in your family *always* give in to *all* the men in your family?" Or, "You're saying that *everyone* in your ethnic group is *always* late and that's why you can't keep to the visitation agreement?" Explicitly labeling such contentions sometimes moves the mediation process forward. If there are family values that affect the problem we are working on, then specific behavioral changes can be incorporated into the mediation agreement in such a way that the disputants believe they can carry them out.

Conflict between different generations of a family may reflect ethnic and cultural issues and "should be examined in light of those conflicts that are normal and those that come out of people born at different points in time yet are within the same ethnic groups. . . . [W]e help clients see that one person is not right and one is not wrong. There are just differences. It's being a mediator, to help people understand values and then help them find the compromises they can handle" ("A Major Change: Therapy and Ethnicity [II], 1984, p. 4). Joseph Giordano's comments about the role of family therapists seeking to be sensitive to cultural causes of conflicts apply to family mediators as well. He cites intermarriage as another issue that can provide families with a wide range of coping behaviors if they deal successfully with the racial and cultural implications.

One traditional counterpart to family mediation is the Hawaiian ho'oponopono, the setting to right and restoration of maintenance of good relationships among the members through a family conference that involves discussion, mediation, arbitration, prayer, fasting, mutual restitution, and forgiveness (Pukui, Haertig, and Lee, 1980). Children participate in this conference, giving them an idea of how to act when they grow up. This is how the children learn that adults have troubles too and how they resolve conflicts and do better in the future. Other families may have particular traditions or procedures that may be important for the mediator to learn about.

Acknowledging the Power of Adolescents

One of the benefits of mediation between parents and children, especially as the child reaches adolescence, is an awareness that the child has increasing power. Some parents are frustrated that they can no longer simply put their children in their rooms or physically move them about as they could when they were smaller. Even if they have relied on such strong-arm methods, they may be at a loss when confronted with a teenager. If they can still physically dominate them, they no longer can control where the child goes.

I once worked at a residential children's center that had 250 kids between the ages of three and eighteen. The most frequent age was fifteen. Staff who learned early on to adopt a mediative stance did well. Specific orders to adolescent kids were often openly or passively defied. By definition, these children were living at this home because their parents had not done a good job of taking care of them no matter whose fault it was. Listening to their side of the story, acknowledging what they felt was valid, working on specific agreements based on objective criteria, writing them down, and developing consequences made a great deal of sense to them. These children were willing to run away repeatedly, get up on the roof and jump off if threatened, cut themselves with shards of glass bad enough to require hospitalization, and take drugs requiring their stomachs to be pumped, often just to get someone to take them seriously.

Dating points up the shifting balance of power between parents and children. The parents cannot physically restrain teenage children to prevent their going out with youngsters undesirable from the parents' point of view. Moreover, whatever techniques the parents do use successfully may backfire.

Consider the problems faced by sixteen-year-old Beth and her mother. Beth wants to leave school and live with Victor, whom Beth's mother disdains. The mother wants Beth to stay in school, but she cannot force her to attend and even if she could, Beth cannot be made to study. The mediator might help Beth and her mother begin to talk by having them look at photographs of Beth as a young child; this approach can remind the disputants of happier times, when both felt more certain about their roles and the issue of control was simpler. In addition, this experience may reawaken their feelings of mutual love, allowing them to negotiate their present conflict successfully.

Beth Gets Pregnant

The U.S. Supreme Court has said that any minor sufficiently mature to become pregnant has the right to decide whether or not to have the child or seek an abortion; parents do not have a say (*Belotti v. Baird*, 96 S. Ct. 2857, 1976). What does Beth really want? What does Victor want? What influence can Beth's mother have in this situation? Mediation is a good forum for helping these folks to work out a positive plan in the context of the law concerning teenage pregnancy, the rights of unwed fathers, partial and total emancipation, and services available. The mediator can help Beth, the child's father, and Beth's mother decide what each really wants in terms of what is possible. Meeting separately with the disputants may give the mediator an opportunity to help them talk about their worst fears, and the solution that most appeals to them. Realistic solutions can then be explored in joint problem-solving sessions. Mediating when pregnancy is the issue definitely has a deadline.

Remarried Families

Remarried persons may treat a new spouse according to assumptions formed in previous relationships. They may also be paying child and/or spousal support and sharing custody of any children. The remarried family tends to move through four stages, taking at least four years to do so ("Stepfamilies," 1983).

Fantasy. At first, both adults think that since they have found the right mate, this marriage will be successful. New stepparents may think that either the children will not be a problem, because they will not be involved significantly in the new relationship, or that they will be living exclusively in the new family, without any interference or entanglements from their other biological parent. Children may like the new person but be worried about what's going to happen with their other parent. They may feel disloyal. They may resent having to share their parent with another adult if they had them all to themselves before.

Pretending. When reality begins to intrude upon it, the remarried family will at first tend to ignore any indications that its fantasies are not entirely accurate. In both the fantasy phase and the pretending phase, families will seldom seek outside help.

Panic. About two years after the marriage, the spouses begin to confront what they really need. As Judy Osborn says, "Many adults are desperate to make a second partnership work and they're desperately afraid to get into conflicts again. Another broken relationship will bring further loss to adults and children. Conflict means divorce to many" ("Stepfamily," 1983, p. 3). She suggests that this is the point when issues that were disregarded during the fantasy phase are consciously confronted. "Perhaps I don't want to rescue any child. Maybe I don't like her children. Maybe the ex-spouse was right to leave" (p. 3). This may be when family mediation is sought.

Conflict Resolution. Osborn suggested that the issues in conflict must be identified before they can be considered in terms of both the fantasies the family has been working under as well as what they feel they individually need. Only then can they move on to accept their losses and gains.

What are the issues that need to be worked on? *Marriage and Divorce Today* newsletter did a survey of their subscribers to find out what problems their remarried clients were seeking to resolve ("What Problems . . .," 1983). These family therapists saw remarried families as trying to strengthen relationships with one another, working out what the stepparent relationship would be like, trying to realistically appraise the new spouse as well as working out the acceptable relationships with the new extended family. Helping them to work together in dealing with children was considered to be a major issue. These families appeared to be working on both how to find time for each other and how to allow more space for each family member. Learning how to resolve conflicts was a major issue for a number of these families. Money problems were often mentioned. After the two years of feeling safe enough to take on some of these issues, it takes two more years to accumulate enough shared history for members to trust the new family.

Stepmothers

A Sunday *New York Times* editorial (1983) captures the problem. On the occasion of Mother's Day, they note that there are no greeting cards for stepmothers, although there are lots of women attempting to make this role work. Stepmothers are the villains in fairy tales, and there is no good term for the second or subsequent marriage whether it's called a stepfamily, blended family, reconstituted or meta-family. In fact, the better the stepmother is at nurturing, the more she may be resented by the children and their biological mother for evoking feelings of disloyalty. Constantly being asked to do the work of raising children without receiving the credit may tempt stepmothers to start acting like their counterpart in Hansel and Gretel. If her best efforts at mothering don't result in the children essentially feeling committed to her in the new family, the stepmother may consider putting pressure on her husband to move away from these children psychologically, economically, or geographically and focus on her and on any children of their current relationship.

Stepfathers

Men traditionally have a greater age range to choose from in selecting a new mate. They may try to avoid picking a woman who has children because of the financial and emotional entanglements. They are less likely than women to have children living with them and more apt to be able to start anew by taking a younger woman who has never been married or, at least, has no children.

Some stepfathers who have never been married or had children may seek a woman with children because they are looking for both a sexual partner and a mother, according to Martin Cohen (1982). These men may have avoided making a commitment to a relationship up until now.

This set of needs may trigger Oedipal conflicts. The step-father may compare himself to his wife's ex-husband both in terms of sexual prowess and who the children really consider as their father. Such a stepfather may try to get his wife not to have contact with her ex-husband, which hampers any sharing of custody or even traditional visitation. Another problem of having a ready-made family is that the stepfather and step-mother never have time of at least a period of a year or so totally alone, so the stepfather may come to resent the time his wife must spend with her children. Cohen also suggests in his therapy work with stepfathers that they often want to have a child of their own in order to be a real father, while the wife may already have had as many children as she wants. Two common conflicts that these families bring to mediation are: "I'm her husband now, she should have nothing to do with her ex-spouse," or "I want us to have our own children." If the family does have their own biological children, the number of potential conflicts multiply with the possibility of his, hers, and our children. Some of these children may not live with the family all the time.

Ahrons (1984) pointed out that it is most realistic to think of ex-spouses as kin after divorce because families are expanded, rather than replaced, when parents remarry. The issue is complicated because there are no generally understood names for the current partners of former spouses. Ahrons' research suggests that remarriage may be even more distressing than divorce for the children. Her findings also reveal that fathers and stepfathers do not care much if they get along with each other, but mothers and stepmothers do, perhaps because the women are more involved in caring for the children. Although major family events such as graduations, weddings, and funerals may be awkward for all members of remarried families, the guests usually manage to get along with each other.

Ahrons also noted that children often lose access to their paternal grandparents after the divorce and remarriage of their parents. This development deprives the children of what Kornhaber (1984) called an emotional sanctuary, as well as a sense of past, present, and future. According to Kornhaber, grandparents and grandchildren get along because "they have the same enemies." Kornhaber suggested that grandparents having difficulty staying in touch with their grandchildren after a divorce try mediation. While grandparents can sue for visitation in forty-nine states and a law establishing this right is under consideration by Congress, unless the family members involved work out an agreement that is satisfactory to them, access may be effectively denied.

Old People and the Family Life Cycle

Two other issues come up for most old people that require negotiation with their families. What are they going to do about a will and estate planning? Where are they going to live and with whom? As parents get older, they may begin thinking about who they would like to leave their belongings to. Dr. Sheila Akabas, who directs the Columbia University School of Social Work Industrial Social Welfare Center, found that, in a study of prepaid legal services, even poor people were very worried about whom they were going to leave possessions to (1982). In the novel *Old Money*, Lacey Fosburgh tells the story of the anguish of deciding whether or not to contest a father's will. Mediation would be especially useful whenever older people have been married several times and have grown children from more than one of these relationships because they could then be peaceful in their old age and avoid further battling by their children and spouses after they're dead.

Where to Live

The first issue may come up in a situation such as Vroom, Fassett, and Wakefield (1981) describe. The husband may be a bit older than his wife and ready to retire and move to someplace in the sunbelt. His wife may have just resumed her career and not want to move. A mediator may help to work this out between them. Another problem many of us may face will be where our elderly parents will live if they begin having trouble taking care of themselves. Since people live longer now, the frail elderly may develop a number of chronic diseases, and it may take tremendous physical energy to take care of them. Their children may have teenage children of their own and have conflicting demands on their time and money. What happens if grandpa dies of a heart attack and grandma has trouble taking care of herself? Should she be institutionalized? Should she come to live with her children? If so, which child? Is one permanent home preferable or should the parent rotate between the children? Mediation can provide a forum for family members to say honestly what they want rather than leave such a painful subject to default and risk hard feelings all around. Resolution is particularly useful for the middle-aged children because usually our parents die before us and our children live on after us, but the family members we know longest in our lives are our brothers and sisters (Bank and Kahn, 1982).

Elder Abuse

Like abused wives and children, older people who are abused by their families are relatively powerless. Abuse also may involve a neighborhood dispute, fear of being threatened by younger people in the street, or fear of having their Social Security check stolen as they come from the mailbox or go to the bank. Similarly, older people may be bullied by bill collectors or others taking advantage of their age. Such psychological abuse can be as debilitating as physical violence. Court-connected or private mediation may provide old people with a chance to tell their story to a greater extent than any court appearance or arbitration proceeding would permit.

Conclusion

Mediators who work with families throughout the life cycle will find many of the family therapy techniques described earlier in this book helpful. This chapter reviewed the legal context and consequences of family disputes. Families usually know their own needs best. If they can be helped to talk about what they need and what is possible, then the conflicts they face can be resolved more effectively than by instituting court action or ignoring the situation.

CHAPTER 6

Mediation Between Neighbors or Unmarried Cohabitants

Mediating Personal Relationships

SOME OF THE PEOPLE we spend most of our waking hours with and who know us best would not be traditionally considered to be part of our family. An exclusive relationship with a lover in which details of each person's day are eagerly shared comes to mind. Even if these lovers decide to live together, they are not yet considered family by tradition or by law. Once folks who like one another get to a certain stage, they begin to search for a word that describes the nature of their relationship to the other person. They may borrow the Census Bureau's acronym POSSLQU-persons of the opposite sex sharing living quarters. In a foreshadowing of any difficulties in working out any differences that may come up in the future, they may introduce the other person as their Marvin or say that what they are doing by living together is Marvinizing, after the court case involving an unwed couple. They may call their counterparts spice, rather than spouse. The term "partner" may leave the impression of a business arrangement only.

Mate has a good sound; it may not be the first mate, but it certainly conveys a sense of bonding.

What these relationships share are less perceived commitment and permanence by both the people involved and by society. They also lack a legal structure in which to resolve the inevitable differences that come up. Family mediation can be especially useful in such situations.

Why Don't They Just Get Married?

There seem to be three major reasons why two million couples in the United States just live together rather than get married. The first is that they may prefer cohabitation rather than marriage for their own reasons related to values, a previously bad experience with marriage, or that they don't intend to have children together. The second reason is that they may simply drift into it and find they like spending time together. Gradually, one person gives up his or her own place to live.

However, the most frequent reason for living together is that it is a way to try out marriage. Living together may also reflect a compromise in which one person wants more of a commitment than the other and will settle for cohabitation rather than marriage. Maybe the man is happy with things the way they are, while the woman is more eager to be able to announce to family and friends that they are getting married. She may be nearing the end of her prime reproductive years, so if she wants children in the present relationship, or any children at all, she may feel pressure. Or it may be the other way around, in which she has been through a marriage and has no desire to leave herself vulnerable to the pain of a divorce again. She wants to avoid too much psychological or economic dependency and prides herself on self-sufficiency in these areas.

How About a Contract?

Warner and Ihara (1983) wrote a living together kit that offers both legal information for nonmarried cohabitants and specific forms for completing an agreement. The couple may want to consider what they are going to do about income, generally choosing to keep separate checking and savings accounts. Similarly, what are they going to do about property? This all gets very sticky once life goes on for a while and people buy a stereo or bring home a pup together. There is a tendency for money issues to get all entangled.

Children of such couples may have uncertain legal status. One of the best things an unwed father can do is to acknowledge paternity by filing a form with the county clerk. This would help both parents have access to the child if they split up later as well as helping the child to receive Social Security survivorship benefits if the father is killed.

Writing a will is important for unmarried couples. They may have spent many years together and intend to leave their possessions to each other. However, since their relationship is not legally recognized, their property will generally go to blood relatives, as specified by state law.

What About the Children?

Parents who start living with someone new may need to negotiate how to balance their relationships with their mate and with their own and each other's children. Couples also may need help planning how they are going to take care of the children and to pay for their care and support.

Both adults and children may get messages from other family members and from neighbors that marriage is more desirable than cohabitation. If adults cannot come up with a name for their new relationship, think how difficult it is for children to explain to a teacher or friend what to call the new person. Children can learn from seeing adults cautiously build a relationship and sometimes move away from a commitment they have made. While children cannot get too much love, and love from different sources is welcome, it may be difficult for children to meet someone who apparently is going to be in their life permanently and then to lose that individual not too long afterward because the relationship between the adults did not go well. Mediation may help such couples to either stay together or preserve contact with the children.

The Law of Living Together

Are We Married?

One of the common myths is that people who live together for a certain period become common law spouses. However, only Colorado, Alabama, the District of Columbia, Georgia, Idaho, Iowa, Kansas, Montana, Ohio, Oklahoma, Pennsylvania, Rhode Island, South Carolina, and Texas continue to recognize common law marriages. If a common law couple from one of these states moves to a state that does not recognize such marriages, they would still be married.

Problems of proof exist in either case, which may result in the loss of Social Security payments, pension benefits, or inheritance from a mate who dies intestate. If you are not married, what happens when you turn to the courts with a property dispute involving your partner? Some states follow the reasoning of the *Marvin* case: unwed cohabitants may attempt to prove the existence of an oral or implied contract to share property. Other states require a valid marriage certificate in order to consider such a claim, otherwise they recognize no such right.

The Case for Contract

Weitzman (1981) noted that marriage

> has not changed from a relationship based on status—its rights and obligations flow from one's position—to a contractual relationship in which rights and obligations are freely negotiated by the parties. Rather, marriage has moved from a status to a status-contract. That is, while the individuals who entered marriage have the same freedom of choice that governs entry into other contractual relations, once they make the decision to enter the contract, the analogy fails because the terms and conditions of the relationship are dictated by the state. The result is that marital partners have lost the traditional privileges of status and, at the same time, have been deprived of the freedom that the contract provides. [P. xix]

Legal scholars have suggested that the distinction between marriage and cohabitation is becoming blurred. According to Weitzman (1981), most people would do better to negotiate a contract with their future mate than either to get married or to live together without such a contract. Her book is useful for family mediators because it considers real situations in which people choose to live together. She also provides sample contracts for both married and unwed couples.

If It Looks Like a Duck

Without a contract, unmarried cohabitants have difficulty sorting out their disputes in court. Nevertheless, even a state that does not recognize common law marriage may recognize an interest in property in unwed partners whose relationship resembles a marriage (*In re Marriage of Cary*, 34 Cal. App. 3d 345 [1973]). People who live together a long time, say that they are husband and wife, use the same last name, hold property listed as husband and wife, or file joint tax returns are acting as though they are married. Three years after *Cary*, the California Supreme Court held in *Marvin v. Marvin* (18 Cal. 3d 660, 557, P.2d 106, 134 Cal. Rptr. 815 [1976]) that property would not be divided 50–50 as a matter of law, but courts still have discretion to award property to unwed cohabitants where the relationship resembles that of a married couple.

Marvinizing

The California Supreme Court held in a widely discussed case that express oral agreements or implied agreements to share property are enforceable unless such an arrangement was made in consideration of sexual services (*Marvin v. Marvin*, 18 C. 3d, 660 [1977]). When this case was subsequently tried, it was found that the two disputants had not entered into an agreement to share property. An attempt by the trial court to grant the petitioner $104,000 to rehabilitate her so that she could be employed was held by a court of appeal to be improper because she had not asked for such rehabilitation (*Marvin v. Marvin*, 122 C.A. 3d, 871 [1981]).

A number of commentators have suggested that the California Supreme Court holding under *Marvin*, that unwed cohabitants may seek to prove their case in court, might actually extend the power married people have over their private affairs by honoring any such contracts and allowing people who either choose not to get married or cannot legally be married to make legally enforceable agreements between themselves as well. One attempt by a gay man to attempt to claim one-half of the estate of his lover based on an alleged oral agreement failed because he himself said that the arrangement was in part based on sexual services, which is explicitly barred under the *Marvin* case (*Jones v. Daly*, 122 C.A. 3d, 500 [1981]). While a sexual relationship is assumed to be part of marriage, homosexual couples cannot be legally married anywhere in the United States.

Same-sex couples and heterosexual partners who are not married simply do not have the same rights as spouses. Adams and Sevitch (1984) summarized a number of the differences. A Marvinizer cannot sue if his or her partner is killed and it is clearly somebody's fault, while a spouse can recover under a wrongful death statute. Marvinizers may have difficulty collecting worker's compensation and other benefits because of difficulty of proof that the relationship existed.

Children

It may be more difficult for an unwed mother to collect spousal and child support than if the parents were legally married. Unwed fathers have fewer rights of access to their children than do married fathers. Under California law, only a father who is either married to the child's mother or has acknowledged the child as his has the right to consent to an adoption (CCC Section 7017[b]). The U.S. Supreme Court has held that an unwed father who cannot demonstrate a relationship with his child may not bar adoption by a subsequent stepfather (*Lehr v. Robertson*, 103 Supreme Court 2985, 1983) even if the father has tried to visit, offered to support the child, and initiated a paternity suit.

The lack of legal structure that would enable parties who have a personal relationship but are not married to predict what the court would do to resolve any disputes makes mediation appropriate. Weitzman has noted that law is too traditional to reflect the realities of most marriages. The law simply does not take into account or handle well the complexities of personal relationships in which the parties are not married. Yet these couples may also own property together, contribute to each other's economic as well as psychological well-being by pooling income, and they may very well have children together.

Radical Psychiatry's Approach

A number of couples who have either chosen not to get married or who are legally barred from marrying have sought mediation. Mediators who describe themselves as radical therapists have mediated couples whose philosophy led them to avoid the courts. The mediation techniques used in this context are different from those described previously, and the disputants typically share values to allow such a directive and intimate approach.

Jenkins and Steiner (1980) describe the radical psychiatry approach in mediation. They tell disputants that they will be working toward an agreement with (1) no lies or secrets (distorted or withheld information), (2) no rescues (doing more than your share, or something you don't want to do), and (3) no power plays (any action intended to get people to do things against their will) (p. 5). In deciding whether to mediate, Jenkins and Steiner try to make sure that everyone involved wants to participate; consequently, they do not contact people but wait for all parties involved to get in touch with them. They also want to make sure that everyone involved in the dispute will be at the mediation. This may be hard to determine if the dispute involves more than a couple, say, a number of people living together in a house or an entire family. They also clarify that all the people involved have accepted the fact that the mediator will determine the procedure. Radical psychiatry's mediation is an active process in which mediators offer a number of opinions; however, they make clear when discussing the possibility of mediation that they are not arbitrators, no disputant is bound by their opinions, and any participant can leave the mediation at any point.

Homework

Goals. Before the first mediation session, each disputant is asked to write down the goals she would like to accomplish during mediation.

Held Feelings. The mediator also asks the disputants to write down anything that has been bothering them but that they have not expressed to the person with whom they are in conflict. Participants are asked to complete this sentence: "When you _____, I feel _____."

Demands. The third homework assignment is to write down things the disputants must have in order to continue in the relationship. Jenkins and Steiner (1980) might ask people who know about their work to include any "paranoid fantasies (a current fear about what another is feeling or doing that is a secret or, at least, not obvious) and rescues (things clients have done or said they want to do or say)" (p. 9). However, most of the time Jenkins and Steiner explain paranoid fantasies and rescues at the session. The final aspect of setting up the mediation is arranging for payment. This approach is radical, but not *that* radical.

The Session

CHECKING IN

After making sure that everyone is settled into a seat, the mediator asks each person how he is feeling. This is a good time to illustrate Jenkins and Steiner's (1980) notion of paranoid fantasies by responding to any fears of bias—"I'm afraid you'll take my mate's side because men always stick together." Since the radical psychiatry approach to paranoia includes heightened awareness, Jenkins and Steiner suggest that there may be a bit of truth to all such fears and that the mediator should respond honestly to participants' concerns. Disputants are asked to point out whenever they feel the mediator is acting biased. Once all the participants have had the chance to talk about what they are concerned about and what their feelings are at the moment, the mediator asks if everyone is ready to deal with the dispute.

CLEARING THE BOARDS

The mediator then helps the disputants exchange their held feelings, paranoias, and rescues. The mediator uses three techniques—asking, taking turns, and avoiding rescues—to elicit this information; parties can apply these techniques themselves when solving conflicts that arise in the future.

Asking. Each disputant is asked to preface any comment with this question: "I have a held feeling [paranoia, or rescue]; do you want to hear it?" If disputants have gone to the trouble to engage in mediation, they are likely to say yes. Sometimes it is necessary to defer a particular discussion until the other disputants are ready to listen and respond. This is a valuable lesson that participants can learn to apply outside the mediation sessions.

Taking Turns. The mediator makes sure that each party gets a chance to talk before someone who has already spoken speaks again. Since much of what is said tends to be unpleasant and may make the listeners angry, they may begin to lash out in response. The mediator must control the session and make sure each party feels protected and certain that he will get a chance to speak without interruption. The mediator may attempt to keep people responding to the subject at hand rather than allow them to bring up a new topic. Mediators also try to use the paranoid fantasy concept to separate how people feel from their worries about what they think the behavior that hurts them means. "When you come home late I think it means you don't want to be with me." The mediator may encourage the person hearing this worry to think about whether there might be some truth to the other person's perception.

Rescues. Rescues are useful to bring out into the open when the mediator is trying to balance disputants' power. Since rescuing means disregarding both parties' feelings and rights, both the rescuer and the person being rescued feel resentful.

MEDIATOR ANALYSIS

In the radical psychiatry model, the mediator suggests what seems to be the major issues and recommends aspects of the agreement that disputants might reach. Disputants are asked whether they agree with the mediator's analysis of the situation and how they might negotiate any general agreement that the mediator is proposing.

DURATION

Radical psychiatry mediation usually is limited to one session that lasts between two and six hours. Jenkins and Steiner suggest that the mediator avoid any temptation to try to make everything better. They recommend letting the people in conflict do more work themselves in the immediate future. The mediator may schedule a future session in a few months to assess how things are going.

STROKES

At the end of a radical psychiatry mediation session, time is set aside for the disputants to pay compliments to one another. It is advisable to let participants know before mediation begins that the session will end this way in order to assure them that their emotional well-being will be preserved. The mediator might begin this final process by paying compliments to a couple for how hard they have worked and for the information they have shared. However, Jenkins and Steiner recommend that it is best for the mediator to wait to do this until other people have been exchanging such strokes. They also suggest that it is important for the mediator to get some strokes, although they are not specific about how to elicit them other than by doing a good job.

The radical psychiatry mediation model appeals to people who seek consensus decisionmaking. However, even members of groups philosophically committed to a nonadversarial approach may resort to the courts in trying to work out disputes. One such group, despite the best efforts of many of the members, ended up changing the locks and filing suits and countersuits in court while communicating with each other by notes on the door of the first largest and longest running women's bookstore in the country (Moore, 1982). One such note read: "This collective is not a collective, it is a collection of women completely at odds with each other to the extent that the meetings are emotionally battering; there is hardly any time to actually think about the bookstore; and no one in the collective is getting what she needs" (p. 3). This was responded to by a note from the other group: "How does the majority of a collective get locked out?" (p. 3). "[A]s each of us came into the collective we were told that . . . legal ownership . . . was 'held in trust' for the group as a 'legal fiction' because the laws did not recognize a collective structure" (p. 3). Despite the lock change and exchange of lawsuits in the county court "both parties have also expressed desire for mediation and arbitration outside the judicial system" (p. 3). Subsequently, a judge issued a temporary restraining order providing for an impartial manager to supervise all seven women involved in the dispute.

Two points are important about this story. The first is that it is difficult for a true collective to operate by law because the requirement that any incorporation papers filed with the state by a nonprofit organization name officers makes some members of the group more equal than others. Second, mediation must be sought by all the parties involved, while court action can be initiated by anyone involved in the conflict. Mediation has a better chance before disputants start down adversarial avenues.

Consensus Decisionmaking

A number of organizations have attempted to reach a consensus on all important decisions. They pay attention to the process by which a number of alternatives are generated and considered. The pure form of this model permits one person to forestall a decision, even if all others in the group are agreed. A mediator may be asked to chair such a meeting in order to insure that the procedures endorsed by the group are followed. Consensus decisionmaking requires time and an agreement on basic principles. Modified models exist in which consensus is tried first and, if such total agreement cannot be reached, then a two-thirds majority of the group can make a decision.

A student of mine who is an advocate of consensus decisionmaking noted that there are difficulties if the rules are not clear to all members or if there are severe time limits (Bundy, 1982). The results show that any mediator attempting to work with a group that has chosen consensus decisionmaking must be alert to attempts by a powerful member to bulldoze others either in the mediation sessions or elsewhere. Bundy notes that, as much as he likes the process, people are often unable to understand it, are often initially confused by it or don't have the time to devote to it, so only relatively well-off people who have lots of time and interest in paying attention to relationships may actually use this method. Still, any process that keeps people talking directly seems preferable to changing the locks on the door and communicating by note while filing court documents against one another, especially if the people involved are committed to similar goals and their interaction is a large and meaningful part of their lives.

Community Boards Models

There are a number of community conflict resolution programs around the country. They reflect their neighborhoods in both the people and issues involved. From New Haven, Connecticut, to Minneapolis, Minnesota, to Honolulu, Hawaii, these programs are developing their communities. Mediation is the major technique used.

Community Boards of San Francisco

We will take an extensive look at the pioneering program started by Ray Shonholtz in 1976. Starting in one neighborhood, Community Boards has now branched out to cover about a third of San Francisco and these ideas have been adapted in seven other cities and by two Indian tribes. His model evolved from an alternative neighborhood criminal justice program to a variety of roles undertaken by community volunteers who address issues that includes conflicts familiar to family mediators. While community boards programs do get a number of complaints about barking dogs and blocked driveways, they also help to resolve a number of issues between family members, roommates, and lovers.

Shonholtz (1984) believes that the neighborhood should be the primary conflict-resolution forum while the alternative should be the legal system. He is attempting to develop neighborhoods by creating a sense of responsibility for community members to work out conflicts themselves rather than abdicating to the legal system and its representatives, judges and lawyers.

Outreach workers let the community know about the program, how it works, and how they might both use it to
solve their own conflicts and to help solve their neighbor's disputes.

Case developers go see the person who called with the
complaints and then all other persons involved in the
dispute, trying to determine what the issues are. They
then select panelists who are trained community volunteers equipped to help settle the conflict.

Panelists are three to five trained members of the community who hear the disputants. Initially, this was the only
role played by community volunteers, but, subsequently, the San Francisco model has expanded so that
community members hold all roles.

Follow-up workers check to see how any agreement
reached is working. Since the emphasis is on the voluntary compliance of the agreement rather than legal enforceability, consumer satisfaction is the primary index
by which the follow-up worker judges the effectiveness
of the process.

The Hearing Process

The panelists, who have been roughly matched for age, race,
and sex with the disputants, meet with the case developers to
get an idea of the problem. Then each person in the dispute
gets a chance to tell his or her story. They are encouraged to
say whatever they think is important to the issues, without
initial concern for narrowing the focus.

Next, each person in the dispute is asked to tell the other
what brought them there that evening. Panelists help the disputants hear each other's concerns by repeating, clarifying,
and validating the statements made by each participant. The
next question each disputant is asked is, "What could you do
to avoid being here?" Asking each disputant to consider their
individual responsibility for the problem prepares them for
helping to solve the conflict.

Shonholtz (1984) says that disputants are then asked,
"How do you want the world to look tomorrow?" This emphasis on positive behavior helps the disputants work toward an
agreement. Any such agreement is written up and signed by

all parties, who each receive a copy. The community boards hearing is then over. The process is free and available for almost any dispute that's not currently in the courts. The hearings are generally conducted as open meetings and limited to a single evening. The San Francisco Community Boards program takes no diversion referrals. They feel strongly that court-connected conflict-resolution programs are coercive and actually increase the number of court cases that are opened.

Getting to the Real Issues

Shonholtz says that the formal justice system disregards differences in language or cultural values that may be the real reasons for disputes or misunderstandings. Community Boards explicitly builds respect for differences among neighborhood members. In San Francisco, the predominantly gay Castro district has been expanding into the primarily Latin Mission district. When I was consulting at Legal Services for Children, they had several cases referred where teenage Latin women had simply walked up and bashed strangers who they thought were gay. A number of conflicts between the Latin and gay communities have been referred to Community Boards. "If the conflict involves Latin youth and gay community members, it is important that the case worker encourages and the panelists explore the fullest expression of cultural differences and attitudes. Might not the youth's behavior mirror deeper family and cultural teachings? Isn't the parents' attitudes about the changing neighborhood and gay behavior relevant to the actions of the youth? And what are gay and Latin attitudes about one another? While difficult, case and panel workers are urged to make these deeper probes. No lasting resolution is possible if hard issues remain unexpressed" (Shonholtz, 1984, p. 21).

Conflict Resolution in the Schools

The San Francisco Community Boards program has begun training young people from kindergarten through high school to use their conflict-resolution process. In one school, teams of children, who wore T-shirts that read "Conflict Manager," were available at lunch and during breaks to help other children settle disputes. Teachers found that the level of squabbling and violence decreased considerably.

More Violent Disputes Referred

Neighbors usually know about family violence. Instead of letting it continue and build until something tragic happens, increasingly such situations are being referred to Community Boards in San Francisco. Disputants are sometimes roommates, others are family members or neighbors. Once again, the positive influence of having this sort of situation worked out by the people involved with the help of three to five neighbors may produce a more lasting solution than simply ignoring the problem or seeking help through the courts. Community members may be influential in preventing future outbreaks of such violence.

Community Boards staff report that a number of family therapy and family law professionals who sign up for the training to assume one of the roles in the process are usually interested because they would like to practice mediation privately. However, there is a great need for family mediators to help to develop their community as a neighbor. Community Boards participation might be best viewed as complementary to the professional practice of family mediation. Shonholtz points out that community boards staffs only have twenty-seven hours of training. Their strength comes from the fact that they live in the neighborhoods where they are mediating. They range in age from fourteen to seventy and have the other demographic characteristics of their community. Shonholtz notes that the strength of the community boards model is that it demonstrates that conflicts can be resolved through mediation even if neighbors have very different values, despite Auerbach's (1983) view to the contrary.

Conclusion

While an experienced family mediator may be a very good community boards member, such specialized expertise may not be necessary to help roommates work out which one is going to move out and how to get the security deposit back, or what a neighbor should do about a tree that is on one side of the fence and hangs over the property next door. The family mediator who participates in community conflict resolution comes to know the neighborhood and makes it a better place to live. Doing a good job as a trained volunteer may also lead to referrals for more complex disputes that require the expertise of the family mediator.

CHAPTER 7

Business and Professional Applications of Family Mediation

Two MEMBERS of your local mediation council have asked you to mediate a dispute between them. They are business partners who founded the Family Mediation Group. The business has done well; the practice is about one-third mediation of families in conflict; one-third supervision of beginning mediators; and, the most lucrative third, contracts with state and local government to train child and adult protective service workers in mediation. The problem is that one partner has just had a baby and wants to spend more time with her family, while the other partner would like to expand the business and hire associates. Their differences seem irreconcilable to them and they have agreed to dissolve the partnership. However, they both think that the name of their business, the Family Mediation Group, is a major asset and each wants to keep the name.

You applaud their acknowledgment that even mediators have disputes that need third-party help to untangle. Conflicts between individual mediators and even mediation groups have too often been seen as a sign either that this approach does not work or that people choose to offer the services they themselves need most. Either view ignores the positive, as well as inevitable, aspects of conflict.

This morning you are concerned about the specific assistance you might offer. A name does not seem easily divisible or subject to split-the-difference concepts of justice. You have also heard through

169

the grapevine that these two partners are acting suspiciously like feuding family members precisely because they have been so close while building their business together. If they cannot settle this difficulty privately, their practice will suffer and so will the reputation of mediation in the community. You know that even though these two disputants are experienced mediators and understand the process, your job will not be easy. It is the similarity of the relationship between business partners to that between family members that makes such disputes so hard to resolve.

This chapter explores family mediation that goes beyond purely personal conflicts to business, professional, and other disputes. Some of the conflicts considered are a natural extension of family difficulties. Fights between parents and children over a family-owned business is one example. The chapter also discusses mediation of family disputes in new settings, such as employee assistance programs sponsored by corporations. A major theme of this chapter is that the expertise of the family mediator can be applied to conflicts within organizations—agencies, small businesses, and larger companies—as well as to disagreements between organizations.

Employee Assistance Programs

A number of progressive companies, including over half of the Fortune 500, offer their employees help with personal problems. Many employee assistance programs (EAPs) started out to help employees with drinking problems. A number of these programs have expanded to help address the abuse of other drugs. Recently, EAPs have begun to offer assistance with "emotional problems, legal issues, financial concerns, family discord, single parenting, job-related problems, substance abuse, difficulty with aged parents, and other issues that when unresolved could affect work performance" (Eichler, 1983, p. 31). EAPs are also moving beyond identification, assessment, and referral of such problems to offering a number of treatment sessions. Just as with medical benefits and, more recently, prepaid legal services, mediation could be offered by companies to increase the productivity and well-being of their employees.

People spend most of their waking hours at work. Major difficulties with their families will affect their productivity.

Family mediators may want to approach corporations who have included family counseling as a service of their EAPs. If they see the benefits of family counseling, mediation should prove to be attractive to them. Mediation's brevity, sharp focus on the present and future, and development of a written plan appeal to good business practice. Many executives in business are also familiar with the notion of mediation from its labor management applications. Family mediators negotiating with a corporation may choose to be paid a certain sum per employee eligible for mediation or to be paid an hourly rate only when the service is used. The former arrangement provides them with a predictable income, which is especially valuable to the beginning mediator. The latter provides a source of referrals and enables mediators to diversify their practice.

Mediation sponsored by an EAP brings up the same concerns as other services provided by sponsoring organizations. Confidentiality is essential. Employees want to be reassured that their jobs will not be at risk if they use the service, especially if they have been referred by management rather than coming in on their own or at the request of a family member. Family mediators have to decide in such circumstances who the client is: management, who pays their fee, or the family receiving the service. This dilemma comes up for any professional employed by an organization, including court-based mediation programs for child custody disputes. For this reason, I recommend a consultant contract with the corporation rather than being employed by them. Mediation away from the workplace also reassures the disputants about confidentiality.

Mediators have to decide what to do when the number of prepaid sessions have been exhausted and there is still no agreement. Should the disputants be able to continue at their own cost at the family mediator's hourly rate? Any paperwork sent to the corporation should be limited to the fact and frequency of participation by the employee or perhaps followed by a general statement that an agreement was reached. Any other records remain with the family mediator.

More and more companies are deciding that giving employees services they request increases productivity. It is better to retain employees and keep them happy than to either write them off as deadwood or to try to fire them and then have to train new workers. Benefits that employees have asked to be made available include financial planning and exercise equipment as well as family counseling. Not all companies are as far along as a leading real estate syndication and investment firm. "Where else can you go to get a fifteen-minute massage in the middle of the morning, nutritional and exercise counseling at lunch, see a psychological or recreational counselor in the afternoon, eat free company-provided fruit all week long, and go whitewater rafting every spring" (Mitchell, 1983, p. 33). Still, mediation is a logical addition to an employee assistance program and an excellent way for family mediators to build their practice.

Business as a Family

"People have to understand that working with others for eight hours a day is a very intense situation. It is natural that individuals will fall into familiar family roles with coworkers since that is a significant portion of their interaction with others. It is, therefore, understandable that individuals play out family issues in the office" ("Family Therapist Addresses Corporation Problems," 1983, p. 2). Now we are going to consider how family mediators may help to resolve conflicts that come up at work.

People who are in business with one another may re-enact family roles. They may have gotten together with the classic combination where one of them had an idea and another had money or perhaps they are in business together because of perceived common interests. Then a bit further into the partnership, each feels the other should be more like them. One may be an early rising lark, the other a work-into-the-night owl; one may be concerned with neatness and detail, the other may want to run the business out of their pocket and only be concerned with outcome.

Mamis (1984) notes that most business partnership breakups are between men simply because over 90% of businesses are male-owned and run, and men typically don't pay much attention to relationships. When things are not going well they may resort to changing the locks on the office and retaining an attorney to go after their partner in court. Simple silence and avoidance may not work. Mamis quotes Grothe and Wylie, who do what they call business therapy and have thought of calling it marriage counseling for business: "The problems in a marriage as in business develop very slowly, so slowly that they are almost imperceptible" (p. 43). Grothe and Wylie often involve wives in business partner disputes because they are usually good at relationships. Family mediators who are aware of such dynamics can help partners to see the advantages of complementarity to their personality and business styles or to help them dissolve their partnership if that seems indicated. Mamis notes that "business therapists [and I would suggest mediators as well] may hold the best hope for partner reconciliation, and their fees are tax deductible, provided that the business, not the individuals, pay for the treatment" (p. 48).

The Family Business

Family members who work together are the most apt to play out their family roles at work. Common problems include sibling rivalry; unprofessional behavior from a family member, which would not be tolerated from other employees; and valuation of family loyalty above good business practice. The process of turning a business over to children is so difficult that only a third of family businesses survive to the second generation and only a tenth remain by the third generation (Topolnicki, 1983).

Members of the generation that started the business may have a more intense interest in it than do their children. The founders may not want to give up any power to their children yet desperately want them to keep the enterprise going. Topolnicki (1983) noted that parents may choose to give all their children equal shares of voting stock in order to avoid the appearance of partiality, although the children who are not working for the company usually vote for current income rather than growth. She suggested that it is better for children who run the business to get voting stock while their nonparticipating brothers and sisters inherit nonvoting stock or assets.

Peter Davis of the Wharton Applied Research Center in Philadelphia reported that at least half of the gross national product of the United States is produced by family businesses

(Goldstein, 1983). He suggested that family businesses work well because they are committed to long-range survival, are able to make quick decisions, and can provide for the total needs of workers. Davis also suggested that the particular needs of family-owned businesses be addressed through family councils. Somewhere in formality between a directors' meeting and a family meal, the family council can address questions such as those proposed by Kathleen Wisman, who has studied both emotional and economic issues in family-owned businesses. She recommended that family members review the following topics:

> (1) What were the original reasons for starting the business? (2) What major events cause anxiety or unity among family members? (3) Are those who are qualified assuming responsibility? (4) Do spouses influence decisions? (5) Are there strong feelings in the family that affect the business, such as a child who feels "jilted" by his father, a father determined to given his children 'a better deal' than he had? (6) Are there jealousies among the spouses and siblings? (7) Are those not in the actual work force wanting to share the profits? (8) Can you talk about expansion, profits, failure, and success without feeling anxious? How does your family respond when you bring up such issues? (9) Are your children showing an interest in learning the business? (10) Considering the family dynamics, are there plans for succession of the business which everyone is aware of? [Goldstein, 1983, p. 30]

These issues might best be faced in terms of planning when everyone is getting along. Perhaps there is a crisis and a major decision must be made or perhaps there is a major dispute and the family members need help mediating an agreement that will meet their individual needs.

Family mediators need to be aware of the intergenerational conflicts that often fuel family business disputes. Mediation can help the family avoid fighting in court about issues that should be settled around the kitchen table.

When only one parent is involved in a business, divorce may still adversely affect the business. Financial counseling firms in California's Silicon Valley are being asked to assess the personal situation of the owner of a company before it goes public. If the owner becomes a major stockholder and then goes through a divorce, the stock may have to be sold, depressing its price. These financial counselors appear to be acting like family therapists, if not mediators, by arranging for housekeeping help or vacations for the company president's spouse in order to hold the marriage together (Joselow, 1983). This is to avoid situations such as the one in which the husband of an executive in a high-tech company, was awarded $20 million in a divorce settlement and the firm had to make secondary stock offerings to raise the money to pay him.

Labor Relations

Grievances

Conflicts between individual employees and their employers may also be resolved through mediation. Some of these disputes may be caused in part because the disputants treat each other the way they do because they remind each other of family members. So far, we have considered mediation in organizational environments that provide the EAPs or include family businesses. Now, let's look at complaints by individuals in the context of the traditionally adversarial relationship between labor and management. The coal mining industry is noted for a high number of grievances. Disputes are usually over minor disciplinary actions. The national contract calls for arbitration to settle these disputes.

Goldberg and Brett (1983) studied mediation of such grievances compared to arbitration. They chose two districts in the Appalachian coal fields; one in which labor relations were relatively good and another with a high rate of wildcat strikes and grievances. The mediators had served as arbitrators in the coal industry. They were given a one-day training session about this particular experiment.

The techniques were typical of negotiations between labor and management in terms of separate caucusing and active participation by the mediator in making suggestions. One unusual feature was the rendering by the mediator of an advisory decision; what would happen if the grievance went on to arbitration, according to the mediator's best assessment. Goldberg and Brett note that this prediction usually did not lead to further negotiation but to a decision to either accept a solution or to go on to arbitration. There were also cases in which the mediators did not make an advisory decision to both parties, but told each one privately their opinion. They were able to go on with negotiations with this assessment. A final difference in techniques with this procedure was whether or not the mediators brought up any perceived underlying problems that might have prompted the grievance in order that they might be dealt with in mediation.

Some screening of disputes occurred in that only grievances that both the employer and union agreed to submit to mediation were included. However, data collected after the experimental period suggested that the settlement rate of 84%–100% occurred even when either party could unilaterally submit a grievance to mediation. What were the findings of this study?

> Grievance mediation proved substantially faster and less expensive than arbitration, according to a 1980 test of the mediation procedure in the Appalachian coal fields. Of 37 grievances submitted to mediation during the six-month experimental period, 32 were resolved—a success rate of 86%. And, on average, mediation consumed only about one-fourth of the time and cost normally required to obtain the final resolution of a grievance in binding arbitration. [Goldberg and Brett, 1983, p. 23]

Both labor and management participants preferred mediation over arbitration. It appears that once again the chance for the disputants to tell their story and to focus on the problems that might underlie the presenting complaint are the advantages of mediation over arbitration. Arbitration also leads to the notion of winning or losing the grievance.

Two criticisms of mediation by participants also illustrate its unique nature. Twenty-five percent of the management representatives felt that mediation did not provide a final resolution to the grievance, as did 12% of the union representatives and 28% of the miners themselves. Twenty-five percent of the management representatives and 7% of the miners also noted that the parties sometimes made agreements other than would have resulted from the bargaining endowments created by the contract. People who choose to mediate commit themselves to a process that may be ongoing and seldom can be captured entirely in a document.

A newspaper account of this program (Franklin, 1983) provides some telling quotes. In one session mediated by Goldberg, he asked management representatives, when he was meeting with them separately, if they thought that the grievant who had been with them for a long time was a good employee. They said yes and he suggested that they tell him so. They did and said that although he had been laid off they could promise to return him to work because he had been with the company so long. He said, "Well, I'll tell you it's not a grievance I want, it's a job." As one labor management director said, "That's the trouble with 95% of these grievances—they don't say what people really want. That's why we're using mediation to get these things out." Hobgood, former Assistant Secretary of Labor for Labor Management Relations, says, "The most valuable aspect is the healing process. Mediation has the flexibility to go behind the mere recitation of contract clauses and find the real 'grief.' In arbitration you don't have that luxury."

Federal and State Labor-Management Mediation Compared

Most mediation between labor and management is done by full-time federal or state employees. "The Federal Mediation and Conciliation Service (FMCS), an independent federal agency, has jurisdiction over disputes in industries engaged in interstate commerce, private non-profit health facilities, and agencies of the federal government. State agencies or boards of conciliation are empowered in some 25 states to provide mediation services to state, county and municipal parties within the jurisdiction of the respective state and to small companies not covered by FMCS" (Kolb, 1983, p. 7).

FMCS receives notification within thirty days of a contract expiration. A field mediator typically contacts both parties twenty days before contract expiration to see if mediation will be required. About half of the cases are settled without mediation. Mediators who start the process to resolve the dispute with the parties typically stay with the case until it is settled either with or without a strike.

If a state has a mediation service, it will be notified by the parties at the same time they give their thirty-day notice of contract expiration to FMCS. The state agencies usually cover public sector disputes for workers not included under federal legislation. Kolb studied both federal and state mediators to determine their techniques. She notes that they work with different categories of disputes. Federal mediators are usually working with disputants in the private sector: private companies and large unions, both of whom may employ professional negotiators as representatives. Private employees have the right to strike, which is costly to both labor and to management. Kolb suggests that these parties are dependent upon one another.

State mediators are working with relatively inexperienced negotiators, usually public employees who do not have the right to strike. So, the federal mediators may be working with national companies and unions while the state agency may be working with local teachers or fire fighters. Most federal and state mediators are full-time civil service employees with many years of experience. Occasionally "stars" from law or mental health professions come in to mediate highly visible disputes.

Kolb found that mediators often discount their influence, suggesting that it is an art rather than a science. She notes, however, that experienced mediators tend to have a definite idea of what their role is. They then formulate a strategy and analyze how they are doing. This is the opposite of the more amorphous view of mediation as an art in which first an analysis would be done, strategy formulated, and then a role emerge. Another way to put this is that just as with experienced family mediators, labor mediators are pretty clear on what they are going to be doing, can assess where they would like to go, and can tell how well they are doing during the process.

Kolb makes a distinction between orchestrators, primarily federal mediators who have highly interdependent professional negotiators to mediate, and dealmakers, state mediators who are working with inexperienced negotiators who need help on substantive issues and may expect a great deal of persuasion from the mediator.

Orchestrators see themselves continuing negotiations in this new setting of mediation. The mediator is there to help disputants to explore their differences to assist in the process of continuing the dialogue, keeping them in joint meetings, and forcing the parties to educate the mediator as a way of continuing the process (Kolb, 1983, p. 39). Dealmakers think they are brought in to mediate when negotiations are stalemated and the parties need help. The mediator should apply pressure, give them information on substantive issues, help them make a deal, carry messages for them, and bang heads until they reach agreement.

The federal mediators think that the state mediators push so hard to make a deal that they make bad agreements, pushing their own preferences on the parties. State mediators say, "The private sector is easier. You know that one side will eventually cave in—it is inevitable. Parties do not really need a mediator but they are required to use them by law. So all the mediator does is let the parties negotiate. In the public sector, we do not let the parties off the hook; we hammer away. We are part of the settlement process" (Kolb, 1983, p. 44).

Building or Narrowing Strategies

Kolb notes that both federal and state mediators have a cycle to their strategies. They first gather information, then make an assessment, then they encourage movement by the parties. However, state and federal mediators have different strategies. State mediators attempt to build an agreement bit by bit so they "actively sought information about priorities and diagnosed these issues according to their conformity with certain patterns of practice. These mediators freely gave their opinions, advice and suggestions about moves the parties should make on these issues. The federal mediators had less interest in identifying the priority issues during the early iterations of the strategic cycle and used movement tactics that encouraged the parties to narrow the differences between them on whatever issues they chose. Although they continually diagnosed a potential settlement, the federal mediators rarely made direct use of this insight in their movement tactics until requested to do so" (Kolb, 1983, p. 74).

Both federal and state mediators prepare to assess the power, people, and patterns involved. Patterns refer to both what has happened in the past and standards for what ought to be. Previous contracts and current standards for this sort of work setting are considered. Mediators also assess bargaining power by determining how much the organization needs the employees, whether or not the employees could strike, and how management could hold up if they did.

People involved in negotiating the dispute often determine whether or not agreement can be reached. Family mediators know from their emphasis on interpersonal relations that negotiators often decide what they want to do and then choose objective criteria to justify their position. Labor mediators in Kolb's study liked working with "pros," experienced negotiators who they knew and who were pleasant to deal with.

Movement Tactics

Kolb suggests that both federal and state mediators use communication tactics, substantive tactics, and procedural tactics. Communication tactics may vary from the mediator acting simply as a human tape recorder to adding his or her own views of the situation. The mediator may suggest what the costs are to a particular course of action, how certain positions deviate from typical patterns in the field. The mediator may give an opinion whether asked to or not, and may finally make a recommendation. Procedural tactics may include caucusing, the strategic use of timing, or threats to stop mediation. The distinction between procedural tactics and communication tactics often blurs.

Mistakes

One of the most valuable contributions of Kolb's research is a description of the mistakes made by federal and state labor mediators. Too little is written about mistakes in mediation. These mistakes have implications for family mediation practice, although they were committed by federal and state labor mediators. Some mediators misread the role the disputants wanted them to play. This can be done either by being too active in pushing for an agreement without listening to what the parties really wanted, or by being too passive when the parties needed substantive consultation on information. Too much pressure often makes disputants balk. A pushy mediator who has never had a failure may be so zealous in attempting to elicit certain responses from the parties that they can no longer use the mediator. However, Kolb (1983) reported that in general parties prefer aggressive to passive mediators and that aggressive mediators are more likely to help the disputants reach an agreement.

The second mistake was failing to identify all the issues in dispute. Limited fact-finding and premature closure may result in failure to determine the priorities of the disputants. This is a particular danger among very active mediators who try to build an agreement piece by piece. The most important aspects of the dispute may not become clear until the middle stages of the mediation process. These new needs or demands may be viewed as an irritation by the mediator rather than as the crux of the negotiations.

Kolb's (1983) research suggests that labor-management mediation has only a limited influence. Only if there are communication problems does mediation play a significant role in averting strikes. In fact, mediation may maintain the existing labor-management situation, which in Kolb's view grants more power to management than to labor. She also noted that mediators tend to be more expert in money issues than in other concerns. We will return later in this chapter to this tendency for mediators to cash out disputes, that is, to assign a monetary value that is easy to measure and incorporate it into the major part of the agreement.

Conflicts Between Corporations

Major companies in the United States each average $5.2 million in legal fees annually (Cullinan, 1983). In addition, they are increasingly employing their own attorneys, creating a legal department within the corporation to handle litigation. There are several reasons why companies are beginning to seek alternative ways to settle disputes. Litigation is expensive. Litigation typically takes a long time, with an uncertain end date and result. Litigation often includes the discovery process, forcing companies to disclose information they would rather keep private whether it has to do with profits or trade secrets.

Recently, there has been a movement to bypass the court system with private alternatives. Often a continuum of services is offered from mediation to arbitration, to rent-a-judge, a private trial before a retired judge who has been hired by the disputants.

Is the Mini-Trial Mediation?

One of the pioneers of the mini-trial procedure (Green, 1982) describes the process as one in which

> after a foreshortened period of pretrial preparation, the lawyers on each side (and experts, if desired) make informal, abbreviated and confidential presentations of their best case. A more distinctive characteristic of the mini-trial is that these presentations are not made to a judge, arbitrator or to any third party with binding decision-making authority, but rather to the principals themselves. In the classic mini-trial where corporations are involved, the principals are generally business executives with settlement authority . . . in the classic format, mini-trials have been presided over by a jointly selected 'neutral advisor.' The advisor's role is to moderate the proceedings, pose questions and highlight crucial facts and issues but not to preside like a judge, arbitrator or, at the information exchange part of the proceedings, even as a mediator. If settlement is not quickly reached by the principals after the information exchange portion of the mini-trial, the neutral advisor is asked to provide a non-binding opinion as to how the advisor thinks a court or jury would handle the case and why. With these views in hand, the parties then resume direct negotiations. The parties state that the mini-trial is successful because it promotes a dialogue on the merits of the case rather than just dollar values and reconverts what has become a 'lawyers' dispute' back into a business problem. [P. 5]

This process certainly has many elements of mediation. Green, a professor of law at Boston University, and another attorney, Jonathan Marks, founded EnDispute as a profit-making business venture to offer mini-trials and other alternative dispute resolution options to corporations. Marks and Green make presentations both to law firms specializing in corporate matters and to major companies describing the advantages of a mini-trial or any other process that may help the parties resolve their dispute out of court. In an article by Pollock (1983), in *The American Lawyer*, Marks says that he and Green "are litigators. We understand the litigation process, and yet we have carved out a niche for ourselves as neutrals" (p. 70). Green says, "We're not touchy-feely mediator/psychologist types. We're first and foremost litigators" (p. 72). They were both formerly partners in a major law firm, where they arranged the first mini-trial. The case was a patent dispute between two companies who wanted to settle quickly and avoid further legal fees and discovery.

Marks and Green incorporated EnDispute in January of 1982. They have offices in Washington, D.C., Los Angeles, Chicago, San Francisco, Hawaii, and Boston. The operation is small and piggybacked on a management consulting firm. They estimate that they earn about 10% of their income in training in-house lawyers about alternative dispute resolution, 30%–40% consulting to companies that are involved in disputes or want to know how to use alternative dispute resolution, and 50%–60% acting as a neutral consultant to companies in conflict (Pollock, 1983). They charge $150 per hour and give detailed bills about their services, including estimates. In Southern California, they have a seventeen-member panel, including a number of former judges, so that disputing parties can choose whether they want a mediator or a judge to preside over a mini-trial. They say that Section 1141 of California's Code of Civil Procedure mandates that nonbinding arbitration be used to attempt to settle most cases involving less than $25,000, which generates business for them. Such a law would be helpful to alternative dispute resolution programs in other states.

Marks and Green do caucus with each side. A lawyer who represented one major company in a dispute where they were called in to set up a mini-trial said that their strength was to keep the process moving and avoid the tendency of litigators to focus on details rather than on the major issues. Marks and Green report the same experience with alternative dispute resolution that many family mediators have found: People who use their services like the process. They are personally persuasive. However, even though they don't have as much business as they would like, since EnDispute is a national corporation they can't mediate or design mini-trials for all disputes that are referred to them. So the question becomes, will people choose the process rather than simply a few charismatic stars and will investors put up venture capital for expansion? Lawyers employed full time as in-house counsel with companies would seem to be most apt to retain them since outside counsel are in competition with them.

Marks suggests that in the future bringing in an expert on settling disputes out of court will be like using any other specialist in a case (Pollock, 1983). Certainly, using the top executives of two firms in settling a dispute to their satisfaction in two days is an improvement over the typical court process in terms of both time and money. Family mediators considering doing such work should note that Marks and Green are lauded for their ability to learn what the issues are quickly rather than that they have expertise on the particular problems facing their corporate clients.

Recently, there has been some suggestion that corporate attorneys have a duty to estimate the potential costs of litigation so clients can make informed choices about settlement. Family mediators who would like to learn more about settling disputes with companies may want to read *Alternatives*, a monthly journal published by the Law and Business Section of Harcourt, Brace, Jovanovich.

Helping people, who have decided they have a problem, to work out a solution remains the strength of mediation versus arbitration or adjudication. Parties are free to go back to court as if mediation never happened, which is also a feature of most mini-trials. One attorney who has participated in them says that mini-trials bring top management back into the dispute. "Too often the businessman walks away from a lawsuit once he starts it. He tells the general counsel, 'It's your problem now, handle it.'" (Jenkins, 1983, p. 30). Business executives have more incentive to increase their profits by settling the dispute than either their own attorneys or any outside counsel hired who will be paid win or lose. In fact, lawyers on each side may have an incentive to demonstrate their worth by continuing litigation. Although family mediators considering doing this sort of work must be eager to learn about major issues, priorities, and laws affecting disputes, they may not need expertise in the particular complexities of each case. Their skills in helping people to tell their side and work toward generating alternatives are valuable in and of themselves in the corporate arena.

Rent-a-Judge

In Southern California, a former judge established the Judicial Arbitration Service, which has handled 700 private cases, half in arbitration and half in mediation. The reported success rate for mediation is 80%–90%. Retired judges act as referees, so sessions may be more formal and agreements may seem to be more binding than in family mediation or other forms of alternative dispute resolution. This might confuse the differences between mediation and arbitration in the minds of both participants and referees.

Small Claims Mediation

One research project undertook to determine whether disputes that are typically settled in small claims court could be successfully mediated (McEwen and Maiman, 1981). McEwen and Maiman noted that much of the literature on mediation suggests that this method works when the disputants have an ongoing relationship and there is considerable social control from family, neighborhood, or government. They asked, "How can mediation be applied in American communities that are open and fluid and have fairly weak systems of informal control, and in cases where significant relationships between disputants have broken off or have never existed?" (p. 240).

Several small claims courts in the state of Maine began to offer mediation in 1977. The program was subsequently expanded, and in 1980, state law gave district courts the authority to mandate mediation before cases can go forward to adjudication.

The mediators, who were described as academic humanists with some training in dispute resolution, describe the process to litigants who have chosen the procedure or who have been ordered to participate. Then the mediators ask each disputant, starting with the person who filed the claim, to tell his or her story. The process has an informal, conversational tone, with mediators asking questions, parties interrupting each other, and the mediators chairing the session. The mediators usually do not caucus. After both parties have told their story, some of the mediators summarize what has been said and suggest an agreement. Other mediators simply continue to referee the process. Some mediators, upon discovering that the conflict has more to do with personal relationships than with the money claim that brought the parties to the attention of small claims court, may try to get the disputants to talk about the real reason for their dispute. However, other mediators simply choose to help the litigants resolve the dispute that they identify as the problem. If the parties agree, the mediator writes down an agreement and both parties sign it. The written agreement is reviewed by the judge, and if approved, as virtually all are, the agreement becomes the court's decision.

McEwen and Maiman (1981) compared three courts using mediation with three courts that adjudicated all small claims cases. They found that litigants who had a past relationship of long duration or one that was likely to continue beyond the conflict were no more likely to select mediation than were people who did not know each other. Two-thirds of the mediations succeeded. Another high rate of success (85%) occurred in cases involving unpaid bills and private sales. Up to 85% of these cases were successfully resolved. It appeared that the reason for the high rate of settlement was that either the defendant admitted the debt but said he didn't have the money to pay, so that a payment plan was established as part of the agreement, or that the defendant made a counterclaim saying he should not have to pay.

The lowest settlement rate involved traffic accidents. These folks were angry with one another and the facts were difficult to determine. Sixty-four percent of landlord-tenant disputes were successfully mediated; 65% of contracts, 62% of personal loans, 57% of consumer complaints about services, and 55% of consumer complaints about products. The highest success rate involved business plaintiffs and individual defendants, with 94% settlement. Eighty-three percent of tenants who brought a claim against a landlord also saw the case settled. However, one of the lowest settlement rates, 50%, occurred when the landlord was plaintiff and the tenant was the defendant. Mediated agreements were also more likely than adjudication to result in some immediate payment and a subsequent plan. Some judges point out how difficult it is to collect money even if they hand down a judgment that the money is owed.

Only 12% of the mediation agreements involved any conditions other than payment of money. McEwen and Maiman note that, although other issues were presented, they were usually converted into money to be incorporated into the settlement. This tendency to "cash out" may be pervasive in dispute resolution. It is simply easier to use the principle of split the difference and determine enforceability with a measurable unit. It is also easier for people to pay money than to change their behavior.

Another factor in this study was that, while the average adjudication time was 14.4 minutes, the average mediation only took 25.7 minutes. Exploration of emotional issues would be difficult to cover in that period of time, while money issues may be easier. Eighty-one percent of the people who went to mediation thought the mediator completely or mostly understood what the conflict was about, while only 71% of the disputants who went to litigation felt that the judge completely or mostly understood what their disagreement was about. This may explain the higher compliance rate for mediated disputes than for judgments by the court after trial. Even people who did not reach an agreement during mediation later complied better than those who had not gone through the process.

There does appear to be some sense of responsibility generated by mediation. Once they have agreed, people like to think of themselves as ethical, so if they say they will do something they try to do it, which they well may prefer to having a decision imposed by a stranger, the judge. McEwen and Maiman speculate that mediation works in small claims for these reasons as well as the fact that "the kinds of resolutions appropriate to disputes among strangers may be more tangible and thus easier to reach and abide by than those appropriate to disputes between parties with continuing relationships" (p. 267). This finding may encourage family mediators to broaden the scope of their practice to include the sorts of issues often brought to small claims courts.

Landlord-Tenant Mediation

A number of cities administer landlord-tenant mediation pro-grams. Some community groups and apartment associations have established private mediation boards as well. Since most of these boards have been established to protect tenants from excessive rent charges by landlords, they have sometimes found that such a voluntary procedure does not attract the worst offenders. A few cities have a provision that if a tenant files for mediation within a certain period of time after receiv-ing notice that the landlord intends to raise the rent, the in-crease cannot take effect until mediation has occurred. These programs seldom focus on the problems landlords face. I use the terms "owner" and "renter" when mediating such issues because they are neutral names.

San Mateo County, California, has a voluntary mediation program to resolve conflicts between landlords and tenants. Mediators are chosen based on where they live in the county, and there is an attempt to balance the number of landlords, homeowners, and tenants among them. Volunteers need not have previous experience as a mediator or know about land-lord-tenant issues before undergoing training. In addition to standard communication and mediation procedures, tech-niques are taught that are appropriate for settling disputes by telephone.

Landlord-tenant mediation is sometimes controversial be-cause it may be suggested to replace rent control. Since it is voluntary, advocates of rent control do not trust the process. Opponents of rent control may be against any such program, from mediation up through binding arbitration.

Business Mediation Techniques

Laborde (1983) published guidelines for conducting success-ful business meetings. The seven procedures she recom-mended, identified by the acronym PEGASUS, are useful in every kind of mediation.

Present Outcomes. Write down on a flip chart the out-come you expect from the meeting. This technique is familiar to family mediators, some of whom never go anywhere without their flip charts. Having a specific goal is the first step toward knowing whether you have reached it.

Explain Evidence. Fisher and Ury (1981) might call this procedure the search for objective criteria. After you have written down the outcome, write on the flip chart how you will know when you have reached the result you are seeking. While ordinarily you may want to make both the outcome and the evidence as specific as possible, there may be times when you want to be vague in order to secure agreement by all disputants at this early stage.

Gain Agreement on Outcomes. You want each disputant to look at the outcome written on the flip chart, say that that's agreeable to him, and indicate agreement by a nod. It is important to have disputants take responsibility for working on their conflict. Having them agree to the outcome will enable you to remind them later that they want to be addressing that problem.

Activate Sensory Acuity. Watch and listen when seeking agreement on the outcome of each mediation session. If a disputant says yes hesitantly or demonstrates by body language that no is the real message, you may want to ask her directly whether she really agrees about what everyone is doing.

Summarize Each Major Decision. You want to communicate some sense of movement as the session proceeds, indicating what progress has been made and what work remains to be done.

Use the Relevancy Challenge. Ask "How is this relevant?" when a disputant begins to wander from working on the desired outcome of the mediation session. Challenge only the information the person is delivering and avoid any appearance of a personal attack. If you point to the outcome written on the flip chart when you ask how the information is relevant, after a while you may be able simply to glance at the chart whenever anyone strays from pertinent topics in order to bring them back to more appropriate content.

Summarize the Next Step. Since most business as well as family mediations need more than one session in order to reach an agreement, the next step may consist of any work to be completed by the disputants between meetings and the topic for the next session. You will find the PEGASUS procedures useful each time you meet with disputants.

Laborde has boiled down important aspects of neurolinguistic programming into usable tools that you first demonstrate for your clients and then help them use themselves. She uses the fingers of the hands to illustrate what she calls "pointers."

Nouns. She notes that we don't know what others mean when they use unspecified nouns such as "bottom line." Every time we hear such words, we want to ask ourselves, "What specifically do they mean?"

Verbs. Similarly, when someone says, "I will do that," we don't know what they mean by such unspecified verbs so we ask, "How? How will they do that? How will we know when they have done that?"

Rules. Laborde suggests that a good business negotiator who hears, "We should, we must, we have to, or we can't," asks, "What would happen if the rule were not followed?" Mediators hear lots of such rules, especially in family disputes.

Generalizations. Most of us rely on generalizations. I just did. It saves us time. However, any time you hear someone say "all" or "never," Laborde suggests that simply repeating the word in a questioning tone may show the speaker that it's not always true.

Comparators. Here Laborde helps you to deal with comments such as "It's better to do this" or "It's easier to do that." If you ask, "It's better or easier than what?" you begin to get specific information to fit the situation of the disputants.

Laborde suggests that you can use these pointers while negotiating with others. Her acronym for this process is UNICORN. Using pointers for outcomes enables you to communicate with disputants in their language. Then you can nudge the see-hear-feel fantasy. Remember Bandler and Grinders' work on primary representational systems from the art and technology chapter? Once you have discovered, by listening to the verbs each disputant uses, whether they primarily experience the world by seeing, hearing, or feeling, try to get them to experience a fantasy of what a desirable outcome would be like.

If, as If, and Future Planning. Here you begin to say, "If we can reach an agreement then at some specific time in the future, this is what reality looks like." Laborde suggests one way to get people to do this is to have them pretend they are in the future and ask themselves how they achieved the result they are now enjoying.

Conditional Close. Since Laborde trains people in major corporations in sales techniques, she uses this term. Here she is suggesting that if we can make the fantasy just a rehearsed reality by these certain behaviors, then we have an agreement. This involves *outcome* dovetailing so that each disputant is getting what he or she wants from the agreement. You want to ask them how they will know if they are satisfied. Laborde suggests that *rapport* and *next step and summary procedures* can prevent you from bulldozing disputants into an agreement that does not really meet their needs.

Laborde summarizes other useful techniques in negotiations, such as stating reasons for any proposal first and then making the proposal so listeners will attack the reasons rather than the proposal. You can then generate other reasons, if necessary. "Chunking up" or "chunking down" is a manipulation of the level of generalization that successful mediators seem to do instinctively. She says that if you are trying to find the intention behind a demand, you might try to get more specific. If someone says, "I need more money," you can say, "You want a raise" in order to check their intentions. You might get more general, so that when they say, "I need more money," you might say, "You could use additional resources." Additional resources might mean benefits rather than salary increases or simply indications of appreciation or prestige.

She also suggests that paying attention to people's hierarchy of values will lead you to their intentions. She suggests that after basic survival needs, most of us put first either identity, connectedness, or feelings of power. You may then be able to help forge an agreement with disputants by helping each to fulfill their most important values. I have mentioned several times what I see as an unfortunate tendency to "cash out" conflicts by reducing the resolution of the dispute to dollar terms. This seems to happen most often when mediation blurs with arbitration or adjudication as in the small claims examples earlier in this chapter and the mandatory child custody and visitation mediation illustrations. While it is true at some level that "money is money" whether characterized as property or income, child support or spousal support, media-

tors who are alert to how the disputants view different categories of the conflict may help them to reach the most satisfactory agreement.

Conclusion: Similarities Among Mediation Applications

Mediation techniques are useful regardless of the nature of
the conflict. The techniques described in the second and third
chapters of this book work well with business and professional disputes, while most of the procedures that we have
talked about in conjunction with the specific application of
mediation in a business or community context may work in
family disputes at some point. Knowing techniques and procedures for helping people to resolve disputes seems to be more
important than being expert on the nature of that particular
conflict.

CHAPTER 8

Ethical Codes and Standards of Family Mediation

THE LACK OF REPRESENTATION and legally enforceable rules during family mediation have led to criticism about the impact on less powerful people involved in the process or affected by the results. Women who don't know as much about money as their husbands or who don't make as much or have as much income afterward are often cited. Less often mentioned are children whose futures are being decided, although they don't get to vote and are seldom included in the mediation process except to be told what's going to happen. Another ethical question has to do with what to do if emerging ethical codes for mediators conflict with existing ethical codes for mental health professionals or attorneys or other groups. Attorneys have had difficulty with their bar associations around this. Mental health people have been concerned but have not been brought to task by their peers. They have been criticized by attorney groups.

What should you do if disputants in mediation are lying? I have heard suggestions along the lines of either having disputants sign statements saying they are going to tell the truth or assuming that they are going to do so. Finding out they are not is then grounds for calling off the mediation. More specific guidelines would be useful. Can secrecy be distinguished from lying? What is the nature of the lie? Hidden property at the time of doing a budget should be brought to light or the mediation stops. However, what if the reason parents are divorcing is that one of them has a new love? The literature on the trust necessary to continue some aspects of a relationship in this case—perhaps shared care of their children—versus the respect and protectiveness also considered to be essential suggests that this may not be as good an idea to push for disclosure. However, even this rough guideline of financial implications or personal reasons for the dispute may not be as easy in real life.

Let's say that you are using a labor-management mediation technique in family mediation. You believe that caucusing or meeting separately with each party early on gives you additional information quickly that you otherwise may not get at all or, at least, you have early enough to determine what the parties real interests are rather than their positions. This has worked well for you in the past. Now, however, you learn in a caucus with the divorcing wife that the reason she is being so difficult around distributional issues is that their year-old daughter was not fathered by her husband, although he thinks he is the father.

Now, what to do? What purpose would be served by revealing to him this painful truth and how would it serve reaching a fair and effective agreement? There are financial implications. Under California law, although the husband who is living with his wife at the time of birth of the child is presumed to be the father, for up to two years afterward he may challenge that presumption in court. If he knew that little Amy was not his biological child, he might choose to challenge any attempt to make him pay child support. So, there are seventeen years of economic implications to what seems to be simply an emotional issue that might better be left undisclosed.

Is Mediation Ethical?

Without individual representation of each disputant as well as any children involved, are we "silently sacrificing one member of a family under the guise of a systems approach?" (Lemmon, 1983b, p. 845). However, "advocacy is not difficult when the issue is clear, or if the advocate either adopts a hired gun mentality or sees the world in absolute terms. For most of us, however, our curse as well as our skill is the ability to see several sides of a given conflict (Lemmon, 1983b, p. 845). I was referring to psychotherapists when I wrote that passage, but it applies even more to mediators.

Ethics or Turf Protection?

Are we protecting the public or ourselves with all this concern about ethics and standards? Probably a little of both. Most of us would want an experienced mediator who knows about relevant family dynamics and family law to help us settle our own issues concerning the future of our children and the division of our marital property.

Yet, in mediation as with many other fields, there is a lack of evidence that more training is better. Respected commentators argue that attempts to regulate mediation will simply produce credentials based on educational attainment rather than competence. We need to determine what it is that mediators need to know and then make sure that they know it. Sander (1983) suggested several ways for divorcing couples to get adequate advice. He reviewed the options of either involving attorneys throughout the process as advisors as Samuels and Shawn (1983) have suggested or to submitting any tentative agreement to their own attorney for review. Sander also cited the study done by the *Yale Law Journal* in 1976 of people doing their own divorces. Lawyers said they thought that their profession was necessary in divorce to handle the tax consequences and complicated issues such as the interstate custody jurisdiction act. However, divorcing clients who had an attorney said that very few of their representatives handled those issues. If family mediators need to know about taxes, we need to make sure they are trained to do so and don't presume based on the originating profession that people will know how to do it.

ABA Standards for Family Mediators

Adopting standards of ethical conduct may educate both potential consumers and potential service providers (Bishop,

1984). In 1984, the House of Delegates of the American Bar Association (ABA) approved the following standards of practice for family mediators developed by its family law section:

Standards of Practice for Family Mediators

PREAMBLE

For purposes of these standards, family mediation is defined as a process in which a qualified person helps family members resolve their disputes in a consensual and informed manner. It is essential to this process that the mediator be qualified and impartial; that the participants reach decisions voluntarily; that their decisions be based on sufficient factual data; and that each participant understands the information upon which decisions are reached. While family mediation may be viewed as an alternate means of conflict resolution, it shall not be a substitute for the benefit of independent legal advice.

I. *The mediator has a duty to define and describe the process of mediation and its cost before reaching an agreement to mediate.*

Specific Considerations

A. Before the actual mediation sessions begin, the mediator shall conduct an orientation session to give an overview of the process and to assess the appropriateness of mediation for the participants. Among the topics covered, the mediator shall discuss the following:

1. The mediator shall define the process in context so that the participants understand the differences between mediation and other means of conflict resolution available to them. In defining the process, the mediator shall also distinguish it from therapy or marriage counseling.

2. The mediator shall obtain sufficient information from the participants so they can mutually define the issues to be resolved in mediation.

3. The mediator and the participants shall agree upon the duties and responsibilities that each is accepting in the mediation process. The participants should understand that either of them or the mediator has the right to suspend or terminate the process at any time.

4. The mediator shall assess the ability and willingness of the participants to mediate. The mediator shall

also assess his or her own ability and willingness to undertake mediation with these particular participants and the issues to be mediated. This is a continuing duty.

5. The mediator shall explain the fees for mediation and reach an agreement with the participants for payment. It is inappropriate for a mediator to charge a contingency fee or to base the fee on the outcome of the mediation process.

6. The mediator shall inform the participants that each should employ independent legal counsel for advice throughout the mediation process. In the event the mediator is a lawyer, the lawyer-mediator shall inform the participants that the lawyer-mediator cannot represent either or both of them in a marital dissolution or in any legal action.

7. The mediator shall discuss the issue of separate sessions and shall reach an understanding with the participants as to whether and under what circumstances the mediator may meet alone with either of them or with any third party.

II. *The mediator shall not voluntarily disclose any information obtained through the mediation process without the prior consent of both participants.*

Specific Considerations

A. At the orientation session the parties should agree in writing not to require the mediator to disclose to any third party any statements made in the course of mediation. The mediator shall inform the participants that the mediator will not voluntarily disclose to any third party any of the information obtained through the mediation process.

B. The mediator shall inform the participants of the mediator's inability to bind third parties to an agreement not to disclose in the absence of any absolute privilege.

C. At this orientation session, the mediator must discuss with the participants the potential outcome of their disclosure of facts to each other during the mediation process.

III. *The mediator has a duty to be impartial.*

Specific Considerations

A. A lawyer-mediator shall not represent either party during or after the mediation process in any legal matters. In the event the mediator has represented one of the parties beforehand, the mediator shall not undertake the mediation.

B. A mediator who is a mental health person shall not provide counseling or therapy to either party or both during or after the mediation process. If the mediator has provided marriage counseling to the participants or therapy to either of them beforehand, the mediator shall not undertake the mediation.

C. The mediator shall disclose to the participants any biases relating to the issues to be mediated both in the orientation session and also before those issues are discussed in mediation.

D. Impartiality is not the same as neutrality. While the mediator must be impartial as between the mediation participants, the mediator should be concerned with fairness. The mediator has an obligation to avoid an unreasonable result.

E. The mediator has a duty to promote the best interest of the children. The mediator also has a duty to assist parents to examine the separate and individual needs of their children and to consider those needs apart from their own desires for any particular parenting formula. If the mediator believes that any proposed agreement between the parents does not protect the best interests of the children, the mediator has a duty to inform them of this belief and its basis.

F. The mediator shall not communicate with either party alone or with any third parties to discuss mediation issues without the prior consent of the mediation participants.

IV. *The mediator has a duty to assure that the mediation participants make decisions based upon sufficient information and knowledge.*

Specific Considerations

A. The mediator shall assure that there is full financial disclosure, evaluation, and development of relevant factual information in the mediation process, such as each would reasonably receive in the normal discovery process.

B. In addition to requiring this disclosure, evaluation, and development of information, the mediator shall promote the equal understanding of such information before any agreement is reached. This consideration may require the mediator to recommend that either or both obtain expert consultation in the event that it appears that additional knowledge or understanding is necessary for balanced negotiation.

C. The mediator who is a lawyer may define the legal issues. The lawyer-mediator shall not direct the decision of the mediation participants based upon the lawyer-mediator's interpretation of the law as applied to the facts of the situation. The mediator shall endeavor to assure that the participants have a sufficient understanding of appropriate statutory and case law as well as local judicial tradition, before reaching an agreement by recommending to the participants that they obtain independent legal representation during the process. This recommendation shall be made whether or not the mediator is a lawyer. If the participants or either of them choose to proceed without independent counsel the mediator shall warn them of the risk involved in not being represented including the possibility that any agreement they submit to a court may be rejected as unreasonable in light of both parties' legal rights or may not be binding on them.

V. *The mediator has a duty to suspend or terminate mediation whenever continuation of the process would harm or prejudice one or more of the participants.*

Specific Considerations

A. If the mediator believes that the ability or willingness of either of the participants to meaningfully participate in the process is lacking, the mediator has a duty to suspend or terminate the process.

B. If the mediator believes that the agreement being approached is unreasonable, the mediator has a duty to suspend or terminate the process.

C. The mediator should assure that each person has had the opportunity to fully understand the implications and ramifications of all options available.

D. The mediator shall inform the participants that emotions play a part in the decision-making process. The mediator shall attempt to elicit from each of the participants a confirmation that each understands the connection between one's own emotions and the bargaining process.

E. The mediator has a duty to assure a balanced dialogue and must attempt to diffuse any manipulative or intimidating negotiation technique utilized by either of the participants.

    F. If the mediator has suspended or terminated the process, the mediator should suggest that the participants obtain additional professional services as may be appropriate.

VI. *The mediator has a continuing duty to advise each of the mediation participants to obtain legal review prior to reaching an agreement.*

Specific Considerations

    A. Each of the mediation participants should have independent legal counsel before reaching final agreement. The mediator shall recommend that the participants obtain legal advice at the beginning of the mediation process and before the participants have reached any accord to which they have made an emotional commitment. In order to promote the integrity of the process, the mediator shall not refer either of the participants to any particular lawyer. When an attorney referral is requested, the parties should be referred to a Bar Association list, if available. In the absence of such a list, the mediator may only provide a list of qualified family law attorneys in the community.

    B. The mediator shall obtain an agreement from the participants in the orientation session as to whether and under what circumstances the mediator may speak directly and separately with each of their lawyers during the mediation process.

    C. The mediator shall obtain an agreement from the husband and the wife that each lawyer, upon request, shall be entitled to review all the factual documentation provided by the participants in the mediation process.

    D. Any agreement which is prepared in the mediation process should be separately reviewed by independent counsel for each participant before it is signed. While the mediator cannot insist that each participant have separate counsel, they should be discouraged from signing any agreement which has not been so reviewed.

The primary drafter of these standards noted that the requirement that mediators instruct participants at the first session to employ separate legal counsel for advice throughout the mediation process might appear to be lawyer-enrichment to people who are not attorneys (Bishop, 1984). Lande (1984) contended that the ABA standards unnecessarily promote use of outside attorneys, as well as intrusiveness by the mediator. Again, the question is whether such standards are primarily protecting the public or unnecessarily restricting the practice of mediation. The standards call for the mediator to be qualified. However, qualifications are not specified. There is an emphasis on making sure that attorneys are involved when people get divorced rather than attempting to identify what either the mediator or those attorneys should know. This bias is not surprising in a statement from a professional organization concerned about the livelihood of its members.

Other Recommendations

Outside counsel before, during, and after mediation along the lines suggested by Samuels and Shawn (1983) can be useful. It is best to find a family law specialist who is also knowledgeable about the mediation process so that her work can complement the sessions. Lande (1984) suggested that the following principles better meet the needs of practicing mediators than do either the ABA standards or its 1983 Model Rules of Professional Conduct:

Competence. Individuals providing services for resolution of disputes should be competent to perform the services offered for each dispute in which they are involved.

Confidentiality. Participants in dispute resolution processes need an opportunity to communicate privately and confidentially so they can feel able to communicate honestly and completely. Dispute resolution service providers have a duty to develop explicit agreements as to what communications are confidential as to third parties and as to individual participants.

Honest and Complete Communications. Disputants and service providers should provide all accurate and materially complete information needed to understand and resolve the dispute.

Careful Consideration of Options. Every process of dispute resolution should be designed to analyze all possible options, resolving the dispute within the time, financial, and other practical limitations of each situation.

Choice of Processes. Each analysis should begin with a consideration of the possible processes for resolving the dispute, including: (1) discussion between the parties without outside intervention; (2) mediation; (3) negotiation through representatives; (4) arbitration; (5) litigation; and (6) variations of the above, especially considering the actual service providers in the local area who might be used.

Procedures Within the Chosen Process. When parties are selecting a particular mode of conflict resolution, they should consider the procedure choices available within alternative processes taking into account the scope of services, areas of protection covered and excluded, and the fees and costs. Before parties become committed to any process of dispute resolution, service providers should make explicit agreements with their clients about the scope of services and protection and estimated total expenses.

Responsibility. Disputing parties are the primary decision-makers. They should assume as much responsibility as feasible for making decisions and accepting the consequences of their decisions.

Participants' Principles of Fairness and Perceptions of Need. The goals of dispute resolution system should be to provide procedures which produce resolutions as close as possible to each party's perception of fairness. In evaluating fairness, parties should consider: (1) how to satisfy each party's real needs and interest for the present and future; (2) the full range of issues involved, including financial, emotional, and relationship issues; (3) the law and the values embodied in the law as significant though not necessarily determinant factors; and (4) a priority for fair substantive results over procedural regularity.

Respect for Others. Parties should respect the legitimate needs and interests of others including other parties and those not represented in the dispute. Dispute resolution processes should involve continuing efforts to identify the mutual overlapping and complementary interest of the parties. These processes should recognize explicitly the effects of disputes and their resolutions on others, especially minor children.

> *Minimizing Negative Behavior.* Every person involved in the dispute resolution process should take whatever steps are appropriate to avoid or minimize negative behavior, such as (1) violence; (2) psychological warfare, including intimidation, threats, and the infliction of mental distress; (3) unnecessarily increasing costs, risks, or delays; (4) denying or avoiding responsibility for one's acts; (5) unnecessary blaming or other judgmental behavior; (6) using positional pressure tactics; and (7) bluffing and deception.

Lande's (1984) concern is to empower the participants rather than let either the mediator or outside attorneys take over the dispute. Balancing what the participants say they want and need with the mediator's values and knowledge has a number of aspects that we will consider later in this chapter.

The English Solicitors Family Law Association developed a Code of Practice that recommends a conciliatory approach for attorneys (solicitors) advising clients.

Solicitors Family Law Association

CODE OF PRACTICE

The Association recommends that members and any solicitor practising family law should adopt the following Code of Practice.

General

1.1 The solicitor should endeavour to advise, negotiate and conduct proceedings in a manner calculated to encourage and assist the parties to reconcile their differences and should inform the client of the approach he intends to adopt.

1.2 The solicitor should encourage the client to see the advantage to the family of a conciliatory rather than a litigious approach as a way of resolving the disputes. The solicitor should explain to the client that in nearly every case where there are children, the attitude of the client to the other party in any negotiations will affect the family as a whole and may affect the relationship of the children with the parents.

1.3 The solicitor should encourage the attitude that a family dispute is not a contest in which there is one winner and one loser, but rather a search for fair solutions. He should avoid using words or phrases that imply a dispute when no serious dispute necessarily exists, for example "opponent," "win," "lose," or *Smith v. Smith.*

1.4 Because of the involvement of personal emotions in family disputes the solicitor should where possible avoid heightening such emotions by the advice given; and by avoiding expressing opinions as to the behaviour of the other party.

1.5 The solicitor should also have regard to the impact of correspondence on the other party when writing a letter of which a copy may be sent to that party and should also consider carefully the impact of correspondence on his own client before sending copies of letters to the client.

1.6 The solicitor should aim to avoid or dispel suspicion or mistrust between parties, by encouraging at an early stage where possible, full frank and clear disclosure of information and openness in dealings.

1.7 The solicitor should aim to achieve settlement of differences as quickly as may be reasonable whilst recognizing that the parties may need time to come to terms with their new situation.

Relationship with Client

2.1 As a rule the solicitor should explain to the client at the outset the terms of his retainer and take care to ensure that the client is fully aware of the impact of costs on any chosen course of action. The solicitor should thereafter at all stages have regard to the cost of negotiations and proceedings.

2.2 Where appropriate, the solicitor must advise the client of his right to apply for Legal Aid. He should bear in mind and explain the impact of costs where the client or the other party is in receipt of Legal Aid, and the particular effect of the statutory charge.

2.3 The solicitor should create and maintain a relationship with his client of a kind which will preserve fully his independent judgement and avoid becoming so involved in the case that his own personal emotions may cloud his judgement.

2.4 Whilst recognizing the need to advise firmly and guide the client the solicitor should ensure that where the decision is properly that of the client, it is taken by the client and that its consequences are fully understood, both as to its effect on any children involved and financially.

Dealing with Other Solicitors

3.1 The solicitor should in all dealings with the other solicitor show courtesy and where possible endeavour to create and maintain a friendly relationship.

3.2 The solicitor should seek wherever possible to foster in his own client a trust in the other party's solicitors so tending to reduce distrust and suspicion between the parties.

3.3 The solicitor should in financial negotiations make use of without prejudice discussions, that is to say discussions involving conditional offers and conditional admissions that are withdrawn and not disclosed to the Court in the event of those negotiations failing. The solicitor should be mindful that an unrealistic offer may be counter productive and delay settlement.

3.4 The solicitor should generally avoid offering or receiving comments or information "off the record," where this phrase is intended to mean that the client should not be informed.

Dealings with the Other Party in Person

4.1 In dealings with another party who is not legally represented the solicitor should take particular care to be courteous and restrained. Especial care should be taken to express letters and other communications clearly, avoiding technical language where it is not readily understandable to the layman or might be misunderstood.

4.2 Wherever proceedings are taken or negotiations conducted that may adversely affect the other party's interests, the other party should, in the interests of both parties, be advised to consult a solicitor.

Petitions and Proceedings

5.1 The solicitor should avoid allegations or procedures which may cause or increase ill-will between the parties without producing any benefit for the client.

5.2 Before instituting proceedings which make allegations about the other party's conduct, the solicitor should consider whether the other party or his solicitor should be consulted in advance as to the particulars to be alleged or the grounds to be relied on.

5.3 Where the purpose of taking a particular step in proceedings may be misunderstood the solicitor should consider explaining it in advance to the other party or his solicitors.

Children

6.1 The solicitor should treat his work in relation to children as the most important of his duties.

6.2 The solicitor should, in advising, negotiating and conducting proceedings, assist both his client and the other parent to regard the welfare of the child as the first and paramount consideration.

6.3 The solicitor should aim to promote cooperation between parents in decisions concerning the child, both by formal arrangements (such as orders for joint custody); by practical arrangements (such as shared involvement in school events) and by consultation on important questions.

6.4 The solicitor must keep in mind that the interests of the child do not necessarily coincide with the interests of either parent, and that occasionally the child should be separately represented. In such case his duty is to bring the matter to the attention of the Court.

6.5 The solicitor should take care to keep separate issues of custody and access on the one hand and money on the other. It is often helpful to deal with these two topics in separate letters.

6.6 "Kidnapping" of children both results from and creates exceptional fear, bitterness and desperation in the parents. The solicitor should therefore take what steps he can strongly to discourage kidnapping a child, that is to say, removing a child in breach of an Order of a Court of any country, or in such a manner as to preempt or preclude a decision by the proper Court (wherever that Court may be) as to the child's custody or access.

The guidelines set out in this Code cannot be absolute rules in as much as the solicitor may have to depart from them if the law or his professional obligations so require. They are a restatement of principles, objectives and recommendations which many solicitors practising family law already seek to follow and to which they seek to aspire in serving their clients.

October 1983

Members of the National Council of Family Conciliators in England receive referrals from solicitors (attorneys) regarding child custody and visitation disputes as well as financial conflicts when children are involved.

AFCC Symposia on Standards and Ethics in Family Mediation

The Association of Family and Conciliation Courts (AFCC) sponsored a series of meetings on standards and certification in divorce mediation in 1982 and 1983. Over forty delegates from thirty professional organizations participated. They decided it was too early to consider certification or licensure, especially since there was no consensus on whether mediation is emerging as a separate profession or will be viewed as an adjunct technique used by attorneys and mental health professionals. Moreover, there is still a lively debate on the minimum credentials. The chairperson of the mediation committee of AFCC summarized the work of the symposium group (Milne, 1984). General goals agreed upon included the promotion of family relationships and the minimization of state intervention, management of conflict, protection of the best interests of children, and knowledgeability of practitioners in the areas in which they are mediating.

Who is the client? Attorneys have attempted to deal with mediation in terms of whether to say that they represent all of the participants, such as they would in the creation of a partnership, or none of the participants. Mental health professionals may choose to say that they advocate only for the children and are impartial with the adults or that they represent the family in a family systems theory based notion of therapy. The AFCC group did agree on certain client rights, such as self-determination, confidentiality, being informed about both the mediation process and the mediator's biases, the right to independent legal advice, and the right for the client to have only the services that they are seeking.

This group defined divorce mediation as involvement with both child custody and financial issues. They stated that minimal education should be a graduate degree. They went on to specify knowledge and skills essential for divorce mediation. Their final recommendations had to do with assessing whether or not to enter into an agreement to mediate with a couple. Are both spouses smart enough to understand the process? Do they have the emotional capability to make decisions? Will they bargain in good faith with one another? Is the mediator the right person to work with this couple in terms of knowledge and biases? Are they freely choosing mediation after being told about other options?

The AFCC group agreed on the following specific principles:

(1) Full disclosure of financial and factual information will be required of the parties. (2) The process may or may not be confi-

dential and no attorney-client privilege exists in the event that the mediator is a lawyer. If, in the course of mediation, the mediator becomes aware of child abuse or an indication of ongoing criminal activity, the mediator may have either a legal or professional responsibility to report this to third parties. (3) The mediator shall clarify the appropriateness of indicating his or her own judgment about the issues. (4) Self-determination is the bedrock of a successful mediation. (5) A determination shall be reached regarding the right of any of the participants or the mediator to withdraw from the process and whether the right to disagree shall be included within this. (6) The needs and interests of children are to be protected in mediation. (7) The mediator should explain the rights and responsibilities of all participants in the process. (8) The mediator should explain the fees and the costs of mediation. This group agreed that contingency fees or lump sum fees based on asset valuation should not be the basis for establishing mediator fees. There was no consensus on whether a flat fee would be unethical. (9) The mediator should define the involvement of third parties in the mediation process (children, experts, attorneys, extended families).

This group also agreed that whether the agreement to mediate was written or oral, the couple should clearly understand the scope of the mediation. They also felt that this agreement should include that neither party would make any changes regarding children or assets while mediation was proceeding. The third and final meeting of this group in 1984 resulted in the following model standards for practice.

Model Standards for Practice: Family and Divorce Mediation

PREAMBLE

Mediation is a family-centered conflict resolution process in which an impartial third party assists the participants to negotiate a consensual and informed settlement. In mediation, where private or public, decision-making authority rests with the parties. The role of the mediator includes reducing the obstacles to communication, maximizing the exploration of alternatives, and addressing the needs of those it is agreed are involved or affected.

Mediation is based on principles of problem solving which focus on the needs and interests of the participants, fairness, privacy, self-determination, and the best interests of all family members.

These standards are intended to assist and guide public and private, voluntary and mandatory mediation. It is understood that the manner of implementation and mediator adherence to these standards may be influenced by local law or court rule.

I. *Initiating the Process*
A. *Definition and Description of Mediation.* The mediator defines mediation and describes the differences and similarities between mediation and other procedures for dispute resolution. In defining the process, the mediator shall delineate it from therapy, counseling, custody evaluation, arbitration, and advocacy.
B. *Identification of Issues.* The mediator shall elicit sufficient information from the participants so that they can mutually define and agree on the issues to be resolved in mediation.
C. *Appropriateness of Mediation.* The mediator shall help the participants evaluate the benefits, risks, and costs of mediation and the alternatives available to them.
D. *Mediator's Duty of Disclosure.*
1. *Biases.* The mediator may have biases. These should be made known to the participants at the outset.
2. *Training and Experience.* The mediator's education, training, and experience to mediate the issues should be accurately described to the participants.
E. *Procedures.* The mediator shall reach an understanding with the participants regarding the procedures to be followed in mediation. This includes but is not limited to the practice as to separate meetings between a participant and the mediator, confidentiality, use of legal services, the involvement of additional parties, and conditions under which mediation may be terminated.
F. *Mutual Duties and Responsibilities.* The mediator and the participants shall agree upon the duties and responsibilities that each is accepting in the mediation process. This may be a written or verbal agreement.
II. *Impartiality and Neutrality*
A. *Impartiality.* The mediator is obligated to maintain impartiality toward all participants. Impartiality means freedom from favoritism or bias either in word

or action. Impartiality implies a commitment to aid all participants, as opposed to a single individual, in reaching a mutually satisfactory agreement. Impartiality means that a mediator will not play an adversarial role. The mediator has a responsibility to maintain impartiality while raising questions as to the fairness, equity, and feasibility of proposed options for settlement.

B. *Neutrality*. Neutrality refers to the relationship that the mediator has with the disputing parties. If the mediator feels or any one of the participants states that the mediator's background or personal experience would prejudice the mediator's performance, the mediator should withdraw from mediation unless all agree to proceed.

1. *Prior Relationships*. A mediator's actual or perceived impartiality may be compromised by social or professional relationships with one of the participants at any point in time. The mediator shall not proceed if previous legal or counseling services have been provided to one of the participants. If such services have been provided to both participants, mediation shall not proceed unless the prior relationship has been discussed, the role of the mediator made distinct from the earlier relationship, and the participants have been given the opportunity to freely choose to proceed.

2. *Relationship to Participants*. The mediator should be aware that post-mediation professional or social relationships may compromise the mediator's continued availability as a neutral third party.

3. *Conflicts of Interest*. A mediator should disclose any circumstance to the participants which might cause a conflict of interest.

III. *Costs and Fees*

A. *Explanation of Fees*. The mediator shall explain the fees to be charged for mediation and any related costs and shall agree with the participants on how the fees will be shared and the manner of payment.

B. *Reasonable*. When setting fees, the mediator shall ensure that they are explicit, fair, reasonable, and commensurate with the service to be performed. Unearned fees should be promptly returned to the clients.

    C. *Contingent Fees.* It is inappropriate for a mediator to charge contingent fees or to base fees on the outcome of mediation.

    D. *Referrals and Commissions.* No commissions, rebates, or similar forms of remuneration shall be given or received for referral of clients for mediation services.

IV. *Confidentiality and Exchange of Information*

    A. *Confidentiality.* Confidentiality relates to the full and open disclosure necessary for the mediation process. A mediator shall foster the confidentiality of the process.

        1. *Limits of Confidentiality.* The mediator shall inform the parties at the initial meeting of limitations on confidentiality, such as statutorily or judicially mandated reporting.

        2. *Appearing in Court.* The mediator shall inform the parties of circumstances under which mediators may be compelled to testify in court.

        3. *Consequences of Disclosure of Facts Between Parties.* The mediator shall discuss with the participants the potential consequences of their disclosure of facts to each other during the mediation process.

    B. *Release of Information.*

        1. The mediator shall obtain the consent of the participants prior to releasing information to others.

        2. The mediator shall maintain confidentiality and render anonymous all identifying information when materials are used for research or training purposes.

    C. *Caucus.* The mediator shall discuss policy regarding confidentiality for individual caucuses. In the event that a mediator, upon the consent of the participants, speaks privately with any person not represented in mediation, including children, the mediator shall define how information received will be used.

    D. *Storage and Disposal of Records.* The mediator shall maintain confidentiality in the storage and disposal of records.

V. *Full Disclosure*

The mediator shall require that there is disclosure of all relevant information in the mediation process as would reasonably occur in the judicial discovery process.

VI. *Self-Determination*
  A. *Responsibilities of the Participants and the Mediator.* The primary responsibility for the resolution of a dispute rests with the participants. The mediator's obligation is to assist the disputants in reaching an informed and voluntary settlement. At no time shall a mediator coerce a participant into agreement or make a substantive decision for any participant.
  B. *Responsibility to Third Parties.* The mediator has a responsibility to promote the participants' consideration of the interests of children and other persons affected by the agreement. The mediator also has a duty to assist parents to examine, apart from their own desires, the separate and individual needs of such people. The participants shall be encouraged to seek outside professional consultation when appropriate or when they are otherwise unable to agree on the needs of any individual affected by the agreement.

VII. *Professional Advice*
  A. *Independent Advice and Information.* The mediator shall encourage and assist the participants to obtain independent expert information and advice when such information is needed to reach an informed agreement or to protect the rights of a participant.
  B. *Providing Information.* A mediator shall give information only in those areas where qualified by training or experience.
  C. *Independent Legal Counsel.* When the mediation may affect legal rights or obligations, the mediator shall advise the participants to seek independent legal counsel prior to resolving the issues and in conjunction with formalizing an agreement.

VIII. *Parties' Ability to Negotiate*
  The mediator shall assure that each participant has had an opportunity to understand the implications and ramifications of available options. In the event a participant needs either additional information or assistance in order for the negotiations to proceed in a fair and orderly manner or for an agreement to be reached, the mediator shall refer the individual to appropriate resources.
  A. *Procedural.* The mediator has a duty to assure balanced negotiations and should not permit manipulative or intimidating negotiation techniques.

B. *Psychological.* The mediator shall explore whether the participants are capable of participating in informed negotiations. The mediator may postpone mediation and refer the parties to appropriate resources if necessary.

IX. *Concluding Mediation*

A. *With Agreement.*

1. *Full Agreement.* The mediator shall discuss with the participants the process for formalization and implementation of the agreement.

2. *Partial Agreement.* When the participants reach a partial agreement, the mediator shall discuss with them procedures available to resolve the remaining issues.

B. *Without Agreement.*

1. *Termination by Participants.* The mediator shall inform the participants of their right to withdraw from mediation at any time and for any reason.

2. *Termination by Mediator.* If the mediator believes that participants are unable or unwilling to meaningfully participate in the process or that a reasonable agreement is unlikely, the mediator may suspend or terminate mediation and should encourage the parties to seek appropriate professional help.

3. *Impasse.* If the participants reach a final impasse, the mediator should not prolong unproductive discussions that would result in emotional and monetary costs to the participants.

X. *Training and Education*

A. *Training.* A mediator shall acquire substantive knowledge and procedural skill in the specialized area of practice. This may include but is not limited to family and human development, family law, divorce procedures, family finances, community resources, the mediation process, and professional ethics.

B. *Continuing Education.* A mediator shall participate in continuing education and be personally responsible for a ongoing professional growth. A mediator is encouraged to join with other mediators and members of related professions to promote mutual professional development.

XI. *Advertising*

A mediator shall make only accurate statements about

the mediation process, its costs and benefits, and about the mediator's qualifications.

XII. *Relationships with Other Professionals*

    A. *The Responsibility of the Mediator Toward Other Mediators.*

        1. *Relationship with Other Mediators.* A mediator should not mediate any dispute which is being mediated by another mediator without first endeavoring to consult with the person or persons conducting such mediation.

        2. *Co-Mediation.* In those situations where more than one mediator is participating in a particular case, each mediator has a responsibility to keep the others informed of developments essential to a cooperative effort.

    B. *Relationship with Other Professionals.* A mediator should respect the complementary relationship between mediation and legal, mental health, and other social services and should promote cooperation with other professionals.

XIII. *Advancement of Mediation*

    A. *Mediation Service.* A mediator is encouraged to provide some mediation service in the community for nominal or no fee.

    B. *Promotion of Mediation.* A mediator shall promote the advancement of mediation by encouraging and participating in research, publishing, or other forms of professional and public education.

These standards provide the best guidance for family mediators now. Guidelines will continue to evolve reflecting the practice of mediation. These standards are being further refined for review and possible adoption by the forty-three organizations who participated in their development. Participants of this group raised many more questions than they were able to answer. Both this document and the ABA Standards leave practitioners without clear guidelines in some areas. There are complicated issues that each group has identified but failed to offer guidance specific enough to help the practitioner who is mediating daily. The open nature of standards in such a new field is to be applauded, but what should practitioners do in the meantime?

Can Mediators Be Both Neutral and Fair?

All of the laundry lists that we have considered above suggest that a good mediator is an impartial mediator. However, the ABA Standards say that "impartiality is not the same as neutrality." While the mediator must be impartial as between the mediation participants, the mediator should be concerned with fairness. The mediator has an obligation to avoid an unreasonable result. Everyone also wants the mediator to promote the best interests of the children.

While this all sounds desirable, how does it work in practice? Just as with family therapists, there are mediators who maintain they are value-free. They claim to have no biases that creep into their work with clients. However, most mediators recognize that they do have biases and make it part of the process to explain the ones that they know about to their clients in the beginning as part of the agreement to mediate. They also note any point in the process whenever they become aware that they are promoting a result out of their own values. How mediators feel about conflict, the proper role of families, and self-determination may influence the strategies they choose in mediation (Bernard et al., 1984).

Should mediators strive to be as neutral as possible or should they seek to impose their view of reasonable result on the participants? Bernard et al. suggest that trying to remain neutral may help clients meet their own needs more than a more intrusive attitude. They suggest two strategies that are somewhere in between the extremes of strict neutrality and high intervention. First, the mediator who is disturbed by the way things are going might suggest some alternatives. The second strategy is to suggest that the clients obtain additional information either on their own or from other professionals.

The phrase "in the best interests of the child" often emerges in the impartiality-neutrality debate. What are the guidelines for promoting the best interests of the children? Knowledge of family development, including relevant research, might lead to general principles such as the need for access to both parents. Children may need contact with both parents even if one is not a good parent. I formerly worked in the field of children and family services. Daily, our staff made decisions on behalf of the state. They knew better than some neglectful or abusive parents what was best for children. What I bring to mediation from the experiences with the children at the residential institution where I once worked suggests to me that children like to know about both their parents.

Seldom do I know best about what the specific plan should be for a child affected by mediation. I may have an opinion. I am not shy about telling participants what I think. However, I also say that I do not know their children. They know their children; they probably know best where the child should live when, what religion if any the child should be raised in, and whether the child should go to private or public school. And, probably, no one cares more about their children than they do. So, beyond a general admonition to parents to consider the children and an attempt to lead them more toward continued access for both parents if they are moving away from that, the specifics of custody and visitation plans seem best generated by the participants.

Just because parents decide to divorce does not mean that they become incompetent at caring for their children. The mediator should not recommend which home the child should live in or suggest other socialization decisions based on a few contacts if the parents appear to be adequate. Hugh McIsaac, director of the Los Angeles Conciliation Court has developed a policy of using evaluation as fact-finding during mandatory child custody mediation. This report by a separate staff member is shared with the parents during mediation, which preserves the impartiality of the mediator and gives the family the information before it is submitted to the court.

It may be helpful to bring in the children after an agreement has been reached so that both parents can explain what is going to happen. The children have a chance to hear the parents saying in front of each other what the plan is going to be, so there are fewer problems of misunderstandings or divided loyalties. Just as before the divorce, the parents are making decisions for their children and notifying them. This is preferable to the parents' abdicating and trying to leave what to do up to the mediator or the children themselves or fighting in court and relying on a court-appointed child custody evaluator.

Fairness is also an elusive concept. Is the agreement about to be reached fair in comparison with what is relevant law in the state? Is it fair in terms of how happy each party is with the proposed result? What about the private value that each participant puts on the issues under mediation versus the economic value with which they might be valued by outsiders? Dibble (1984) refers to the danger that bargaining in mediation may encourage sole economic valuation over the personal concerns that are essential to ongoing relationships in families. He suggests a Socratic questioning of the ethical assumptions that seem to underlie each of the party's statements of interest.

The ease with which most couples divide personal property suggests that they do have some sense of fairness that simply can't be made known to an outside person, and that they will act in a fair way with one another. I certainly cannot balance grandmother's soup tureen against the blues records collection for them. I can tell people who are agonizing over who gets the baby pictures to make copies.

The Further Development of Ethical Standards for Family Mediators

There is a considerable resurgence of interest in ethics among the human service professions. The Institute of Society Ethics in Life Sciences (the Hastings Center) has encouraged members of a number of professions to develop guidelines for teaching ethics to help students to "(1) realize that professional decisions have moral consequences; (2) recognize ethical issues; (3) develop skill in analysis from an ethical point of view; (4) develop more responsibility that is reflected in behavior; and (5) learn when to tolerate and when to resist ambiguity and disagreement" (Lemmon, 1983, p. 862b). Law professors have recently been asked to include in their curricula consideration of ethical issues and asked to encourage adherence to ethical standards by setting examples with their own behavior.

Modeling an approach to the profession may be the most powerful way to encourage future practitioners to consider ethical consequences of their own behavior. Mediators can give a high priority to visibly ethical practice. They can keep in touch with what appears to be emerging typical good practice and make sure their own work conforms to relevant law as well as draft standards in order to provide the most effective mediation service as well as to avoid any malpractice charges. They should also compare the code of ethics of their originating professions as well as any professional licenses they hold with any need for different practice as a mediator in order to shape the field. Society is increasingly concerned with ethics. Mediation has touted itself as being especially ethical. Maintaining such a superior posture is common for emerging professions. However, if we are indeed to be better than existing alternatives, we must move from general ethical admonitions and pronouncements toward specific principles for practice to which we can be held accountable. Only then can we sort out what works and what doesn't and advance the practice of mediation.

Confidentiality in Mediation

A number of the statements about guidelines for mediators say that confidentiality is essential to the process. However, confidentiality, the professional duty of the practitioner to handle information gained through the relationship with the client in a responsible manner, must be differentiated from privileged communication, a right by the client to prevent the professional from disclosing information in court should he or she be subpoenaed. This latter right has a common law basis for some professions, such as the clergy and attorneys. Privileged communication must be created by state statute for others, such as most mental health professions.

Since attorneys are particularly careful to distinguish their mediating from their lawyering roles, it is not clear whether or not the privilege would cover their mediating activities. Mental health professionals who are mediating cannot promise that their clients have the privilege either. So, while the agreement to mediate may contain a promise that the mediator will not disclose information to third parties, the court might require disclosure if one of the parties in mediation subsequently is in litigation. What principles should a mediator follow in such a murky area?

First, written ethical standards have prevailed in court. One psychotherapist with an M.S.W. cited both the National Association of Social Workers' code of ethics as well as that of the American Association of Marriage and Family Therapy to persuade a judge in a child custody hearing that she should not testify since her client had not given her permission. Some mediators recommended obtaining a written agreement from all the participants in mediation that they will not call you to testify and also explicitly listing what information may be divulged to others, such as their attorneys or other professionals that might be consulted during the mediation process. The Society of Professionals in Dispute Resolution held a conference in 1984 on ethical issues in dispute resolution that recommended confidentiality in mediation. The Federal Mediation and Conciliation Service has some confidentiality protection in the code of federal regulations. A leading case, reproduced as Appendix C, supports their privilege not to testify (*NLRB v. Joseph Macaluso, Inc.*, 618 F. 2d 51 [1980]). Maxine Baker-Jackson, a lawyer and social worker who serves as senior mediator for the Los Angeles Conciliation Court, noted that this case argues for the mediator's privilege not to testify based on the need for impartiality rather than on the need for confidentiality. The Community Relations Service of the United States Department of Justice also has a confidentiality provision in its originating statute.

Others have noted the general tendency in the law to encourage settlement that might also be cited in an attempt to create a privilege in the absence of a state statute specifically addressing mediators. Mediators attempting to create a privilege might want to cite Wigmore's four criteria: "(1) The communications must originate in a confidence that they will not be disclosed. (2) This element of confidentiality must be essential to the full and satisfactory maintenance of the relation between the parties. (3) The relation must be one which in the opinion of the community ought to be sedulously fostered. (4) The injury that would inure to the relation by the disclosure of the communications must be greater than the benefit thereby gained for the correct disposal of litigation" (8 Wigmore, Evidence, McNaughton, Revised, 1961, Section

2285, p. 527. Cited in Brieland and Lemmon, 1977, p. 287). Privileged communication has nearly thirty exceptions (Wilson, 1978), so that even creation of a clear mediator-client privilege would not be absolute, even less so if it followed the mental health statutes rather than the attorney-client privilege tradition. Issues related to suspected child abuse, other domestic violence, or the commission of crimes are examples that may come up in the mediator's practice

Can the Mediator Own the Privilege?

The Los Angeles Conciliation Court was able to persuade a judge that a mediator should not be compelled to testify, even though the parents had signed a waiver permitting a recommendation, if mediation failed and both parents wanted the mediator to testify regarding a dependency matter. (In re Jessica Y., Los Angeles County Juvenile Court, J957290, March 15, 1982, unpublished.) The Los Angeles Superior Court subsequently adopted a local rule that the privilege not to testify could be invoked by the court-connected mediator. This rule is a guide for private mediators as well because it recommends what action to take when the mediator witnesses the commission of a crime, or hears allegations of child abuse or threats against others.

The Los Angeles Superior Court Local Rule

The local rule is given in each inset paragraph with a clarification of intent commentary given in the paragraph that follows:

A. Except as provided herein, it is the policy of the Los Angeles County Superior Court that all Conciliation Court marriage counseling and family mediation services be confidential. Such confidentiality is essential to the effective functioning of the Conciliation Court.

Staff members of the Conciliation Court of the Los Angeles County Superior Court shall not disclose information to persons other than participants and their counsel, or produce records in violation of this policy. No counselor, party, counsel, or participant shall be compelled to testify concerning any information acquired—including, but not limited to, communications, or observation made in connection with the provision of Conciliation Court services.

B. Exceptions

    1. Nothing in this section shall restrict any person from reporting or serving as a witness where a crime has been committed, or is alleged to have been committed, in his, or her, presence.

This provision means if a crime is committed in the presence of the mediator, the mediator may testify regarding the crime but may not reveal other information not related to the criminal act. This provision applies only to acts committed in front of the mediator and not to admissions regarding past criminal behavior.

    2. Nothing in this section shall restrict any Conciliation Court staff member from complying with any law requiring reporting of child abuse.

The counselor must report the child abuse to the Protective Service Unit of the Department of Public Social Services, and not to the trial court hearing the custody dispute. It is the responsibility for the Protective Services Unit to investigate the allegation, and if warranted to carry the information forward.

    3. Nothing in this section shall restrict a Conciliation Court staff member from complying with the requirements of *Tarasoff v. The Regents of the University of California*, 17 Cal. 3d 425.

The mediator has the duty to inform intended targets of threats made against them when the threat has been made in the presence of the mediator. Again, the report is made to the intended target and not to the trial court hearing the custody dispute.

    4. The fact that the Conciliation Court session took place, the time and place of that session, and the identities of participants shall not be deemed confidential.

The Conciliation Court referrals are contained in the divorce file, which is a public record. Therefore the fact a Conciliation session took place is not confidential, while the contents of these sessions are protected.

    5. The fact that an agreement was, or was not, reached and the contents of any stipulation and order resulting from a Conciliation Court session shall not be deemed confidential.

When agreements are made into court orders, they are filed in the divorce file, which is a public record. The agreement, itself, is not confidential but all transactions and negotiations leading to the final agreement are protected.

6. Nothing in this section prevents the Conciliation Court from recommending that a matter be referred for a child custody evaluation, or that an attorney be appointed for a child, or children.

When no agreement is forthcoming, the mediator may recommend to the trial court a child custody evaluation be conducted or an attorney be appointed for the children. This recommendation is made to protect the best interest of the child and does not in itself reveal anything adverse about either of the parties.

7. Nothing in this section shall prevent the Conciliation Court counselor from meeting with the judicial officer hearing a contested custody matter in an in-chambers conference with both attorneys and the parties when the parties themselves have both requested and consented to such a conference following the parents' having completed the mediation process.

When both parents request and consent to an inchambers conference, the mediator may participate in the settlement conference, but the agency reserves the right to assert absolute privilege even if the parents so request and under no circumstances will the mediator participate in the trial process should the effort toward settlement fail. (McIsaac, 1984, pp. 14–18.)

Ethical Code for Child Custody Mediation

Since California has mandatory mediation of child custody and visitation disputes, court connected mediators in that state see a wider range of clients than do private mediators. The clients think of themselves as involuntary. They may include more poor people and more disturbed people than the clients of a private family mediator. The certification committee of the California chapter of the Association of Family and Conciliation Courts developed a draft code of ethics and suggested knowledge, base, skills, abilities identified, as well as education and training methods, as a start toward a certification process. They note in a committee report (Baker-Jackson et al., 1983) that while any such certification should address all mediators, their committee's document addresses only court-connected mediators.

Code of Ethics for Mediators in Child Custody Disputes

PREAMBLE

1. The mediator believes in the intrinsic dignity, worth and right to self-determination of human beings.
2. Mediation is a process towards conflict resolution in which an impartial third party intervenes in a dispute with the consent of two parties as an assist to the parties in the negotiation of a mutually satisfactory settlement of the issues in dispute.
3. The process of mediation is goal-oriented. It is separate and distinct from arbitration, evaluation, adjudication or litigation and therapy. The client should be informed of the distinctions and the right to pursue the alternatives of arbitration, litigation or therapy as deemed necessary.
4. The mediator accepts responsibility to practice according to the highest ethical standards of his/her profession.
5. The mediator recognizes the magnitude and responsibility, therefore, of maintaining at all times a high standard of competence.
6. The mediator informs the client of the scope and limits of the mediation process.
7. Mediation is not intended to replace or compete with other professionals. It is an additional area of expertise open to all those professionals who are qualified.
8. Mediation is a tool which should be flexible and adaptable to the individual's changing needs in a dynamic complex society. The mediator is dedicated to an interdisciplinary approach. And, agreements are finalized in accordance with proper legal standards of the court.

I. *Impartiality*

Comments: The mediator shall remain impartial and objective during the mediation process. The mediator shall strive to be aware of any biases he/she may have regarding the parties or regarding possible outcomes. The mediator must disqualify him/herself if there is a conflict of interest that might affect impartiality. Being impartial does not mean that the mediator will abrogate his/her responsibility to help the parties reach a resolution that is in the best interest of the child.

II. *Confidentiality*

Comments: The mediator shall be aware and adhere to all requirements of the law pertaining to the issue of client confidentiality (state, county or jurisdictional). This shall include confidentiality in the storage and disposal of records accumulated during the mediation process. Mediators shall inform and gain consent (preferably written) from the parties before consulting or discussing their case with other agencies.

III. *Goal of the mediation process*

Comments: The mediator shall describe and explain the mediation process in the initial session. The goal of the mediation process is to reach an agreement between the parties that would be in the best interest of all concerned, if possible, with primary consideration being what is in the best interest of the child.

IV. *Referrals*

Comments: The mediator shall make referrals when appropriate. This may take the form of psychological, educational, medical, financial or legal resources to serve the mediation process or post-resolution state. It is the responsibility of the mediator to keep informed of the resources available in the community.

V. *Training and Education*

Comments: The mediator has the responsibility to upgrade his/her skills, knowledge and information on a consistent basis as it relates to the mediation process. This can be accomplished through formal education, workshops/conferences/seminars or supervision. Maintaining knowledge of professional literature should be a continuing and ongoing process.

VI. *Impropriety*

Comments: The mediator shall not use his/her position for personal gain or advantage. Mediators shall not accept, give or solicit gratuities in the performance of their duties. The mediator shall disqualify him/herself when a conflict of interest is or may be involved. This may take the form of monetary, psychological, emotional or any other affiliations with the parties involved that might result in or appear to result in a conflict of interest. The mediator shall not be involved in activities that may interfere with the professional performance of his/her duties.

VII. *Integrity and Competence of the Mediation Process*

Comments: Mediators shall assist in maintaining the integrity and competence of the mediation process by adhering to the above code of professional conduct, and acting with honor and dignity. Mediators should cooperate with other officials and organizations within legal and ethical means to achieve the goal of the mediation of child custody disputes. Mediators shall not participate in areas that are beyond, or above, their levels of competence that might result in psychological, legal, financial or physical harm to the parties.

A draft of professional standards for mediation developed by the Mediation Council of Illinois combined adherence to the American Bar Association Standards with sections on unethical conduct and consequences adapted from the American Psychological Association Guidelines. They include other mandates specific to mediation, such as the mediator's duty to insure noncoercive negotiations, to terminate mediation if power imbalances persist, and, finally, to indicate in writing if the mediator does not concur with the decision the parties have reached (Schneider, 1984).

Conclusion

What kind of ethical standards do family mediators need? Several law professors have opposed the imposition of legal regulation on mediators. They fear that such regulations would focus on the degrees held by applicants, not their capabilities. The interdisciplinary nature of the mediator role complicates the determination of appropriate criteria (Perry, 1980). However, concerns voiced by a number of state bar associations about the mediator's role indicate that state licensure may dictate the scope of the role that private family mediators will play in the future.

There has been an ongoing interdisciplinary collaboration in seeking information and comments from a variety of sources in an attempt to create the most workable standards. This chapter indicates the current lack of consensus on appropriate ethical standards for family mediation. Nevertheless, a variety of disciplines are actively seeking to develop an ethical code for this emerging profession. The task is complicated by the interdisciplinary character of family mediation, but the growth of the field is likely to prompt regulation at the state level through licensing and other requirements.

Family mediators will continue to develop their ethical codes to the point where they can be incorporated into legislation. We can learn from experience what standards of practice we need in order to mediate successfully with clients.

CHAPTER 9

Becoming a Family Mediator

THIS CHAPTER GOES step-by-step through the process of establishing a family mediation practice. First, I look at graduate programs that can serve as a foundation for this career. Next, I consider specific training in the techniques of family mediation. The major section of this chapter addresses the nuts and bolts of building a practice—from defining the scope of services to finding clients. Then I look at several key practice issues discussed previously. This time the concern is what mediators do on a daily basis about confidentiality, supervision, and so on. Finally, the chapter considers how the individual mediator may help shape the future of family mediation.

Preparation

Graduate Programs

All standards for family mediators presume at least a master's degree in a mental health profession or a law degree. A few graduate programs offer coursework in mediation, and this trend is increasing rapidly. A survey on introducing legal topics into the social work curriculum offers a framework for incorporating such material into mental health degree programs (Lemmon, 1983a).

Family mediation requires special knowledge and skills. No one university degree program now offers all the necessary information. As with other innovations in the human services, leading practitioners provide training and develop curricula, which eventually will be incorporated into university programs. Until then, potential family mediators will have to develop their own plans of study, choosing from a variety of courses in the university, followed by specialized training.

Mental Health Graduate Degrees

A few universities now offer master's degrees with an interdisciplinary focus. Courses are taken in schools of social work and law, as well as in psychology, sociology, and human development departments. The degree itself is usually taken under one of the mental health professions, such as social work or human development. An internship with an opportunity to practice family mediation under supervision is a vital aspect of any such program.

Law Schools

Many law schools are now offering a course on alternative dispute resolution. The American Bar Association's Special Committee on Alternative Dispute Resolution published a directory profiling the courses offered in law schools throughout the country, as well as identifying university-based and community-based services for conflict resolution outside the courts. Most of these courses study mediation along with negotiation, arbitration, interviewing, and counseling, but Professor Frank Sander at Harvard University Law School offers a course solely on mediation. An internship is available in conjunction with this seminar.

The American Bar Association spent four years developing a lawyering skills program that features exercises in interviewing, counseling, and negotiation. This package includes a videotape, sample problems, and a teacher's guide. Also, the

National Institute for Dispute Resolution, a new nonprofit organization in Washington, D.C., has established a two-year, $230,000 grant program to enable law professors and students to develop course materials on alternatives to litigation ("Notes on Law Schools," 1984).

Dual Degrees

Joint degree programs in law and mental health have existed since 1970. However, they take a long time to complete because candidates must fulfill most of the requirements of each discipline. By applying electives toward both degrees, the student can save perhaps a semester of a five- or six-year course of study.

There is a lack of faculty members modeling interdisciplinary roles and advising students on how to combine the two degree programs. One dual program in law and social work recommends that first one year in social work school and then one year in law school be completed. Such a plan could mean four years of graduate education without earning either degree.

Nevertheless, dual degree programs in mental health and law are valuable. Particularly important is whether they have good teachers for family therapy and for family law. Family mediation is so new that the best strategy may be to find a few faculty members who are pursuing this area and seek guidance from them about how to complete a joint degree program. It may be possible to pick courses and do independent study appropriate to the student's particular goals.

Specific Training

A number of leading family mediators offer two- to five-day introductory training programs for either mental health practitioners with at least a master's degree or law school graduates. Most such training is limited to divorce mediation. Some trainers address child custody mediation only, while others consider financial issues as well. A few programs limit participation to lawyers.

Participants usually endorse these workshops, which emphasize learning how to mediate. Role-playing and case examples are featured. Some programs have been criticized for offering less than the five-day norm, pressing inexperienced trainers into service, or having only one trainer available at a time if a team is providing the information over the course of several days. As in other fields, persons signing up to take the training want famous mediators to lead their group. Few training programs have made the transition to reliance on the course content rather than on a star instructor.

While trainers agree that brief instruction (up to forty hours on divorce mediation) does not make a seasoned mediator, follow-up has been left primarily to the trainees. Some programs offer a practicum, supervision, and advanced courses while urging the new mediator to pursue an individual plan of study based on unique needs. A lawyer might take more coursework and training on psychological issues related to children and families. Mental health professionals might need to learn more about family law in their state. A certificate program that is completed part-time over the course of a year would allow family therapists and family lawyers to integrate their knowledge of mediation. Such a plan of study could be applied toward a Ph.D. in family mediation for practitioners who want to continue advanced work.

Getting Started

Obtaining Supervision

It is advisable to have someone to talk with about your first few mediation cases. An experienced family mediator can help you develop your practice and provide advice on particular cases. In addition, supervision groups usually enjoy talking about mediation with the supervisor and with fellow participants.

Joining Organizations

Another way to get information about mediation is to join an organization. If you join the Academy of Family Mediators, you will receive a newsletter, as well as *Mediation Quarterly*. The Academy is also developing a mediation referral service to connect its members with clients. Other national and international organizations, such as the Association of Family and Conciliation Courts (AFCC), publish journals like *Conciliation Courts Review*, which often includes articles on mediation. The California chapter of AFCC also has a newsletter. The Society for Professionals in Dispute Resolution has a number of relevant publications. The American Arbitration Association has established a family mediation committee.

Some states have local or statewide mediation councils. Michigan has a statewide council for divorce and family mediation intended to educate the public about the advantages of mediation and to provide a variety of services for members. The council supports legislation that develops mediation, sponsors training, and provides supervision. The Northern California Council of Mediators holds meetings on techniques and applications of mediation and publishes a newsletter. Joining or starting such a state or local group benefits the field because family laws affecting mediation occur state by state. Marketing mediation can be synergistic at the local level.

Mediating for a Living

You have taken relevant courses, undergone specific training, and joined appropriate organizations. Now it is time to establish your family mediation practice. Can you make a career as a family mediator?

Public Employment

The first choice is whether to work as a public employee or to start a private practice. Court-connected mediators are well paid compared to other mental health professionals at the master's degree level. In cities, these jobs tend to be full time. Your work will probably be limited to child custody and visitation disputes. You will probably be busy, perhaps seeing two or three families before lunch. Your biggest problem may be handling your feelings of overload and burnout caused by seeing so many angry people. You probably will not be able to consult with these families for as many sessions or about as many issues as you think they need.

Private Practice

If you decide to go into private practice, you must first determine the scope of your services. Are you going to mediate only child custody and visitation disputes? Are you going to mediate only divorces? Are you going to work with the wide range of disputes reviewed in this book? Perhaps you will specialize in yet other types of problems.

Team or Solo Practice

There are a number of advantages to mediating with a partner. If you are a mental health professional who feels a little uncertain about relevant family law and financial concerns, you might choose an attorney as your co-mediator. If you are a lawyer who needs to learn more about the emotional aspects of family conflicts, you might choose a co-mediator who is a psychotherapist. You also might consider a co-mediator of the opposite sex in order to provide a gender balance for your clients. Team mediation offers an opportunity for you and your partner to "Mutt & Jeff" with families: One partner makes an extreme recommendation while the other allies herself with the family to help them develop a reasonable agreement. In addition, families watching two mediators interact have a chance to observe successful interaction. Team mediation is also a way to serve an apprenticeship and gain experience.

Eventually, both economics and ego will probably lead you to practice alone. Paying both you and your colleague makes mediation prohibitively expensive for most clients. Mediators may feel inhibited in front of a colleague or may be unwilling to share control of the mediation process. So, while mediators may use a team model while supported by a grant or while learning the process, once outside funding stops or they feel comfortable with all aspects of mediating, they tend to stop co-mediating.

Referral Sources

Once you have decided where, what, and with whom to practice, you are ready to tackle the major question for most beginning family mediators in private practice. Where will clients come from? First, let's talk about where they probably will not come from. They will probably not come from the yellow pages even if you decide to call yourself AAA Family Mediation Services in order to get the first listing. Mediation is too new an idea for people to go looking through the phone book for practitioners. Also, the private and intimate nature of disputes that might be appropriate for the family mediator to help resolve usually requires a recommendation from a person known and trusted by the disputants.

Beginning family mediators usually have two mistaken assumptions. They may think their friends who are also family mediators will refer disputants to them, even though the most common problem in the field is a lack of clients. They also expect to receive referrals from attorneys specializing in divorce law. Neither of these sources typically send them clients.

Satisfied Clients

People who go through mediation are usually enthusiastic about the process. After you have mediated a few family disputes, you may find that people who at first appeared to be self-referrals in fact heard about you from someone you previously had mediated. Building a mediation practice is similar to building a practice in psychotherapy or law. A network of satisfied consumers typically leads to a thriving practice.

Corporate Attorneys

Attorneys specializing in corporate work or in other areas of law often do not like divorce work. Even fairly diversified law firms seldom have a domestic relations specialist. Yet the one lawyer with whom a divorcing executive has a long-standing relationship may be a senior partner in the firm that handles the company's business or the executive's own tax attorney, neither of whom knows much about family law. Because lawyers are reluctant to fail to meet the needs of good clients, they are an excellent referral source for the family mediator.

These clients often make good livings; typically, they want to avoid embarrassment in the community, as well as any dispute that could affect their performance on the job or their standing with the company. If they have just been told by their tax lawyer about the advantages of reaching an agreement—minimizing the adverse tax consequences of a divorce or other family dispute—they may be eager for your services.

Physicians

The stress of a divorce or other family dispute often brings people to their family doctor. Many visits to a general medical practitioner may be prompted at least partially by psychosomatic disorders. Board certified family practitioners include marriage counseling among their areas of expertise. Such signs as habitual tiredness, significant weight loss or gain, as well as forthright descriptions of the problem may alert the physician to what really brought the patient in. Educating your own family doctor and other physicians who might be receptive to the notion of family mediation can lead to a steady flow of referrals.

Clergy

Just as people sometimes seek out their family doctor when they have a personal problem, they may also turn to their minister, priest, or rabbi with private concerns. Some clergy now offer secular counseling and welcome the prospect of keeping members of their congregation from harming themselves and their children by a court fight.

Self-Help Groups

Organizations such as stepparent associations and Parents Without Partners may welcome your offer to speak about family mediation. Letting them see who you are and perhaps demonstrating some of the range of problems that you address, as well as some of your techniques, may encourage disputants to approach you. I was once asked to speak to a large meeting open to the public sponsored by another state's bar association and local stepparent association. The night before the public meeting I met with the local family mediation council. Their members told me that they had had virtually no clients. The next day, while I was speaking, a woman stood up and asked what I thought could be done when parents who were sharing custody of their child faced the need for one of them to move out of state. As I began to answer her, her ex-husband stood up beside her and they each held one of their children. They had come to the meeting to be mediated. After the talk had ended, two more couples approached me, asking me if I could help them solve their problems. I told them I had a plane to catch but referred them to local family mediators. The point is that finding a forum where you are visible can help to connect you with the many people who have problems that you can help them resolve.

Court-Connected Referrals

Not all states have full-time employees providing court-based child custody and visitation mediation. Some family courts have no such program at all, yet every community has disputes over these matters. You might offer to accept referrals by speaking to the local judge who hears such cases. Some court-connected mediation programs work by referring clients to a panel of private mediators. Some court-based programs that employ full-time mediators also refer disputants who need more sessions—either because of the psychological issues involved or perhaps because of the need to mediate financial aspects of the dispute—than the staff can offer.

Psychotherapists

Although a number of psychotherapists are beginning to offer mediation themselves, others would welcome the opportunity to refer clients that they have come to know and care about to a nonadversarial option when a family dispute seems to be leading to a court battle. Since much of what is referred to as marriage counseling takes place during the transition to a divorce, psychotherapists are a good referral source. Perhaps you are a psychotherapist considering expanding your practice to include family mediation. Since you probably should not mediate counseling clients of yours, you could work out a referral arrangement with colleagues who agree that persons participating in mediation require an impartial mediator.

Mediation as a Hidden Agenda

Just as clients who come in for counseling may be appropriate candidates for mediation, a number of people who hire you as a consultant or trainer actually are hoping you will settle a dispute. An agency once hired me to provide training on identifying physical and emotional child abuse. As I started my warm up, seeking to engage the group, I suddenly realized that everyone was very angry. I set aside the curriculum I had prepared and asked what was the matter. Seems that they had had some organizational development workshops about six months before and management had told them that "we're all in this together, let us know about any concerns that you have, and we'll work them out."

What happened next was that the agency was told by a funding source that, in order to continue to get their considerable government funding for child welfare services, they had to develop and maintain a twenty-four hour hotline for people to call in and report child abuse. When they told their employees about this problem, they said that everyone would have to start being on call periodically in order to staff the hotline. Being graduates of the organizational development workshop, the employees responded that they would like to see some new people hired to do this full time so that folks that had been there up to eleven years and had never had to be on call would not have to start now. Management was adamant and scheduled the training, which I was hired to provide. I had previously worked out a number of disputes between management and employees at branches of this agency statewide, and I think that was why I was brought in to do this training, and, of course, that's what I did, which was a much better use of the time than simply plowing through the scheduled content before a hostile audience.

Once you are known as a mediative sort of person, you

will find that people will bring you on board, simply hoping you will catch on and solve their problem. They may be embarrassed to say that that's why you have been asked to be there, or they may simply not have a budget that permits them to hire a mediator, but they can hire you to provide some sort of content as a trainer. There is always plenty of work for such a mediator. Listen carefully for a hidden agenda when you are asked to consult or to train.

Employee Assistance Programs

Follow my suggestion in Chapter 7 and seek referrals with EAPS. One or two contracts with major corporations can produce a full-time practice for a family mediator.

Mediation with Low-Income Families

Privately mediating disputes of low-income families seems to be a lot like the weather: everybody talks about it, but few people are actually doing much about it. Coogler (1979) proposed a model for mediating divorces of poor people. He suggested that a client referral network be established through Legal Aid societies, social service agencies, churches, and courts. He also suggested that initial interviews take place as soon as possible after contact by the client. Perhaps the mediator might go to the disputants' neighborhood and meet in some neutral place in an informal manner. He recommended involving relevant third parties in the mediation and having them sign any agreement reached even if these parties, such as extended family members, cannot be legally held to the agreement.

Divorce is the most common problem addressed by Legal Aid for poor people. However, a nationwide survey of the Legal Services Corporation found that 44% of the field offices were no longer handling divorce cases and 18% were no longer taking child custody and visitation cases ("Study Says Poor Hurt . . .," 1983). Family mediators who are willing to work on a sliding fee scale might solicit referrals from Legal Aid attorneys who can no longer provide divorce services, as well as from social service agencies who learn that their clients have a family dispute.

I also repeat my recommendation in an earlier chapter that you consider becoming a mediator of disputes in your neighborhood, either by participating in the present community board program or by starting one if none now exists. Getting experience mediating cases is valuable. Both serving on community boards, panels, and privately mediating disputes of low-income families may not present the complexities of clients with more money. You get experience and are visible as a family mediator. People may then think of you when more complicated issues arrive if they know that family mediation is your profession.

Where Are You Going to Mediate?

At this point you may want to read one of the books on the subject of psychotherapy as a business or managing a law practice. While I recommended in the techniques section of this book that you mediate in an attractive setting and use an answering service rather than an answering machine, you may find yourself with a negative cash flow if you gear up for a full-time mediation practice before the referral sources we just considered have begun to operate for you. "Net is the name of the game," as my tax lawyer reminds me each year. While it is impressive to have an office with your name in gold lettering on the door and a secretary to greet clients and offer them coffee, you are going to have to see a lot of people in order to pay for such an operation.

I often recommend that beginning family mediators ease into private practice with a time-share arrangement for a suite of professional offices. Often such a package includes a secretary and an after-hours answering service, duplicating equipment, and a conference room. If such situations are not common in your area, you might explore with the owners the use of an office that you find attractive. Family mediation often takes place before or after business hours and on weekends, and the owners may welcome the extra income, while you pay for office space and services only when you schedule clients.

How Much Will You Charge?

What must your hourly rate be after you pay the expenses of your practice in order for you to net a decent income? There are other objective criteria, such as the hourly rates of psychotherapists and family lawyers in your community. What is the hourly rate for other services you provide? I recommend that you charge the same hourly rate for mediation as for these. However, certain tasks—for instance, preparation of a memorandum of understanding—might be performed for a flat fee. Mediation differs from psychotherapy in this way because such written work must be done outside the mediation sessions. Preparation of written documents will increase if you decide to provide a written summary to each disputant after each session, as I suggested in the techniques section of this book.

Are you going to ask for a retainer fee? Family lawyers often require potential clients to make a nonrefundable deposit. The typical minimal amount is $2,500 in order even to take the case. Nevertheless, if the client decides to discharge the attorney, he may be able to persuade the court to refund the unearned portion of the retainer ("Unearned Portion of Retainer . . .," 1982). I suggest that a pay-as-you-go principle or advance payment for at most the first several sessions in advance is preferable to requiring a large, nonrefundable retainer.

Clients may be disappointed to learn that their insurance, which covers psychotherapy, will not cover mediation. This is an issue mediators can work to change with insurance companies and legislators. Do not offer to call mediation psychotherapy so that clients can have their insurance company pay for the service. You are trying to teach clients to be honest with each other and to make full financial and emotional disclosure during mediation. You want to model honest behavior in your conduct with them.

Mediation also may not be tax deductible. A number of services provided by family lawyers related to child custody and visitation are not tax deductible either unless they concern tax advice.

For now, you are going to have to assume that neither clients' health and mental health insurance nor prepaid legal services plans will cover mediation and that they cannot deduct the cost except to the extent that tax planning is concerned. One exception is that charges for a dispute mediated between business partners (even in a family-owned business) may be deductible if the business, rather than the individuals involved, pays for the fee.

Whatever you decide to charge, do not offer to provide mediation services for a flat fee. While a number of widely advertised discount law clinics operating in shopping centers and other convenient locations do just that, they both rely on secretaries or paralegals and treat all cases alike. While customers can get an uncontested divorce at a low price, Joel Hyatt, founder of Hyatt Legal Services, one of the largest law firms in the country, cautioned, "What we don't do are the unique cases because we couldn't do those any differently from any other practitioner" (Preston, 1983, p. 204). Mediation is often wrongly compared to low-cost, or flat-rate, legal services. Both to maintain your credibility and to help the disputants realize that they have personal responsibility for their conflict, make it clear that you do not know whether a resolution can be reached at all and you certainly do not know how many sessions such an agreement might take. Therefore, you must charge on an hourly basis.

How Much Boilerplate Can You Use?

This book does not include sample forms because each mediator must tailor his or her paperwork to the scope of the practice. Once you have decided the type of problems you wish to mediate, taking into account both family law in your state and local practice, you will have additional decisions to make.

First, are you going to develop a brochure? Like business cards, brochures are fun for professionals to exchange, but many successful family mediators never produce them. If you do decide to print a brochure, you may want to use it as a handout for potential referral sources rather than as a means of obtaining clients directly. When clients do approach you, you may want to have a handout that describes your services and your rules and procedures for mediation.

Second, should clients sign an agreement to mediate? Attorneys often ask clients to sign a form that describes the scope of issues to be mediated; identifies the costs; and specifies that no legal advice will be given to either party, that separate attorneys are advised; that the disputants may each be asked to consult a lawyer before, during, and after mediation; that all proceedings are confidential; and that the parties are to disclose fully all financial information requested and to share the costs in a prescribed manner, with payment either in advance or at each session. Some mediators, most prominently John Haynes, say that the parties' presence in your office means that they have agreed to mediate. Confronting them with a detailed form does not enhance the chance that mediation will proceed. The relevant information can be told to the parties by the mediator in the first session and constitute an oral contract. Experienced mediators know that the real reason for the dispute may not be apparent during the first session. Family lawyers reflect their legal training by attempting to get the form right, to get a comprehensive agreement to mediate nailed down. Family therapists entering the mediation field reflect their professional training by seeking to enhance the process and engage the disputants for enough sessions to give mediation a chance to work.

Whether you decide to develop a written agreement to mediate or simply to talk about the relevant issues with the parties; such as whether you may want to meet with each of them separately and, if so, what information so revealed will be shared, if you see fit, with the other parties, you may at least write a memorandum of understanding at the end of each successful mediation. At most, you might have working documents to distribute at the end of each session. You will also want to have all disputants sign a standard release form for any photographs, videotapes, or audiotapes that you might include them in during sessions.

How Can a Personal Computer Help You?

Whether you devote all your time to family mediation or practice either family therapy or family law as well, there are at least four ways in which a personal computer can help you. We discussed drafting agreements, financial planning, and legal research in Chapter 3. Here I outline useful features and typical costs so that you can choose a system to meet your needs.

Word Processing

Most people use a personal computer as though it were a smart typewriter. You can see the document on the screen and make sure the text is satisfactory before it is printed. Corrections can be made without leaving a trace, and both margins can be justified. The ability to use standard forms and make only minor changes, such as entering a new client's name, is an especially useful feature. Moreover, original documents can be created for each mediation case with only minimal changes. That is, you can put together an original document composed primarily of standard clauses, but the order and particular words and numbers are customized to fit your latest mediation case's memorandum of understanding. This keeps errors from creeping in and saves either you or your secretary time, which in turn saves money.

Real Men Don't Type, They Keyboard

Real women, as well as real men, who have relied on secretaries to translate their dictation or scrawling on legal pads know how much time and money it takes to get an error-free document out the door and in the mail. One of my colleagues whose correspondence to me often reads "dictated but not read" told his tape machine late one night about an unfortunate case in which a woman was killed by her paramour. His dictation was duly transcribed and mailed without his reviewing it. Later when he was reading the case file he noticed that it said that the woman was killed by her power mower.

If that real-life example doesn't persuade you, let me tell you about a major research university that decided to put personal computers in the office of each dean on campus. The computers were first made part of the secretary's work station. However, one by one, the deans decided to put the personal computer in their inner sanctum. For one thing, the computers were set up so that the deans could "talk" to each other by simultaneously displaying documents on the screens. However, the real reason was that it was fun to fool around with the computer.

You may be able to minimize secretarial time and even avoid becoming an employer by learning a word processing program. If you have tried using a custom secretarial service, you know that the work piles up. You can prepare documents on your personal computer when it fits your schedule, including evenings and weekends, and get the work done on time. This may help you to operate profitably in a solo practice or in association with a few other professionals, which is typical of family mediators.

Office Management

Like the practice of family therapy or family law, family mediation is a business. The product is primarily your time. Accounting software that has been developed for law office use can enable you to do your own billing and other bookkeeping for less money than you could pay someone else to do it. Advocates of computers in law offices say that in-house computerization reduces the cost of billing clients considerably. If you are accustomed to running your practice out of your back pocket, or relying solely on ledger sheets, you may find that as your business increases, computerized bookkeeping can help you keep track of your time.

Can You Afford a Computer?

Estimates of a personal computer system suitable for a law office range from $3,000 to $5,000. If you plan to use the computer solely for your mediation practice rather than for personal applications, you may be able to deduct the entire cost the year that you buy the system. If your financial situation permits, there may be a slight advantage to depreciating all or part of the purchase price over a period of years. You can use your new tax software package to compare the two options. Comparison of this sum to the cost of hiring additional staff for even one year suggests the advantages of buying a computer. You may be able to start your practice with just an answering service or answering machine and a computer, adding staff only when the number of clients permits you to do so, and still make a profit.

What Computer Equipment Should You Buy?

Talk to family mediators who use a computer in their practice. Keep in mind that almost any computer system is better than none, so that most owners are advocates of whatever outfit they have. You can counter this bias by going to a variety of retail computer stores and telling them what your needs are. From these various sources of information, a picture should emerge as to what you should buy.

I recommend buying a computer made by a well-established company so that it does not go out of business, leaving you with a dinosaur. Popular machines also have more software written for them, which lets you get additional features as you need them. Word processing software actually should determine the kind of machine you buy. Again, I recommend well-known software programs because improvements by the manufacturer, as well as add-ons by other companies, enable you to add features. It is also more likely that you can coordinate work done by a word processing service or another mediation office if you have one of the popular word processing software packages.

Try to buy a "what you see is what you get," screen-oriented system. Another consideration is an integrated package that combines word processing, office management, and financial planning. You need two disk drives in order to do the kind of word processing we have been talking about. It is also useful and not much more expensive to get a machine with a considerable amount of memory so you can manipulate book-length documents more easily. You should also get a letter-quality printer. Starting with a cheaper printer is a false economy because you will soon realize that what you and others expect is copy that looks like it came from an expensive typewriter. If you decide to subscribe to a legal database you will also need a modem. Start with a very inexpensive, bare-bones model if you are not sure whether you need this service; if you know you will use it a lot, buy a first-rate, fast modem. Of course, you can add the modem later.

The next step in buying a computer system is to think through what you want it to do. Then, make sure that any system you are considering can solve those problems for you and that you know how to use the equipment before you buy it. Many retail computer stores offer free or inexpensive classes of three hours or so; the cost of more expensive instruction often is applicable to the purchase price of any equipment you buy from the store offering the training. If you are worried that a computer might set the wrong tone for your office, you can balance the high tech with high touch as Naisbitt (1982) suggests we all do. My personal computer is housed in an oak desk designed for it so it fits in well with my rolltop desk. Look into buying a computer. If you get a system that meets your needs and take the trouble to learn how to use it, it will be a valuable tool in your family mediation practice.

Practice Issues

Confidentiality and Privileged Communication

Chapter 8 defined confidentiality as the duty to treat information received in your professional role responsibly, while privileged communication is the legal right not to testify in court if subpoenaed to do so. Some mediators make privileged communication—what they call confidentiality—a provision of the written agreement to mediate that every client of theirs signs. Other mediators assume there is no such right. Adriane Berg says,

> I believe that there is no confidentiality. Until it is tested, I will continue to believe that. Some professionals do not have to testify—mental health professionals, lawyers—but mediators are not on that list of professionals who cannot be subpoenaed to testify. I believe the lawyer who acts as mediator is a mediator and therefore can be subpoenaed to testify. But because my group is so self-selected that rarely troubles them. [Berg, 1983, p. 1]

In the last chapter I suggested ways to create a privilege in the absence of statutory protection.

Malpractice

Following generally accepted standards of practice is the way to avoid malpractice suits. Unfortunately, mediation is so new that it is difficult to identify such standards.

So far, successful malpractice suits against family mediators have been rare, as is the case with mental health professionals. While today's family lawyers can be successfully sued for missing a pension or failing to move forward in a divorce case in timely fashion, headlines such as "An Epidemic of Malpractice Suits" (Porter, 1982) still apply mostly to the practice of medicine, although "no profession is now immune from the threat of malpractice suits . . . associated medical professionals such as hospital administrators, nurses, dentists, X-ray technicians and pharmacists—and also attorneys, architects, engineers, insurance brokers, real estate agents" (p. 44).

Professional liability insurance for mental health professionals or attorneys probably does not cover mediation, but policies that specifically cover the practice of family mediation are now offered by several major insurance companies and sponsored by several mediator organizations. Such coverage promises peace of mind, and the cost is offset by several hours' mediation. Angry people who have family problems may consult friends, neighbors, other family members, or adversarial-oriented attorneys who tell them that they could have done better or that they were had. Someday one of them may sue you. Even frivolous suits must be defended. When obtaining a policy, make sure specifically what coverage is available.

> While many states have a statute of limitations, usually running from two to five years for bringing suit, that time limit is virtually meaningless. Recent court rulings have stated [that] the statute of limitations doesn't start to run until the person realizes that she/he has been "damaged" and in the case of children or adolescents, the statute of limitations runs through one year after they reach maturity. Thus it is possible for a therapist [or mediator] to be forced to justify actions in a case which might have occurred five or ten years previously. ["How to Protect Yourself Against a Lawsuit (I)," 1983, p. 2]

Some policies are cheaper through a professional association, and it may be worthwhile to join just to qualify for low-cost professional liability insurance. Coverage included in a comprehensive liability package may also be cheaper. One item to assess in any policy you are considering is whether it is a "claims made" policy or an "occurrence based" policy; the first means you have to be covered at the time of the claim; the second will provide coverage even if you no longer own the policy ("Malpractice Insurance," 1983).

What would happen if a ten-year-old child sued you when she reached age eighteen or nineteen because she was unhappy with the custody agreement her parents reached with your help? Again, even if she had virtually no chance of succeeding in court, she could still bring the suit and you would have to respond. Incorporating prevailing standards of practice for mediators into your conduct with families and keeping written records to prove that you do so would be essential for defending such a suit many years later.

The Unauthorized Practice of Law

You may want to review the section in the divorce mediation chapter that discusses the potential for unauthorized practice of law by divorce mediators. More generally, Deborah Rhode, associate professor of law at Stanford Law School, did a study of the "data regarding the bar's current enforcement activities in all fifty states as well as relevant statutes and all reported cases involving lay practitioners of the last decade" (1984, p. 8). She found that most such complaints involved a nonattorney giving advice during an uncontested divorce or real estate deal along with the completion of standardized forms. Only 2% of these bar association committee investigations began because of consumer complaints. Rhode states, "My research revealed no convincing evidence that the types of unauthorized practice triggering the greatest bar concern presented serious risk of harm to the public" (p. 8). Over three-fourths of the bar association committees' work was aimed at stopping the preparation of standardized forms.

Much of this work is done in law firms by paralegals or legal secretaries.

Rhode also makes the point that "unauthorized practice constraints implicates First Amendment values by restricting a lay speaker's ability to convey information and the public's opportunity to receive it" (p. 8). She suggests that bar enforcement agencies must be required to prove rather than simply claim the need for sanctions against the unauthorized practice of law. She suggests, "Lay persons providing legal assistance could be held to the same standards of competence, confidentiality and ethical conduct as attorneys and could be granted the same attorney-client privilege" (p. 8).

There are generally three aspects to the unauthorized practice of law. The first is representing clients in court. Family mediators, whether or not they are licensed attorneys, should not be representing their mediation clients in any adversarial proceeding. The second aspect of the practice of law is the preparation of legal documents for a client. Here, the mediator, seeking to avoid bar association committee investigation, may note well Rhode's research. Although current enforcement activities are primarily aimed at typing services in which people are attempting to represent themselves in court, family mediators may choose to prepare informal memoranda of understanding rather than formal marital settlement agreements or other legal documents for clients even if such agreements are to be reviewed by each disputant's own attorney.

Finally, the area of provision of legal advice is the third traditional aspect of the practice of law. Here, attempts to distinguish legal information (what the law is, that everyone is supposed to know) from legal advice (recommending that a particular person follow a specific course of action) present dilemmas for active family mediators. What we need to move toward are treaties exempting the typical practice of family mediation from charges of the unauthorized practice of law, similar to provisions in the state law concerning real estate agents, accountants, and bankers. *Model Rules of Professional Conduct*, adopted by the American Bar Association in 1983, states that a ban on the unauthorized practice of law "does not prohibit lawyers from providing professional advice and instruction to nonlawyers whose employment requires knowledge of the law; for example, claims adjusters, employees of financial or commercial institutions, social workers, accountants, and persons employed in government agencies" (p. 27). Any legal information given by family mediators would be minimal and peripheral to the primary process of mediation.

Those who argue that only attorneys admitted to the bar should act as family mediators might recall that many attorneys who begin their practice by doing divorces did not take family law coursework. In fact, although the California Family Law Specialist Program was continued in 1983, beginning lawyers and general practitioners argued against having a program that granted such a designation even though it did not prevent other attorneys from practicing family law. However, since its inception in 1971, the program has been considered to be successful and the governors of the California State Bar voted to approve the program permanently if it could be financially self-supporting. One board member said, "As a self-regulating body, if we don't step in and identify legal specialists, then others will and what occurs will be less standardized and not done as well" ("Bar Moves Step Closer . . .," 1983, p. 28). Similarly, a California bill that would mandate continuing legal education for all California lawyers was opposed and defeated. This is despite the comments of one malpractice litigator who said that "claims have been coming up in complex fields where lawyers are not adequately trained, primarily in family law" (Sacramento Scene, 1983, p. 48). Still, I believe there is often a role for family lawyers before, during and after their clients undergo family mediation, as Samuels and Shawn (1983) have suggested. Even in surveys showing that the public generally deplores the legal profession, respondents report that they respect the attorneys they know.

Supervision

The standards for membership in the Academy of Family Mediators call for ten hours of supervision of your first fifteen mediated cases. Continuing education requirements include twenty-four hours of case consultation each year. The practice issue here combines prevailing standards in our emerging profession with the opportunity to talk about mediation with other people who care about it as much as you do. You may also learn some new techniques and procedures. My supervision group ranges from role plays to marketing tips for obtaining more clients. Supervision and ongoing consultation is a good idea in an area as new as family mediation.

Continuing Education

The standards for membership in the Academy of Family Mediators require fifteen hours of instruction in the content that the particular member feels, along with his or her supervisor, is the area of greatest need. More specifically, I will tell you what I do to attempt to stay current about family mediation. I subscribe to and read *Family Law Quarterly* and *Family Advocate*, journals published by the Family Law Section of the American Bar Association. I founded *Mediation Quarterly* because I enjoy reading about and helping to shape developments in our field. I look forward to receiving the Academy of Family Mediators' newsletter as well. *Marriage and Divorce Today* newsletter often describes developments in family mediation. I subscribe to *California Family Law Report* in order to track family law unique to my state. *Family Law Reporter* provides a national overview of developments. Remember *Alternatives*, the journal I mentioned in the business and professional applications chapter that tracks alternative dispute resolution with business.

Each year I take twelve hours of coursework offered to California family law specialists, which apprises them of annual changes in the law. Conferences sponsored by the American Bar Association and the Association of Family and Conciliation Courts often include family mediation and related topics. I learn by talking to other family mediators. Consultation, advanced training, and workshops are ways to check in with practitioners who may be a bit further along than you are. They can give you good ideas on building your practice.

Shaping Your Future

Your future as a family mediator is in part up to you. The field is so new that you will help to determine the nature of family mediation practice. What are some of the areas you might consider?

Legislation

Wait a minute, don't we pride ourselves on the alegal-outlaw nature of our field? Aren't we, in part, an alternative to law? Shouldn't we wait until standards of practice reach a consensus before advocating legislation? There are several areas that need legislation now for mediation to prosper. The first may be creation of a mediator-client privilege so that if any of the clients involved in a mediation don't want us to talk in court we cannot be subpoenaed to do so. Given the delicate nature of many family disputes, we want to encourage full disclosure. Professor Rhode's article cited above gives us guidance about how we might do this without deciding educational and training standards for family mediators at this point in our profession's development.

We should work to enact a treaty in state law to prevent the typical practice of family mediation as being characterized as the unauthorized practice of law. This would not prevent dissatisfied consumers from complaining; it would follow the precedent set for real estate agents, bankers, and accountants, as mentioned above, and perhaps prevent a turf battle between attorneys and mental health professionals and others about what profession mediators must come from. We should develop mediation by lobbying for insurance companies to reimburse their clients who mediate with us, just as psychotherapy sessions and prepaid legal services are now covered. Berg (1983) suggests that this is a key factor in the survival of mediation and that both lawyers and mental health professionals who are divorce mediators should work toward this goal.

Standards

How do the standards reviewed in the ethical codes and standards chapter of this book compare with your experience as you mediate family disputes? How should they be changed? Working with professional organizations that are concerned

with mediation standards of practice is a way to have considerable influence.

Techniques That Work

Your colleagues will want to hear about techniques that you
find especially useful. Case examples showing how it's done
are valuable when giving a talk to a public group or to your
peers at a professional conference. Finally, if you find that
your ideas work for you and if they are well-received by your
colleagues, write them up and get them published. Yes, I have
a vested interest because I edit *Mediation Quarterly*. However,
I will also enjoy reading your work in other journals. The
main thing is that we communicate with each other about
what is most important to us, which is, after all, what we ask
of the families whose disputes we mediate.

APPENDIX A

Domestic Relations Tax Reform Act of 1984

P.L. 98–369

Sec. 1041. Transfers of Property Between Spouses or Incident to Divorce.

- (a) General Rule.—No gain or loss shall be recognized on a transfer of property from an individual to (or in trust for the benefit of)—
  - (1) a spouse, or
  - (2) a former spouse, but only if the transfer is incident to the divorce.
- (b) Transfer Treated as Gift; Transferee Has Transferor's Basis.—In the case of any transfer of property described in subsection (a)—
  - (1) for purposes of this subtitle, the property shall be treated as acquired by the transferee by gift, and
  - (2) the basis of the transferee in the property shall be the adjusted basis of the transferor.
- (c) Incident to Divorce.—For purposes of subsection (a)(2), a transfer of property is incident to the divorce if such transfer—
  - (1) occurs within 1 year after the date on which the marriage ceases, or
  - (2) is related to the cessation of the marriage.

(d) Special Rule Where Spouse Is Nonresident Alien.—Paragraph (1) of subsection (a) shall not apply if the spouse of the individual making the transfer is a nonresident alien.

Sec. 71. Alimony and Separate Maintenance Payments.
   (a) General Rule.—Gross income includes amounts received as alimony or separate maintenance payments.
   (b) Alimony or Separate Maintenance Payments Defined.—For purposes of this section—
      (1) In general.—The term "alimony or separate maintenance payment" means any payment in cash if—
         (A) such payment is received by (or on behalf of) a spouse under a divorce or separation instrument,
         (B) the divorce or separation instrument does not designate such payment as a payment which is not includible in gross income under this section and not allowable as a deduction under section 215,
         (C) in the case of an individual legally separated from his spouse under a decree of divorce or of separate maintenance, the payee spouse and the payor spouse are not members of the same household at the time such payment is made, and
         (D) there is no liability to make any such payment for any period after the death of the payee spouse and there is no liability to make any payment (in cash or property) as a substitute for such payments after the death of the payee spouse (and the divorce or separation instrument states that there is no such liability).
      (2) Divorce or separation instrument.—The term "divorce or separation instrument" means—
         (A) a decree of divorce or separate maintenance or a written instrument incident to such a decree,
         (B) a written separation agreement, or
         (C) a decree (not described in subparagraph [A]) requiring a spouse to make payments for the support or maintenance of the other spouse.
   (c) Payments to Support Children.—
      (1) In general.—Subsection (a) shall not apply to that part of any payment which the terms of the divorce or separation instrument fix (in terms of an amount of money or a part of the payment) as a sum which is payable for the support of children of the payor spouse.
      (2) Treatment of certain reductions related to contingencies involving child.—For purposes of paragraph (1), if any amount specific in the instrument will be reduced—

      (A) on the happening of a contingency specified in the instrument relating to a child (such as attaining a specified age, marrying, dying, leaving school, or a similar contingency), or

      (B) at a time which can clearly be associated with a contingency of a kind specified in paragraph (1), an amount equal to the amount of such reduction will be treated as an amount fixed as payable for the support of children of the payor spouse.

   (3) Special rule where payment is less than amount specified in instrument.—For purposes of this subsection, if any payment is less than the amount specified in the instrument, then so much of such payment as does not exceed the sum payable for support shall be considered a payment for such support.

(d) Spouse.—For purposes of this section, the term "spouse" includes a former spouse.

(e) Exception for Joint Returns.—This section and section 215 shall not apply if the spouses make a joint return with each other.

(f) Special Rules to Prevent Excess Front-Loading of Alimony Payments.—

   (1) Requirement that payments be for more than 6 years.— Alimony or separate maintenance payments (in excess of $10,000 during any calendar year) paid by the payor spouse to the payee spouse shall not be treated as alimony or separate maintenance payments unless such payments are to be made by the payor spouse to the payee spouse in each of the 6 post-separation years (not taking into account any termination contingent on the death of either spouse or the remarriage of the payee spouse).

   (2) Recomputation where payments decrease by more than $10,000.—If there is an excess amount determined under paragraph (3) for any computation year—

      (A) the payor spouse shall include such excess amount in gross income for the payor spouse's taxable year beginning in the computation year, and

      (B) the payee spouse shall be allowed a deduction in computing adjusted gross income for such excess amount for the payee spouse's taxable year beginning in the computation year.

   (3) Determination of excess amount.—The excess amount determined under this paragraph for any computation year is the sum of—

    (A) the excess (if any) of—
        (i)   the amount of alimony or separate maintenance payments paid by the payor spouse during the immediately preceding post-separation year, over
        (ii) the amount of alimony or separate maintenance payments paid by the payor spouse during the computation year increased by $10,000, plus
    (B) a like excess for each of the other preceding post-separation years. In determining the amount of the alimony or separate maintenance payments paid by the payor spouse during any preceding post-separation year, the amount paid during such year shall be reduced by any excess previously determined in respect of such year under this paragraph.

(4) Definitions.—For purposes of this subsection—
    (A) Post-separation year.—The term "post-separation year" means any calendar year in the 6 calendar year period beginning with the first calendar year in which the payor spouse paid to the payee spouse alimony or separate maintenance payments to which this section applies.
    (B) Computation year.—The term "computation year" means the post-separation year for which the excess under paragraph (3) is being determined.

(5) Exceptions.—
    (A) Where payments cease by reason of death or remarriage.—Paragraph (2) shall not apply to any post-separation year (and subsequent post-separation years) if—
        (i)   either spouse dies before the close of such post-separation year or the payee spouse remarries before the close of such post-separation year, and
        (ii) the alimony or separate maintenance payments cease by reason of such death or remarriage.
    (B) Support payments.—For purposes of this subsection, the term "alimony or separate maintenance payment" shall not include any payment received under a decree described in subsection (b)(2)(C).
    (C) Fluctuating payments not within control of payor spouse.—For purposes of this subsection, the term "alimony or separate maintenance payment" shall not include any payment to the extent it is made pursuant to a continuing liability (over a period of not

less than 6 years) to pay a fixed portion of the income from a business or property or from compensation for employment or self-employment.

Sec. 215. Alimony, Etc., Payments.
    (a) General Rule.—In the case of an individual, there shall be allowed as a deduction an amount equal to the alimony or separate maintenance payments paid during such individual's taxable year.
    (b) Alimony or Separate Maintenance Payments Defined.—For purposes of this section, the term "alimony or separate maintenance payment" means any alimony or separate maintenance payment (as defined in section 71[b]) which is includible in the gross income of the recipient under section 71.
    (c) Requirement of Identification Number.—The secretary may prescribe regulations which—
        (1) any individual receiving alimony or separate maintenance payments is required to furnish such individual's taxpayer identification number to the individual making such payments, and
        (2) the individual making such payments is required to include on such individual's return for the taxable year in which such payments are made.
    (d) Coordination With Section 682.—No deduction shall be allowed under this section with respect to any payment if, by · reason on section 682 (relating to income of alimony trusts), the amount thereof is not includible in such individual's gross income.

Sec. 423. Dependency Exemption in the Case of Child of Divorced Parents.
    (e) Support Test in Case of Child of Divorced Parents, Etc.—
        (1) Custodial parent gets exemption.—Except as otherwise provided in this subsection, if—
            (A) a child (as defined in section 151[e][3] receives over half of his support during the calendar year from his parents—
                (i) who are divorced or legally separated under a decree of divorce or separate maintenance,
                (ii) who are separated under a written separation agreement, or
                (iii) who live apart at all times during the last 6 months of the calendar year, and

(B) such child is in the custody of one or both of his parents for more than one-half of the calendar year, such child shall be treated, for purposes of subsection (a), as receiving over half of his support during the calendar year from the parent having custody for a greater portion of the calendar year (hereinafter in this subsection referred to as the "custodial parent").

(2) Exception where custodial parent releases claim to exemption for the year.—A child of parents described in paragraph (1) shall be treated as having received over half of his support during a calendar year from the noncustodial parent if—

(A) the custodial parent signs a written declaration (in such manner and form as the Secretary may by regulations prescribe) that such custodial parent will not claim such child as a dependent for any taxable year beginning in such calendar year, and

(B) the noncustodial parent attaches such written declaration to the noncustodial parent's return for the taxable year beginning during such calendar year. For purposes of this subsection, the term "noncustodial parent" means the parent who is not the custodial parent.

(3) Exception for multiple-support agreement.—This subsection shall not apply in any case where over half of the support of the child is treated as having been received from a taxpayer under the provisions of subsection (c).

(4) Exception for certain pre-1985 instruments.—

(A) In general.—A child of parents described in paragraph (1) shall be treated as having received over half his support during a calendar year from the noncustodial parent if—

(i) a qualified pre-1985 instrument between the parents applicable to the taxable year beginning in such calendar year provides that the noncustodial parent shall be entitled to any deduction allowable under section 161 for such child, and

(ii) the noncustodial parent provides at least $600 for the support of such child during such calendar year. For purposes of this subparagraph, amounts expended for the support of a child or children shall be treated as received from the noncustodial parent to the extent that such parent provided amounts for such support.

    (B) Qualified pre-1985 instrument.—For purposes of this paragraph, the term "qualified pre-1985 instrument" means any decree of divorce or separate maintenance or written agreement—

      (i)   which is executed before January 1, 1985,

      (ii) which on such date contains the provision described in subparagraph (A)(i), and

      (iii) which is not modified on or after such date in a modification which expressly provides that this paragraph shall not apply to such decree or agreement.

(5) Special rule for support received from new spouse of parent.—For purposes of this subsection, in the case of the remarriage of a parent, support of a child received from the parent's spouse shall be treated as received from the parent.

(6) Cross reference.—For provision treating child as dependent of both parents for purposes of medical expense deduction, see section 213(d)(4).

APPENDIX B

McLaughlin v. Superior Court

140 Cal. App. 3d 473 (March 1983)

[No. AO18674. First Dist., Div. Four. Mar. 1, 1983.]

THOMAS J. MCLAUGHLIN, PETITIONER, v.
The SUPERIOR COURT of SAN MATEO COUNTY, Respondent;
LINDA LEE MCLAUGHLIN, Real Party in Interest.

Rattigan, J.—Civil Code section 4607 requires prehearing mediation of child custody and visitation disputes in marital dissolution proceedings conducted pursuant to the Family Law Act. (Civ. Code. pt. 5, commencing with section 4000.) The statute also provides that, if the parties fail to agree in the mediation proceedings, the mediator "may, consistent with local court rules, render a recommendation to the court as to the custody or visitation of the child or children" involved. Pursuant to this provision, respondent superior court has adopted a "local court rule," or policy, which (1) requires the mediator to make a recommendation to the court if the parties fail to agree in the mediation proceedings, but (2) prohibits cross-examination of the mediator by the parties. We hold in this original proceeding that the policy is constitutionally invalid in significant respects.

The record in the proceeding supports the following recitals:

Petitioner Thomas J. McLaughlin and real party in interest Linda Lee McLaughlin were married in 1969. They have three children, between 6 and 13 years. The following events occurred in 1982: On May 17, petitioner filed a petition in respondent court for dissolution of their marriage. He requested in it, among other things, that he be awarded custody of the children. Real party in interest filed a response in which she requested the court to award "joint legal" custody of the children and their "physical custody" to her.

On June 10, petitioner applied to respondent court for an order granting temporary custody of the children to him and reasonable visitation rights to real party in interest. On the same date, the court issued an order to show cause in which the questions of temporary custody and visitation were set for hearing on June 30. Real party in interest filed a responsive declaration in which she requested an order granting temporary custody to her and "[r]easonable visitation to petitioner."

The hearing on the order to show cause was commenced on June 30 as scheduled. When it was called, petitioner's counsel recited his understanding that the pending issues of temporary custody and visitation were to be "referred for mediation." Counsel also stated his view that "the mediation procedure[,] insofar as it allows the mediator to make a recommendation to the Court, and bars the introduction of any testimony from the mediator about what the parties tell him or her[,] is unconstitutional as a denial of his right to cross-examine." On that ground, counsel in effect moved for a "protective order" which would permit mediation proceedings, but which would provide that if they did not result in agreement by the parties, on the issues of temporary custody and visitation, the mediator would be prohibited from making a recommendation to the court unless petitioner were guaranteed the right to cross-examine the mediator.

Speaking to the motion, the court pointed out that Civil Code section 4607 "required" that "a contested custody or visitation matter . . . be preceded . . . by a session of mandatory mediation . . . under the 1980 law."[1] The court also pointed out that the re-

[1]It is undisputed that the court's reference to "the new 1980 law" was to Civil Code section 4607, which was added to title 4 of the Family Law Act in that year. (Stats. 1980, ch. 48, section 5, pp. 133–134.) The statute reads in pertinent part as follows (italics added):

"4607. (a) Where it appears on the face of the petition or other application for an order or modification of an order for the custody or visitation of a child or children that either or both such issues are contested, as provided in Section 4600, 4600.1 or 4601, the matter *shall* be set for mediation of the contested issues prior to or concurrent with the setting of the matter for hearing. The purpose of such mediation proceeding shall be to reduce acrimony which may exist between the parties and to develop an agreement assuring the child or children's close and continuing contact with both parents after the marriage is dissolved. The mediator shall use his or her best efforts to effect a settlement of the custody or visitation dispute.

quired mediation proceedings were to be conducted "before the court of conciliation."[2] In an exchange with counsel which followed, the court denied the motion on the ground that the "protective order" requested would violate a policy the court had adopted pursuant to Civil Code section 4607, subdivision (e). (See fn. 1, *ante*.)

The exchange produced clarification of petitioner's motion. It also included the only available description of respondent courts policy, which has apparently not been memorialized in a written rule. For these reasons, we quote pertinent passages of the exchange in the margin.[3]

After the court had denied the motion, counsel for both parties agreed to a continuance of the hearing on temporary custody and visitation. They also agreed that custody would remain in "status quo" pending further proceedings. On July 6,

---

"(b) Each superior court shall make available a mediator. Such mediator may be a member of the professional staff of a family conciliation court, probation department, or mental health services agency, or may be any other person or agency designated by the court. In order to provide mediation services, the court shall not be required to institute a family conciliation court. . . .

"(c) Mediation proceedings shall be held in private and shall be confidential, and all communications, verbal or written, from the parties to the mediator made in a proceeding pursuant to this section shall be deemed to be official information within the meaning of Section 1040 of the Evidence Code.

"(d) The mediator shall have the authority to exclude counsel from participation in the mediation proceedings where, in the discretion of the mediator, exclusion of counsel is deemed by the mediator to be appropriate or necessary. . . .

"(e) The mediator *may, consistent with local court rules*, render a recommendation to the court as to the custody or visitation of the child or children. The mediator *may*, in cases where the parties have not reached agreement as a result of the mediation proceeding, recommend to the court that an investigation be conducted pursuant to Section 4602, or that other action be taken to assist the parties to effect a resolution of the controversy prior to any hearing on the issues. The mediator *may*, in appropriate cases, recommend that mutual restraining orders be issued, pending determination of the controversy, to protect the well-being of the children involved. . . . Any agreement reached by the parties as a result of mediation shall be reported to the court and to counsel for the parties by the mediator on the day set for mediation or any time thereafter designated by the court. . . ."

[2]This reference established that respondent court has elected to maintain a "family conciliation court" pursuant to the Family Conciliation Court Law (Code Civ. Proc., pt. 3, tit. 11.5, ch. 1, commencing with section 1730; see *id.*, section 1733); and that mediation proceedings required in respondent court by Civil Code section 4607 are conducted by personnel of its family conciliation court pursuant to subdivision (b) of that statute. (See fn. 1, *ante*.)

[3]"THE COURT [addressing Mr. Brunwasser, petitioner's counsel]: Some counties, as you probably know, do not permit or require a recommendation from the mediator in the event the parties are unable to agree. Some do. This county [i.e., respondent court] does, and therefore, I'm not prepared to give you the protective order you wish. The court feels that in the event the mediator were free to testify as to any of the matters mediated, that is[,] the substance of the matter as gleaned from the mediation session, . . . certainly you would have the right to cross-examine the mediator.

respondent court filed a formal order in which it directed mediation of the pending issues pursuant to Civil Code section 4607, subdivision (a); denied petitioner's motion for a protective order; and continued the hearing on the pending issues to August 11.[4]

On July 30, petitioner commenced the present proceeding by petitioning this court for a writ of prohibition restraining respondent court from "taking any further actions to enforce its order filed July 6, 1982, requiring petitioner and real party to submit their temporary custody dispute to mediation" in the absence of a "protective order" to the effect that the mediator could not make a recommendation to the court unless petitioner were permitted to cross-examine the mediator. (See fn. 4, *ante.*) Petitioner also asked this court to stay the mediation proceedings pending disposition of his petition.

On August 10, this court summarily denied the petition and the request for a stay. In a petition for hearing filed in the Supreme Court on August 16, petitioner again requested a temporary stay of the mediation proceedings in respondent court. In a later communication to the Supreme Court, he stated that respondent court had meanwhile set the hearing on temporary custody and visitation for August 24. Petitioner in effect requested that the Supreme Court make an order temporarily staying the hearing in the absence of a protective order barring a recommendation to respondent court by the mediator.

On August 18, the Supreme Court made an order temporarily staying the August 24 hearing without qualification. On August 25, it made an order in which it granted the petition for hearing; returned the cause to this court with directions to issue an al-

---

"However, our instructions as a matter of court policy to the mediators are that they are not to state the basis for their ... recommendation. .... In short, the recommendation of the mediator is simply ... a recommendation to the court without any statement of underlying basis. .... That's the way we do business here. ...

"MR. BRUNWASSER: ... I have no objection to mediation. What I have an objection to is a procedure which allows the mediator ... to communicate with the court and not be subject to defend [*sic*] his or her opinion by cross-examination.

"THE COURT: I understand that. I hope you equally understand that it is our policy to require a recommendation if the mediation is unsuccessful. It's a starting point which enables the court ...[,] in the absence of other evidence, to make an interim order based upon the opinion of the trained counselor, and it's a procedure we opted for when this law was enacted. We're satisfied that the law permits that, and so your motion for a protective order is denied."

[4]The formal order filed on July 6 read in pertinent part:
IT IS ORDERED as follows:

1. It appearing that there is a contested issue over child custody, the Court orders the parties to report to the Family Conciliation Court for media-

ternative writ; and ordered that the stay granted on August 18 was to remain in effect "pending final determination of this matter."[5]

This court issued an alternative write of prohibition which provided for the filing of "the written return, if any." With leave of this court, the California Chapter of the Association of Family and Conciliation Courts filed a brief amicus curiae. Amicus expressly disclaimed "taking a position in support of either side," but provided us with detailed information showing the practices followed by some superior courts relative to mediation proceedings conducted pursuant to Civil Code section 4607. (See fn. 7, *post*.) Real party in interest did not file a return to the alternative writ. Recognizing the desirability of an adversary proceeding, we requested respondent court to file a return. The court complied, and it appeared through counsel at oral argument. Amicus curiae and real party in interest also appeared at the argument.[6]

REVIEW

It may first be mentioned that we did not state reasons in our order summarily denying the petition in the first instance, but that we denied it on the basis of our views and that the mediation proceedings should be permitted to run their course; that the petition was essentially premature unless and until it were made to appear that a recommendation by the mediator might be forthcoming because the parties had failed to agree; and that the challenge raised in the petition would be rendered moot if

tion pursuant to the mandatory provisions of Civil Code section 4607(a) [i.e., section 4607, subdivision (a)].

2. Petitioner's motion for a protective order barring the mediator from rendering a recommendation to the Court for temporary custody and visitation[,] unless petitioner is afforded an opportunity to cross-examine the mediator, is denied.

3. Further hearing . . . is continued to August 11, 1982, at 9:00A.M. . . .

[5]The Supreme Court's order of August 18 read in pertinent part: "Pending determination of the petition for hearing filed herein, the hearing scheduled for August 24, 1982, in the respondent court in action No. 264286 . . . is hereby stayed."

The order made on August 25 read in pertinent part: "Petition for hearing GRANTED. The matter is transferred to this court and retransferred to the Court of Appeal, First District, Division Four, with directions to issue an alternative writ of prohibition. . . . The stay heretofore granted August 18, 1982 shall remain in effect pending final determination of this matter."

The Supreme Court having stayed only the hearing set for August 24, it appears at this point that the mediation proceedings ordered by respondent court on July 6 (see fn. 4, *ante*) have not been stayed at any time.

[6]It was stipulated at the argument that the petition was to be deemed a traverse of respondent court's return.

the parties agreed in fact. The Supreme Court obviously disagreed with these views, but the possibility of mootness persists because that court did not stay the mediation proceedings. (See fn. 5, *ante*.) The court having nevertheless directed us to consider the petition on its merits, we disregard any possibility of mootness on the ground that the issue presented is one of broad public interest and is likely to recur. (*Libertarian Party v. Eu* [1980] 28 Cal. 3d 535, 539 [170 Cal. Rptr. 25, 620 P.2d 612]; *City of Monterey v. California Coastal Com.* [1981] 120 Cal. App. 3d 799, 806 [174 Cal. Rptr. 798].)

Civil Code section 4607, subdivision (a), clearly requires prehearing mediation of child custody and visitation disputes in marital dissolution proceedings. (See fn. 1, *ante*.) Subdivision (e) of the statute is also clear to the effect that the mediator "may, consistent with local court rules," make a recommendation to the court on either issue, or both, if the parties fail to reach agreement in the mediation proceedings. Subdivision (e) does not require or authorize disclosure to the parties of a recommendation made by the mediator to the court, nor of the mediator's reasons; it neither requires nor authorizes cross-examination of the mediator by the parties, which would necessarily require or bring about disclosure of the recommendation and the reasons for it; and the statute's express deference to "local court rules" has the effect of making disclosure and cross-examination matters of local opinion.

As we have seen, respondent court has exercised this option by adopting a policy which requires that the mediator make a recommendation to the court if the parties have failed to agree on child custody or visitation in the mediation proceedings; requires that the mediator *not* state his or her reasons for the recommendation; and denies the parties the right to cross-examine the mediator on the ground that the reasons have not been disclosed to the court. (See fn. 3, *ante*.) Amicus curiae has shown us that one large metropolitan superior court follows an entirely different procedure, and that another has adopted a policy which is essentially similar to respondent court's.[7]

---

[7]Amicus curiae describes the practice of the Los Angeles County Superior Court without documentation, but without dispute by any party to this proceeding, as follows: Where prehearing mediation proceedings have been conducted in that court pursuant to Civil Code section 4607, and where the parties have not agreed on child custody or visitation (or both), the court (1) neither receives nor permits a recommendation by the mediator and (2) proceeds to hear and determine the contested issue or issues without referring to the unsuccessful mediation process in any way.

Amicus curiae has filed declarations showing the related practice followed in the Superior Court for the City and County of San Francisco. Only one of the declara-

The feature of respondent court's policy which prohibits cross-examination of the mediator is consistent with the provision in subdivision (c) of the statute that the mediation proceedings "shall be confidential." (See fn. 1, *ante*.) The requirement that the mediator not state to the court his or her reasons for the recommendation is consistent with the provision in subdivision (c) which protects the confidentiality of the parties' "communications" to the mediator by making them "official information within the meaning of Section 1040 of the Evidence Code." (See *ibid*.)[8] The facts remain that the policy permits the court to receive a significant recommendation on contested issues but denies the parties the right to cross-examine its source. This combination cannot constitutionally be enforced.

In *Fewel v. Fewel* (1943) 23 Cal. 2d 431 [144 P. 2d 592], the plaintiff had appealed from successive child custody orders made by a trial court in a divorce action. (*Id*., at p. 433.) The order which was "controlling" had been "based exclusively on the *recommendation* of a court investigator. . . ." (*Ibid*. [original italics].) The Supreme Court further described the recommendation, and held, as follows: "The recommendation . . . is a recommendation for an order *and nothing more*. It contains no statement of facts or of *the reasons* for the conclusions suggested. The investigator was *not present for cross-examination*. . . . Such procedure cannot be sustained. By it the plaintiff was *denied the fair trial in open court* to which she was entitled; . . . she was *precluded from cross-examination of adverse witnesses*. . . . Such errors require a reversal of the order." (*Fewel v. Fewel, supra*, 23 Cal. 2d 431 at p. 433 [italics added].) The "errors" had included actions and omissions by the trial court in addition to the denial of the right to cross-examine the investigator. (See *ibid*.) The *Fewel* court nevertheless made it clear that the denial of that right alone was reversible error, holding further: "The reports of . . . investigators should be presented . . . under oath,

---

tions describes what happens when the parties fail to agree in the mediation proceedings. This declaration was executed by the presiding judge of the domestic relations department of the San Francisco court. He states in effect as follows: The mediator is required to make a recommendation to the court in such cases. The mediator first communicates the recommendation to the parties' attorneys, in writing, without stating reasons for it. The attorneys present it to the court, which permits either of them to argue against its adoption. The court thereupon makes an order on child custody and visitation without permitting cross-examination of the mediator. The reasons for the mediator's recommendation are apparently not disclosed to the parties at any time.

[8]The provisions here quoted were apparently adapted from language in the Family Conciliation Court Law (see fn. 2, *ante*) which similarly controls in conciliation proceedings conducted pursuant to that enactment. (See Code Civ. Proc., section 1747.)

and an investigator, upon timely demand by any party, *must appear like any other witness and testify* subject to the rules of evidence and *the right of cross-examination*. It definitely is not the province of investigators to make a *private . . . recommendation* to the judge, or any recommendation independent of the evidence on which it is based." (23 Cal. 2d 431 at p. 436 [italics added].)

The applicability of these holdings to the comparable situation presented in respondent court is obvious. In *Long v. Long* (1967) 251 Cal. App. 2d 732 [59 Cal. Rptr. 790], the Court of Appeal followed *Fewel* as the basis for finding reversible error in a situation which was not materially distinguishable. (*Id.*, at pp. 735–736.) The *Long* court explicitly cited *Fewel* as authority for the statement that "[t]o deny a litigant the right to cross-examine a witness who testifies against him is a denial of due process of law." (*Id.*, at p. 736.) Another Court of Appeal reached the same result on comparable facts and the authority of *Fewel* and *Long*. (*In re George G.* [1977] 68 Cal. App. 3d 146, 156–157 [137 Cal. Rptr. 201]; see also *Wheeler v. Wheeler* [1973] 34 Cal. App. 3d 239, 241–242 [109 Cal. Rptr. 782]; *Dahl v. Dahl* [1965] 237 Cal. App. 2d 407, 414 [46 Cal. Rptr. 381]; on the right of cross-examination as an essential element of due process, see 5 Witkin, Summary of Cal. Law [8th ed. 1974] Constitutional Law, section 293, par. (3), p. 3583 [citing *Fewel*]; see also Evid. Code, section 711; Witkin, Cal. Evidence [2d ed. 1966] sections 1071 [pp. 993–994], 1197 [pp. 1105–1106].)

Respondent court contends that the enforcement of its policy prohibiting cross-examination of a mediator who makes a recommendation to it is constitutionally permissible because only "temporary" child custody and visitation are involved and "due process is not required at every stage of the proceeding." The language of Civil Code section 4607, subdivision (a), fairly imports that the mediation proceedings directed by it will most frequently involve custody and visitation rights which are "temporary" in the sense that they are to be resolved in the underlying marital dissolution proceeding pendente lite. (See fn. 1, *ante*.) The showing made by amicus curiae supports the conclusion that this is true of the mediation proceedings ordered in a typical case.

However, the word "temporary" does not appear in Civil Code section 4607. We are not at liberty to interpolate it, by construction, because in construing a statute "a court is not authorized to insert qualifying provisions not included and may not rewrite the statute to conform to an assumed intention which does not appear from its language." (*People v. One 1940 Ford*

V-8 Coupe [1950] 356 Cal. 2d 471, 475 [224 P. 2d 677]; *Jordan v. Superior Court* [1981] 116 Cal. App. 3d 202, 210 [172 Cal. Rptr. 30]; see also Code Civ. Proc., section 1858.) In all events, any child custody or visitation order made in a marital dissolution proceeding is "temporary" in the sense that it may be modified on an adequate showing of changed conditions. (See, e.g., *In re Marriage of Carney* [1979] 24 Cal. 3d 725, 729–731 [157 Cal. Rptr. 383, 598 P. 2d 36, 3 A.L.R. 4th 1028].) The constitutional infirmities in respondent court's policy are such that it may not be enforced on the theory that only "temporary" custody or visitation are involved. (See *In re George G., supra*, 68 Cal. App. 3d 146 at p. 157.)

Subdivision (a) of Civil Code section 4607 provides that contested issues of child custody and visitation "shall" be referred to prehearing mediation proceedings. (See fn. 1, *ante*.) Subdivision (e) of the statute provides that the mediator "may, consistent with local court rules," make a recommendation to the court if the parties fail to agree in the proceedings. (See *ibid*.) The use of the opposing verb forms in the same statute fairly reflects a legislative intent that the first provision is to be construed as mandatory and the second as permissive. (See Code Civ. Proc., section 1859; *Estate of Mitchell* [1942] 20 Cal. 2d 48, 51 [123 P. 2d 503]; *Lara v. Board of Supervisors* [1976] 59 Cal. App. 3d 399, 410–411 [130 Cal. Rptr. 668].) Construction of the second provision as permissive is also supported by its express deference to "local court rules."

"If 'the terms of a statute are by fair and reasonable interpretation capable of a meaning consistent with the requirements of the Constitution, the statute will be given that meaning, rather than another in conflict with the Constitution.' [Citations.]" (*Metromedia, Inc. v. City of San Diego* [1982] 32 Cal. 3d 180, 186 [185 Cal. Rptr. 260, 649 P. 2d 902].) We are therefore to construe the permissive language of Civil Code section 4607, subdivision (e), in such manner as will comport with the requirements of due process discussed above. It follows that the mediator designated by respondent court may not make a recommendation to the court subject to a "local court rule," or policy, which prohibits either party from calling the mediator and cross-examining him or her at a hearing on the contested issue or issues covered by the recommendation. (*Fewel v. Fewel, supra*, 23 Cal. 2d 431 at pp. 433, 436.) For purposes of the present proceeding, it further follows that the mediator "may" not make a recommendation to respondent court in the absence of the protective order sought by petitioner, which will guarantee him the right to cross-examine the mediator.

These conclusions permit the mediation proceedings which Civil Code section 4607 requires where child custody or visitation are contested. They also permit the mediator to make a recommendation to the court if the proceedings do not produce agreement, but only if the parties are guaranteed—or waive— the right to cross-examine the mediator and other rights essential to due process. (See *Fewel v. Fewel, supra,* 23 Cal. 2d 431 at pp. 433, 436.) Our conclusions are consistent with our duty to harmonize the provisions of subdivisions (a) and (e) of the statute without doing violence to its salutary purposes. (See Code Civ. Proc., section 1859; *In re Bandmann* [1958] 51 Cal. 2d 388, 393 [333 P. 2d 339]; *Marrujo v. Hunt* [1977] 71 Cal. App. 3d 972, 977 [138 Cal. Rptr. 220].) In addition, it has been shown in the present proceeding that disparities among "local court rules" adopted pursuant to subdivision (e) have had the effect of guaranteeing due process in some superior courts but not in others. (See fn. 7, *ante.*) Our conclusions will terminate this effect, which the Legislature obviously did not intend.

Our conclusions also establish that petitioner is entitled to extraordinary relief from the enforcement of respondent court's policy. He has sought a writ of prohibition, which would lie if the infirmities in the policy reflected an excess of jurisdiction. (Code Civ. Proc., section 1102; 5 Witkin, Cal. Procedure (2d ed. 1971) Extraordinary Writs, sections 15 [pp. 3790–3791], 39 [p. 3813].) Enforcement of the policy would be reversible error, but not for want of jurisdiction. (*Fewel v. Fewel, supra,* 23 Cal. 2d 431 at pp. 436–437.) The appropriate remedy is therefore a writ of mandate. (See Code Civ. Proc., sections 1085–1086; 5 Witkin, Cal. Procedure, *op. cit.,* sections 61 [pp. 3838–3839], 69 [p. 3847], 183–184 [pp. 3942–3943].)

The writ of mandate ordered below permits the mediation proceedings to be conducted as previously ordered by respondent court. It also directs that the court *not* receive a recommendation from the mediator, as to any contested issue on which agreement is not reached, unless (1) the court has first made a protective order which guarantees the parties the rights to have the mediator testify and to cross-examine him or her concerning the recommendation or (2) the rights have been waived.

A preemptory writ of mandate consistent with this opinion will issue.

Caldecott, P. J., and Poché, J., concurred.

APPENDIX C

National Labor Relations Board (NLRB) v. Joseph Macaluso, Inc.

(1980) 618 F. 2d 51.

Wallace, Circuit Judge—The single issue presented in this National Labor Relations Board (NLRB) enforcement proceeding is whether the NLRB erred in disallowing the testimony of a Federal Mediation and Conciliation Service (FMCS) mediator as to a crucial fact occurring in his presence. The decision and order of the Board are reported at 231 N.L.R.B. 94. We enforce the order.

I.

In early 1976 Retail Store Employees Union Local 1001 (Union) waged a successful campaign to organize the employees of Joseph Macaluso, Inc. (Company) at its four retail stores in Tacoma and Seattle, Washington. The Union was elected the collective bargaining representative of the Company's employees, was certified as such by the NLRB, and the Company and Union commenced negotiating a collective bargaining agreement. Several months of bargaining between Company and Union negotiators failed to produce an agreement, and the parties decided to enlist the assistance of a mediator from the FMCS. Mediator Douglas Hammond consequently attended the three meetings between the Company and Union from which arises the issue before us. To frame that issue, it is necessary first to describe the history of this litigation.

During the spring and summer of 1978 the Company engaged in conduct which led the NLRB to charge it with unfair labor practices. Proceedings were held and the NLRB ruled that the Company had violated section 8(a)(1) of the National Labor Relations Act (NLRA) by threatening pro-union employees, and section 8(1)(3) of the NLRA by discharging an employee for union activity. At this unfair labor practice proceeding the NLRB also found that the Company and Union had finalized a collective bargaining agreement at the three meetings with Hammond, and that the Company had violated NLRA sections 8(a)(5) and (1) by failing to execute the written contract incorporating the final agreement negotiated with the Union. The NLRB ordered the Company to execute the contract and pay back-compensation with interest, and seeks enforcement of that order in this court. In response, the Company contends that the parties have never reached agreement, and certainly did not do so at the meetings with Hammond.

The testimony of the Union before the NLRB directly contradicted that of the Company. The two Union negotiators testified that during the first meeting with Hammond the parties succeeded in reducing to six the number of disputed issues, and that the second meeting began with Company acceptance of a Union proposal resolving five of those six remaining issues. The Union negotiators further testified that the sixth issue was resolved with the close of the second meeting, and that in response to a Union negotiator's statement "Well, I think that wraps it up," the Company president said, "Yes, I guess it does." The third meeting with Hammond, accordance [sic] to the Union, was held only hours before the Company's employees ratified the agreement, was called solely for the purpose of explaining the agreement to the Company accountant who had not attended the first two meetings, and was an amicable discussion involving no negotiation.

The Company testimony did not dispute that the first meeting reduced the number of unsettled issues to six, but its version of the last two meetings contrasts sharply with the Union's account. The Company representatives testified that the second meeting closed without the parties having reached any semblance of an agreement, and that the third meeting was not only inconclusive but stridently divisive. While the Union representatives testified that the third meeting was an amicable explanatory discussion, the Company negotiators both asserted that their refusal to give in to the Union demands caused the Union negotiators to burst into anger, threaten lawsuits, and leave the room at the suggestion of Hammond. According to the Company, Hammond was thereafter unable to bring the parties together and the Union negotiators left the third meeting in anger.

In an effort to support its version of the facts, the Company requested that the administrative law judge (ALJ) subpoena Hammond and obtain his testimonial description of the last two bargaining sessions. The subpoena was granted, but was later revoked upon motion of the FMCS. . . . [T]he ALJ decided that the Union witnesses were more credible and ruled that an agreement had been reached. The Company's contention in response to this request for enforcement of the resulting order to execute the contract is that the ALJ and NLRB erred in revoking the subpoena of Hammond, the one person whose testimony could have resolved the factual dispute.[1]

II.

Revocation of the subpoena was based upon a long-standing policy that mediators, if they are to maintain the appearance of neutrality essential to successful performance of their task, may not testify about the bargaining sessions they attend. Both the NLRB and FMCS (as amicus curiae) defend that policy before us. We are thus presented with a question of first impression before our court: can the NLRB revoke the subpoena of a mediator capable of providing information crucial to resolution of a factual dispute solely for the purpose of preserving mediator effectiveness?

Statutory authority for NLRB subpoena revocation is found in NLRA section 11(1). 29 U.S.C. section 161(1):

> Within five days after the service of a [subpoena] on any person requiring the production of any evidence in his possession or under his control, such person may petition the [NLRB] to revoke, and the [NLRB] shall revoke, such [subpoena] if in its opinion the evidence whose production is required does not relate to any matter under investigation, or any matter in question in such proceedings, or if in its opinion such [subpoena] does not describe with sufficient particularity the evidence whose production is required.

[1]The company did not challenge the NLRB's finding of unfair labor practices from the threatening and discharge of employees.

We have interpreted this provision broadly, stating:

> The statute in question does not state that petition to revoke subpoenas can only be made on the two grounds therein stated, or that the [ALJ] or [NLRB] may revoke only on those grounds. It does provide that a person served with such a subpoena may petition for revocation of the subpoena and the [NLRB] *shall* revoke it if one of the two specified circumstances exist [sic]. Insofar as the statute is concerned, the [NLRB] may also revoke a subpoena on any other ground which is consonant with the overall powers and duties of the [NLRB] under the [NLRA] considered as a whole.

General Engineering, Inc. v. NLRB, 341 F. 2d 367, 372–73 (9th Cir. 1965) (emphasis in original). We must determine, therefore, whether preservation of mediator effectiveness by protection of mediator neutrality is a ground for revocation consistent with the power and duties of the NLRB under the NLRA. Stated differently, we must determine whether the reason for revocation is legally sufficient to justify the loss of Hammond's testimony. The NLRB's own regulation authorizing revocation states:

> The administrative law judge or the [NLRB] as the case may be, shall revoke the [subpoena] if in its opinion the evidence whose production is required does not relate to any matter under investigation or in question in the proceedings or the [subpoena] does not describe with sufficient particularity the evidence whose production is required, *or if for any other reason sufficient in law the [subpoena] is otherwise invalid.*

29 C.F.R. section 10231(b) (1979) (emphasis added).

The NLRB's revocation of Hammond's subpoena conflicts with the fundamental principle of Anglo-American law that the public is entitled to every person's evidence. *Branzburg v. Hayes*, 408 U.S. 665, 688, 92 S. Ct. 2646, 2660, 33 L. Ed. 2d 626 (1972); *United States v. Bryan*, 339 U.S. 323, 331, 70 S. Ct. 724, 730, 94 L. Ed. 884 (1950); 8 Wigmore, Evidence section 2192, at 70 (McNaughton Rev. 1961). According to Dean Wigmore this maxim has existed in civil cases for more than three centuries, and the Sixth Amendment guarantee of compulsory process was created "merely to cure the defect of the common law by giving to parties defendant in criminal cases the common right which was already possessed . . . by parties in civil cases. . . ." *Id*. at section 2191, at 68.

The facts before us present a classic illustration of the need for every person's evidence: the trier of fact is faced with directly conflicting testimony from two adverse sources, and a third objective source is capable of presenting evidence that would, in all probability, resolve the dispute by revealing the truth. Under such circumstances, the NLRB's revocation of Hammond's subpoena can be permitted only if denial of his testimony "has a public good transcending the normally predominant principle of utilizing all rational means for ascertaining truth." *Elkins v. United States*, 364 U.S. 206, 234 80 S. Ct. 1437, 1454, 4 L. Ed. 2d 1669 (1960) (Frankfurther, J., dissenting), *quoted in United States v. Nixon*, 418 U.S. 683, 710 n. 18, 94 S. Ct. 3090, 3108, 41 L. Ed. 2d 1039 (1974). The public interest protected by revocation must be substantial if it is to cause us to "concede that the evidence in question has all the probative value that can be required and yet exclude it because its admission would injure some other cause more than it would help the cause of truth and because the avoidance of that injury is considered of more consequence than the possible harm to the cause of truth." 1 Wigmore, Evidence section 11, at 296 (1940). We thus are required to balance two important interests, both critical in their own setting.

We conclude that the public interest in maintaining the perceived and actual impartiality of federal mediators does outweigh the benefits derivable from Hammond's testimony. This public interest was clearly stated by Congress when it created the FMCS:

It is the policy of the United States that—

(a) sound and stable industrial peace and the advancement of the general welfare, health, and safety of the Nation and of the best interests of employers and employees can most satisfactorily be secured by the settlement of issues between employers and employees through the process of conference and collective bargaining between employers and the representatives of their employees;

(b) the settlement of issues between employers and employees through collective bargaining may be advanced by making available full and adequate governmental facilities for conciliation, mediation, and voluntary arbitration to aid and encourage employers and the representatives of their employees to reach and maintain agreements concerning rates of pay, hours, and working conditions, and to make all reasonable efforts to settle their differences by mutual agreement reached through conferences and collective bargaining or by such methods as may be provided for in any applicable agreement for the settlement of disputes.

29 U.S.C. section 171(a)(b). Since Congress made this declaration, federal mediation has become a substantial contributor to industrial peace in the United States. The FMCS, as amicus curiae, has informed us that it participated in mediation of 23,450 labor disputes in fiscal year 1977, with approximately 325 federal mediators stationed in 80 field offices around the country. Any activity that would significantly decrease the effectiveness of this mediation service could threaten the industrial stability of the nation. The importance of Hammond's testimony in this case is not so great as to justify such a threat. Moreover, the loss of that testimony did not cripple the fact-finding process. The ALJ resolved the dispute by making a credibility determination, a function routinely entrusted to triers of fact throughout our judicial system.

The FMCS has promulgated regulations which explain why the very appearance of impartiality is essential to the effectiveness of labor mediation.

> Public policy and the successful effectuation of the Federal Mediation and Conciliation Service's mission require that commissioners and employees maintain a reputation for impartiality and integrity. Labor and management or other interested parties participating in mediation efforts must have the assurance and confidence that information disclosed to commissioners and other employees of the Service will not subsequently be divulged, voluntarily or because of compulsion, unless authorized by the Director of the Service.
>
> • • •
>
> No officer, employee, or other person officially connected in any capacity with the Service, currently or formerly shall, in response to a subpoena, subpoena duces tecum, or other judicial or administrative order, produce any material contained in the files of the Service, disclose any information acquired as part of the performance of his official duties or because of his official status, or testify on behalf of any party to any matter pending in any judicial, arbitral or administrative proceeding, without the prior approval of the Director.

29 C.F.R. section 1401.2(a), (b) (1979). This need for the appearance of impartiality, and the potential for loss of that appearance through any degree of mediator testimony, was well ex-

pressed by the NLRB in the decision relied upon by the ALJ when revoking Hammond's subpoena.

> However useful the testimony of conciliator might be to the [NLRB] in any given case, we can appreciate the strong consideration of public policy underlying the regulation [denying conciliator testimony] and the refusal to make exceptions to it, because of the unique position which the conciliators occupy. To execute successfully their function of assisting in the settlement of labor disputes, the conciliators must maintain a reputation for impartiality, and the parties to conciliation conferences must feel free to talk without any fear that the conciliator may subsequently make disclosures as a witness in some other proceeding, to the possible disadvantage of a party to the conference. If conciliators were permitted or required to testify about their activities, or if the production of notes or reports of their activities could be required, not even the strictest adherence to purely factual matters would prevent the evidence from favoring or seeming to favor one side or the other. The inevitable result would be that the usefulness of the [FMCS] in the settlement of future disputes would be seriously impaired, if not destroyed. The resultant injury to the public interest would clearly outweigh the benefit to be derived from making their testimony available in particular cases.

Tomlinson of High Point, Inc., 74 N.L.R.B. 681, 698 (1947). We agree.

During oral argument the suggestion was made that we permit the mediator to testify, but limit his testimony to "objective facts" as suggested by *International Association of Machinists and Aerospace Workers v. National Mediation Board*, 425 F. 2d 527, 540 (D.C. Cir. 1970). We do not believe, however, that such a limitation would dispel the perception of partiality created by mediator testimony. In addition to the line-drawing problem of attempting to define what is and is not an "objective fact," a recitation of even the most objective type of facts would impair perceived neutrality, "for the party standing condemned by the thrust of such a statement would or at least might conclude that the [FMCS] was being unfair." *Id.* at 539. "[N]ot even the strictest adherence to purely factual matters would prevent the evidence from favoring or seeming to favor one side or the other." *Tomlinson of High Point, Inc., supra*, 74 N.L.R.B. at 688.

We conclude, therefore, that the complete exclusion of mediator testimony is necessary to the preservation of an effective system of labor mediation, and that labor mediation is essential to continued industrial stability, a public interest sufficiently great to outweigh the interest in obtaining every person's evidence.[2] No party is required to use the FMCS; once having voluntarily agreed to do so, however, that party must be charged with acceptance of the restriction on the subsequent testimonial use of the mediator. We thus answer the question presented by this case in the affirmative: the NLRB can revoke the subpoena of a mediator capable of providing information crucial to resolution of a factual dispute solely for the purpose of preserving mediator effectiveness.[3] Such revocation is consonant with the overall powers and duties of the NLRB, a body created to implement the NLRA goals of "promot[ing] the flow of commerce by removing certain recognized sources of industrial strife and unrest" and "encouraging practices fundamental to the friendly adjustment of industrial disputes ..." 29 U.S.C. section 151.

The Order of the Board is enforced.

[2]We need not reach the question whether a different result would occur if the FMCS Director granted authority for the mediator to testify pursuant to 29 C.F.R. section 1401.2(b) (1979).

[3]The Company argued that revocation of Hammond's subpoena was improper because communications made to him during the course of the bargaining sessions were necessarily made in the presence of the opposing party and were not, therefore, confidential. Such a contention misapprehends the purpose of excluding mediator testimony which is to avoid a breach of impartiality, not a breach of confidentiality.

APPENDIX D

Academy of Family Mediators

Membership Categories

There shall be five membership categories:

1. *Affiliate*—Anyone may become an affiliate and receive the Newsletter, Journal, and other publications of the Academy.
2. *Student*—Open to students enrolled in a graduate program in the behavioral sciences, law, or conflict resolution.
3. *Associate*—Open to those who have completed the academic requirements and who are in the process of completing the experience and specialized training requirements as set forth below. Additionally, an Associate Member must be in the process of completing the case handling and supervision required for Full Membership. One may not be an Associate Member for longer than twelve consecutive months unless extended by the Membership Committee.
4. *Member*—Open to those who have completed all of the academic, experience, training and case completion, and supervision requirements as set forth below.
5. *Fellow*—Open to those who have been members of the Academy for at least two years, or for the two years prior to becoming a Fellow, one must have met all the standards of Full

Membership in the Academy. In addition, to be a Fellow, one must have completed a total of at least thirty mediation cases and must have demonstrated a significant contribution to the field of family mediation through either research, publication, lecturing, or education as reviewed on an individual basis by the Membership Committee.

The Board of Directors has approved the following Standards of Membership in the Academy. These standards define the appropriate criteria for measuring the development of professional mediators and determining the appropriate levels of Academy membership.

These standards pertain to family mediation, which is not limited to disputes between divorcing or separating spouses. It is not our intent fully to define or describe the conduct of mediation, nor the particular relationship between the ethical requirements of the mediator and one's professional discipline. These standards represent preliminary education, training, experience, and continuing education requirements for membership in the Academy of Family Mediators. Membership in the Academy does not represent certification; in establishing standards of membership, the Academy does not seek to certify the competence of any particular member to the public nor to limit in any way the right of a nonmember to practice mediation.

Standards of Membership

Academic Requirements. Completion of a master's degree in a related behavioral science, a law degree, or an equivalent approved by the Membership Committee.

Experience. Completion of two years of professional work experience following receipt of one's qualifying degree.

Specialized Training in Family Mediation. One must have completed forty hours of training, including a minimum of five hours in each of the following categories:
1. Conflict resolution theory
2. Social-psychological issues in child development, family dynamics, and the divorce process
3. Mediation process and techniques
4. Family law, including support, asset distribution and evaluation, and taxation as it relates to divorce.

Completion of Fifteen Mediated Cases and Ten Hours of Supervision.

Continuing Education. In order for one to continue membership in the Academy, one must report, annually, completion
of the following requirements:
  1. Fifteen hours of instruction in any combination of the
     specialized training categories listed above, with em-
     phasis in the subject area of the member's greatest need
  2. Twenty-four hours of peer review or case consultation

Note

The specialized training need not be forty consecutive hours and
may include lectures, conferences, continuing education programs,
graduate classes, or seminars, as well as more specialized training
programs in divorce mediation.

The supervision required above must be received from a person
who meets all of the specific standards of full membership (Member) whether or not that person is in fact a member of the Academy.

Academy of Family Mediators Referral Directory Application

Name of your Agency/Organization

_____

_____

Phone Number_____

Name of Director(s)_____
Service:
When did you begin offering mediation services?_____

Number of mediation cases to date_____

Please check all other services your agency/organization provides in addition to mediation

__ 1. Marriage counseling
__ 2. Financial counseling
__ 3. Individual divorce counseling
__ 4. Groups for the divorcing
__ 5. Workshop/lectures to inform about divorce and/or custody
__ 6. Divorce-related therapy for children
__ 7. Divorce support groups for children
__ 8. Counseling not related to divorce or marriage
__ 9. Custody investigations
__ 10. Psychiatric investigations
__ 11. Legal services not related to divorce
__ 12. Legal services related to divorce
__ 13. Mediation not related to divorce (landlord/tenant)
__ 14. Mediation of domestic relations issues other than divorce
__ 15. Arbitration of divorce-related issues
__ 16. Other (please specify)

Which best describes the organization of your mediation practice?
__ Private, profit organization
__ Private, nonprofit organization
__ Professional partnership
__ Solo practitioner
__ Government or court-connected

Funding of your service is by:
__ Client fees
__ Private foundation grant
__ Insurance payments
__ State government
__ Other (please specify)

Staff:

Name	Profession	Degree	Number of cases mediated	Full or part-time

Service Format:

Average Length of mediation case _____ hours _____ sessions.

Who drafts the mediated agreement and what becomes of it?_____

_____

References

"A California Experiment: Private Dispute Resolution." *Dispute Resolution*, 1982, no. 9, p. 4.

ADAMS, S. "Mediation: The Private Sector." *California Family Law Report*, 1982, 6(18):1.

ADAMS, S., and SEVITCH, N. *1982 California Family Law Practice*. San Francisco: California Family Law Practice, 1982.

_____. *1984 California Family Law Practice*. Sausalito, Calif.: California Family Law Practice, 1984.

AHRONS, C. "Divorced Families: Complexity and Change." Paper presented at the Twenty-second Annual Conference of the Association of Family and Conciliation Courts, Denver, May 24, 1984.

AKABAS, S. "Prepaid Legal Services." Paper presented at the Annual Program Meeting of the Council on Social Work Education, New York City, March 8, 1982.

"A Major Challenge: Therapy and Ethnicity (II)." *Behavior Today*, 1984, 15(7):4–5.

AUERBACH, J. *Justice Without Law?* New York: Oxford University Press, 1983.

BAKER-JACKSON, M.; BERGMAN, K.; FERRICK, G.; HOVSEPIAN, V.; GARCIA, J.; and HULBERT, R. *Certification Committee Report*. Los

Angeles: California Chapter of the Association of Family and Conciliation Courts, 1983.

BANDLER, R., and GRINDER, J. *frogs into Princes*. Moab, Utah: Real People Press, 1979.

————. *Reframing*. Moab, Utah: Real People Press, 1982.

BANK, S., and KAHN, M. *The Sibling Bond*. New York: Basic Books, 1982.

BARDEN, J. "When Clarity is the Devil's Workshop." *New York Times*, November 21, 1982, p. E9.

"Bar Moves Closer to Legal Specialists." *Los Angeles Times*, August 14, 1983, p. 28.

BERG, A. "The Attorney as Divorce Mediator." In *Successful Techniques for Mediating Family Breakup*, edited by J. A. Lemmon. *Mediation Quarterly*, No. 2. San Francisco: Jossey-Bass, 1983.

BERGER, M. (ED.). *Videotape Techniques in Psychiatric Training and Treatment*. New York: Brunner/Mazel, 1978.

BERNARD, S.; FOLGER, J.; WEINGARTEN, H.; and ZUMETA, Z. "The Neutral Mediator: Value Dilemmas in Divorce Mediation." In *Ethics, Standards, and Professional Challenges*, edited by J. A. Lemmon. *Mediation Quarterly*, No. 4. San Francisco: Jossey-Bass, 1984.

BETHEL, C., and SINGER, L. "Mediation: A New Remedy for Cases of Domestic Violence." In *Alternative Means of Family Dispute Resolution*, edited by H. Davidson, L. Ray, and R. Horowitz. Washington, D.C.: American Bar Association, 1982.

BETTELHEIM, B. *The Uses of Enchantment: The Meaning and Importance of Fairy Tales*. New York: Knopf, 1976.

BISHOP, T. "Mediation Standards: An Ethical Safety Net." In *Ethics, Standards, and Professional Challenges*, edited by J. A. Lemmon. *Mediation Quarterly*, No. 4. San Francisco: Jossey-Bass, 1984.

BLACK, M., and JOFFEE, W. "A Lawyer-Therapist Team Approach to Divorce." *Conciliation Courts Review*, 1978, 16(11):1–5.

BLADES, J. "Mediation: An Old Art Revitalized." In *Reaching Effective Agreements*, edited by J. A. Lemmon. *Mediation Quarterly*, No. 3. San Francisco: Jossey-Bass, 1984.

BLAKE, G. "Child Visitation Rights: A New Twist." *Los Angeles Times*, April 14, 1981, p. 1.

BLUMSTEIN, P., and SCHWARTZ, P. *American Couples*. New York: Morrow, 1983.

BOHANNON, P. "Taking a New Look at Families: Toward a Well-Family Industry." Paper presented at the Twenty-second Annual Conference of the Association of Family and Conciliation Courts, Denver, May 24, 1984.

BRASCH, N. "Legal Aid: The Attorney's PC." *PC Magazine*, February 7, 1984, pp. 297–301.

BRIELAND, D., and LEMMON, J. *Social Work and the Law*. St. Paul: West, 1977.

BUGDANOWITZ, R. "Boxing in the Hostile Witness." *Family Advocate*, 1983, 6(1):12–15.

BUNDY, A. "Consensus Decision Making." Paper presented at San Francisco State University, December 15, 1982.

CARTER, E., and McGOLDRICK, M. *The Family Life Cycle: A Framework for Family Therapy*. New York: Gardner Press, 1980.

"Children's Aid Society Suggests Mandatory Mediation for Juvenile Court Cases." *Marriage and Divorce Today*, 1984,9(38):4.

COLLINS, G. "Helping Couples Stay Married." *San Francisco Chronicle*, December 7, 1983, p. 41.

"Consultants' Consultant Teaches Behavior Strategies for and of Clients." *Behavior Today*, 1982, 13(48):4.

COOGLER, O. J. *Structured Mediation in Divorce Settlement*. Lexington, Mass: Heath, 1978.

_____. "Divorce Mediation for 'Low Income' Families: A Proposed Model." *Conciliation Courts Review*, 1979, 17(1):21–26.

CROSS, J. *The Economics of Bargaining*. New York: Basic Books, 1969.

CULLINAN, T. "A New Approach to Settling Differences Outside the Court." *California Business*, July 1, 1983, p. 14.

DAVIDSON, H. "Family Mediation in Parent-Child Disputes: A Legal Justification." In *Alternative Means of Family Dispute Resolution*, edited by H. Davidson, L. Ray, and R. Horowitz. Washington, D.C.: American Bar Association, 1982.

DAVIS, A., and SALEM, R. "Dealing with Power Imbalances in the Mediation of Interpersonal Disputes." In *Procedures for Guiding the Divorce Mediation Process*, edited by J. A. Lemmon. *Mediation Quarterly*, No. 6. San Francisco: Jossey-Bass, 1984.

DIBBLE, C. "Bargaining in Family Mediation: Ethical Considerations." In *Ethics, Standards, and Professional Challenges*, edited by J. A. Lemmon. *Mediation Quarterly*, No. 4. San Francisco: Jossey-Bass, 1984.

"Divorce Mediation: Does It Have a Future?" *Marriage and Divorce Today*, 1983, 8(45):1–4.

DULLEA, G. "Setting a Diploma's Value in Divorce." *New York Times*, November 21, 1982, "Style" section, p. 44.

————. "The Divorce Lawyer as Amateur Shrink." *San Francisco Chronicle*, September 8, 1983, p. 38.

ECKHOUSE, J. "Bargaining Tool." *San Francisco Sunday Examiner and Chronicle*, October 9, 1983, p. B-2.

EICHLER, S. "Comments on Marketing EAP Services." *Consultation*, 1983 (1):31–32.

EISENBERG, M. "Private Ordering Through Negotiation: Dispute Settlement and Rule Making." *Harvard Law Review*, 1976, 89:637–681.

EKMAN, P.; LEVENSON, R.; and FRIESEN, W. "Autonomic Nervous System Activity Distinguishes Among Emotions." *Science*, 1983, 221:1208–1210.

ELIAS, M. "When We Chuckle, We Show More Than Our Smiles." *USA Today*, December 16, 1983, p. 4D.

————. "Anger at Home Upsets Our Toddlers." *USA Today*, March 14, 1984, p. 1.

ERIKSON, E. *Childhood and Society*. New York: Norton, 1950.

————. "On the Generational Cycle." *International Journal of Psychoanalysis*, 1980, 61:213–223.

EVATT, C., and FELD, B. *The Givers and the Takers*. New York: Macmillan, 1983.

"Family Therapist Addresses Corporation Problems." *Marriage and Divorce Today*, 1983, 8(44):2.

FATIS, M., and KONEWKO, P. "Written Contracts as Adjuncts in Family Therapy." *Social Work*, 1983, 28:161–163.

FEDERICO, J. "The Marital Termination Period of the Divorce Adjustment Process." *Journal of Divorce*, 1979, 3:93–106.

FISHER, R. "Getting to Yes: How Does Negotiation Work?" Address presented at the University of Santa Clara, March 16, 1984.

FISHER, R., and URY, W. *Getting to Yes*. Boston: Houghton Mifflin, 1981.

FOLBERG, J. "The Changing Family: Implications for the Law." *Conciliation Courts Review*, 1981, 19:1–6.

FOSBURGH, L. *Old Money*. Garden City, N.Y.: Doubleday, 1983.

FRANKLIN, B. "Costs and Tensions Cut in Mine Mediation Plan." *New York Times*, July 11, 1983, p. 12Y.

FREED, D. "What the States Say About Prenuptial Agreements." *Family Advocate*, 1984, 6(3):26–29.

FULLER, L. "Mediation: Its Forms and Functions." *Southern California Law Review*, 1971, 44:305–342.

GALBRAITH, J. K. *The Anatomy of Power*. Boston: Houghton Mifflin, 1983.

GALLANT, C. *Mediation in Special Education Disputes*. Silver Spring, Md.: National Association of Social Workers, 1982.

GARDNER, R. *Family Evaluation in Child Custody Litigation*. Cresskill, N.J.: Creative Therapeutics, 1982.

GOLDBERG, S., and BRETT, J. "An Experiment in the Mediation of Grievances." *Monthly Labor Review*, March 1983, pp. 23–30.

GOLDSTEIN, J. "Ma, Pa, and the Kids: Keeping Family and Business Running Along Parallel Lines Makes Life Easier for Everyone." *In Business*, 1983, 5(5):30–31.

GOODE, E. "Divorce and Children—Surprising Findings." *San Francisco Chronicle*, May 3, 1984, p. 23.

GORDON, D. *Therapeutic Metaphors*. Cupertino, Calif.: Meta, 1978.

GREEN, E. "Mini-Trials Now Used in Government Contract Disputes." *Dispute Resolution*, 1982 (11):5.

GREIF, J. "Fathers, Children, and Joint Custody." *Journal of Orthopsychiatry*, 1979, 49:311–342.

HAYNES, J. "Divorce Mediator: A New Role." *Social Work*, 1978, 23(1):5–9.

_____. *Divorce Mediation: A Practical Guide for Therapists and Counselors*. New York: Gardner, 1981.

_____. "The Process of Negotiation." In *Dimensions and Practice of Divorce Mediation*, edited by J. A. Lemmon. *Mediation Quarterly*, No. 1. San Francisco: Jossey-Bass, 1983.

HENRY, W.; SIMS, J.; and SPRAY, S. *The Fifth Profession: Becoming a Psychotherapist*. San Francisco: Jossey-Bass, 1971.

HOWARD, W. "Tax-in-the-Box?" *Family Advocate*, 1982, 4:37–44.

"How to Protect Yourself Against a Lawsuit (I)." *Marriage and Divorce Today*, 1983, 8(37):2–3.

HUNTINGTON, D. "The Needs of Families and Children in the Process of Divorce." Paper presented at the Seventh Annual Family Law Colloquium, Los Angeles, November 18, 1983.

ILFELD, F.; ILFELD, H.; and ALEXANDER, J. R. "Does Joint Custody Work? A First Look at Outcome Data of Relitigation." *American Journal of Psychiatry*, 1982, 139:34–41.

JENKINS, B., and STEINER, C. "Mediations." *Issues in Cooperation and Power*, 1980 (3):4–22.

JENKINS, J. "Day Out of Court." *TWA Ambassador*, July 1983, pp. 28–30.

"Joint Custody of a Dog." *San Francisco Chronicle*, September 9, 1983, p. 3.

JOSELOW, F. "Advice to High-Tech Millionaires." *New York Times*, October 9, 1983, p. 10F.

KIECHEL, W. "Executives Ought to Be Funnier." *Fortune*, December 12, 1983, pp. 205–208.

KOHLBERG, A. "Social and Legal Policy Implications of Domestic Violence." In *Alternatives Means of Family Dispute Resolution*, edited by H. Davidson, L. Ray, and R. Horowitz. Washington, D.C.: American Bar Association, 1982.

KOLB, D. *The Mediators*. Cambridge, Mass.: MIT Press, 1983.

KOOPMAN, E., and HUNT, E. "Divorce Mediation: Issues in Defining, Educating, and Implementing a New and Needed Profession." *Conciliation Courts Review*, 1983, 21(1):25–37.

KORNHABER, A. "Grandparent Rights in America: Now and in the Future." Paper presented at the Twenty-second Annual Conference of the Association of Family and Conciliation Courts, Denver, May 24, 1984.

KORNHABER, A., and WOODWARD, K. *Grandparents/Grandchildren: The Vital Connection*. Garden City, N.Y.: Anchor Press/Doubleday, 1981.

KRESSEL, K., and DEUTSCH, M. "Divorce Therapy: An In-depth Survey of Therapists' Views." *Family Process*, 1977, 16:413–443.

KÜBLER-ROSS, E. *On Death and Dying*. New York: Macmillan, 1969.

LABORDE, G. *Influencing with Integrity*. Palo Alto, Calif.: Syntony, 1983.

LANDE, J. "Mediation Paradigms and Professional Identities." In *Ethics, Standards, and Professional Challenges*, edited by J. A. Lemmon. *Mediation Quarterly*, No. 4. San Francisco: Jossey-Bass, 1984.

LEMMON, J. "Divorce Mediation: Optimal Scope and Practice Issues." In *Dimensions and Practice of Divorce Mediation: No. 1*, edited by J. A. Lemmon. San Francisco: Jossey-Bass, 1983.

_____. Personal Correspondence, February 6, 1982.

_____. "Legal Content in the Social Work Curriculum." *Journal of Education for Social Work*, 1983a, 19(2):71–76.

_____. "Values, Ethics, and Legal Issues." In *Handbook of Clinical Social Work*, edited by A. Rosenblatt and D. Waldfogel. San Francisco: Jossey-Bass, 1983b.

LERMAN, L. "Stopping Domestic Violence: A Guide for Mediators." In *Alternative Means of Family Dispute Resolution*, edited by

H. Davidson, L. Ray, and R. Horowitz. Washington, D.C.: American Bar Association, 1982.

LEWYN, M. "Computers and Psychiatry: These Doctors Are On-Line." *USA Today*, April 6, 1984, p. 3B.

"Malpractice Insurance: What Does It Protect You Against (II)?" *Marriage and Divorce Today*, 1983, 8:2–3.

"Malpractice: Pastoral Counselors and Mediators (III)." *Marriage and Divorce Today*, 1983, 8(39):2.

MAMIS, R. "Sparring Partners." *Inc.*, 1984, 6(3):43–48.

MANUEL, D. "Grandparents' Family Role Grows." *Los Angeles Times*, November 13, 1983, Part VII, p. 14.

"Marital Caution." *Marriage and Divorce Today*, 1984, 9(32):2.

MARKOWITZ, J., and ENGRAM, P. "Mediation in Labor Disputes and Divorces: A Comparative Analysis." In *Successful Techniques for Mediating Family Breakup*, edited by J. A. Lemmon. *Mediation Quarterly*, No. 2. San Francisco: Jossey-Bass, 1983.

MAYER, B. "Conflict Resolution in Child Protection and Adoption." Paper presented at the Twenty-second Annual Conference of the Association of Family and Conciliation Courts, Denver, May 24, 1984.

McEWEN, C., and MAIMAN, R. "Small Claims Mediation in Maine: An Empirical Assessment." *Maine Law Review*, 1981, 33(2):237–268.

McGOLDRICK, M.; PEARCE, J.; and GIORDANO, J. *Ethnicity and Family Therapy*. New York: Guilford Press, 1982.

McISAAC, H. "Confidentiality." Paper presented at the Family Mediation Conference, Dominican College, San Rafael, Calif., July 13, 1984.

MILNE, A. "Divorce Mediation: The State of the Art." In *Dimensions and Practice of Divorce Mediation*, edited by J. A. Lemmon. *Mediation Quarterly*, No. 1. San Francisco: Jossey-Bass, 1983.

_____. "The Development of Parameters of Practice for Divorce Mediation." In *Ethics, Standards and Professional Challenges*, edited by J. A. Lemmon. *Mediation Quarterly*, No. 4. San Francisco: Jossey-Bass, 1984.

MITCHELL, G. "Perks for Corporate Employees." *Bay City Journal*, October 1983, p. 33.

MNOOKIN, R., and KORNHAUSER, L. "Bargaining in the Shadow of the Law: The Case of Divorce." *Yale Law Journal*, 1979, 88:960–997.

Model Rules of Professional Conduct. Washington, D.C.: American Bar Association, 1983.

MOMJIAN, A. "Preserving Your Witness's Stellar Testimony." *Family Advocate*, 1983, 6(1):8–44.

MOORE, J. "Collective Discomfort: The Fight for a Woman's Place." *East Bay Express*, November 12, 1982, p. 3.

NAISBITT, J. *Megatrends*. New York: Warner, 1982.

"New Study Highlights Needs of Child Witnesses to Family Violence." *Marriage and Divorce Today*, 1983, 9(8):1–3.

"New Task Force on Family Violence." *San Francisco Chronicle*, September 20, 1983, p. 6.

NICOLSON, H. *Diplomacy*. New York: Oxford University Press, 1964.

"Notes on Law Schools." *Chronicle of Higher Education*, February 22, 1984, p. 3.

ORENSTEIN, S. "The Role of Mediation in Domestic Violence Cases." In *Alternative Means of Family Dispute Resolution*, edited by H. Davidson, L. Ray, and R. Horowitz. Washington, D.C.: American Bar Association, 1982.

PALENSKI, J. "Some Observations on the Use of Mediation by Police." In *Community Mediation*, edited by J. A. Lemmon. *Mediation Quarterly*, No. 5, 1984.

PATTERSON, G. *Families: Applications of Social Learning to Family Life*. Champaign, Ill.: Research Press, 1971.

PEARSON, J.; RING, M.; and MILNE, A. "A Portrait of Divorce Mediation Services in the Public and Private Sector." *Conciliation Courts Review*, 1983, 21(1):1–24.

PEARSON, J., and THOENNES, N. "Mediation and Divorce: The Benefits Outweigh the Costs." *Family Advocate*, 1982, 4:26–32.

————. "A Preliminary Portrait of Client Reactions to Three Court Mediation Programs." In *Reaching Effective Agreements*, edited by J. A. Lemmon. *Mediation Quarterly*, No. 3. San Francisco: Jossey-Bass, 1984.

PERRY, M. "Divorce Mediation Style." *San Francisco Sunday Examiner and Chronicle*, October 25, 1980, p. 4.

PHILLIPS, B., and PIAZZA, A. "The Role of Mediation in a Litigation Practice." *Civil Litigation Reporter*, 1983, 5(3):45–50.

POLLOCK, E. "The Alternative Route." *American Lawyer*, September 1983, pp. 70–74.

PORTER, S. "An Epidemic of Malpractice Suits." *San Francisco Chronicle*, June 5, 1982, p. 44.

"Premarital Test Can Predict Divorce, New Research Shows." *Marriage and Divorce Today*, 1984, 9(32):2–3.

PRESTON, L. "When to Appeal to a Storefront Lawyer." *Money*, 1983, 12(11):203–206.

"Profile: Judith Jackson." *Dispute Resolution*, 1983 (12):3.

PUKUI M.; HAERTIG, E.; and LEE, C. *Nana I Ke Kumu*. (Look to the Source). Honolulu: Hui Hanai, Queen Lilikokalani Children's Center, 1980.

RAY, L. "Domestic Violence Mediation Demands Careful Screening." In *Alternative Means of Family Dispute Resolution*, edited by H. Davidson, L. Ray, and R. Horowitz. Washington, D.C.: American Bar Association, 1982.

RHODE, D. "The Bar's Monopoly Game: Only Lawyers Can Play." *Nolo News*, Winter 1984, p. 8.

RIOS, D. "A Champion to Act for Neglected Children." *San Jose Mercury-News*, August 8, 1983, p. 1b.

RODBELL, S. "Considerations to Be Given in Mediating Couples in Which There Is Inter-Family Violence." *Marriage and Divorce Today*, 1983, 9(9):4.

ROGERS, M. *Women, Divorce, and Money*. New York: McGraw-Hill, 1981.

ROSEN, S. *My Voice Will Go with You: The Teaching Tales of Milton H. Erickson*. New York: Norton, 1982.

"Sacramento Scene." *California Lawyer*. July, 1983, p. 48.

SAITOW, R. *Insured Support Payments*. New Rochelle, N.Y.: Family Support Systems Inc., New Rochelle, N.Y., 1983.

SAMUELS, D., and SHAWN, J. "The Role of the Lawyer outside the Mediation Process." In *Successful Techniques for Mediating Family Breakup*, edited by J. A. Lemmon. *Mediation Quarterly*, No. 2. San Francisco: Jossey-Bass, 1983.

SANDER, F. E. A. "Family Mediation: Problems and Prospects." In *Successful Techniques for Mediating Family Breakup*, edited by J. A. Lemmon. *Mediation Quarterly*, No. 2. San Francisco: Jossey-Bass, 1983.

SAPOSNEK, D. "Strategies in Child Custody Mediation: A Family Systems Approach." In *Successful Techniques for Mediating Family Breakup*, edited by J. A. Lemmon. *Mediation Quarterly*, No. 2. San Francisco: Jossey-Bass, 1983.

SATIR, V. *Peoplemaking*. Palo Alto, Calif.: Science and Behavior Books, 1972.

SCHNEIDER, C. *Draft: Mediation Council of Illinois Professional Standards of Practice for Mediators*. Park Ridge, Ill.: 1984.

SHAW, M. "Mediating Between Parents and Children." In *Alternative Means of Family Dispute Resolution*, edited by H. Davidson, L. Ray, and R. Horowitz. Washington, D.C.: American Bar Association, 1982.

SHEAR, L. "Drafting Plans Allocating Parental Responsibility." *News-*

letter of the California Chapter of the Association of Family and Conciliation Courts, Spring 1983, pp. 1–2.

SHONHOLTZ, R. *Work, Structure, and Ethics of a Neighborhood Justice System.* In *Community Mediation*, edited by J. A. Lemmon. *Mediation Quarterly*, No. 5. San Francisco: Jossey-Bass, 1984.

SILBERMAN, L. "Professional Responsibility Problems of Divorce Mediation." *Family Law Reporter*, 1981, 7:4001–4012.

SMART, L. "An Application of Erikson's Theory to the Recovery from Divorce Process." *Journal of Divorce*, 1977, 1:67–79.

SMITH, K.; TROHA, M.; KINSEY, K.; and SHENASSA, A. "A Survey of the Membership of the ABA Section of Family Law." *Family Law Quarterly*, 1983, 17(3):225–285.

SOLOMON, B. "Value Issues in Working with Minority Clients." In *Handbook of Clinical Social Work*, edited by A. Rosenblatt and D. Waldfogel. San Francisco: Jossey-Bass, 1983.

"Stepfamilies: The Restructuring Process." *Marriage and Divorce Today*, 1983, 8(40):1–3.

"Stepmothers." *New York Times*, May 8, 1983, p. 18y.

STONE, A. "How Divorce Law Affects Women." *San Francisco Chronicle*, December 5, 1983, p. 2.

"Study Says Poor Hurt by Cuts in Legal Aid." *San Francisco Chronicle*, November 14, 1983, p. 36.

TAVRIS, C. *Anger, The Misunderstood Emotion.* New York: Simon & Schuster, 1982.

TAYLOR, A. "Toward a Comprehensive Theory of Mediation." *Conciliation Courts Review*, 1981, 19:1–10.

TOPOLNICKI, D. "Family Firms Can Leave the Feuds Behind." *Money*, 1983, 4(6):83–89.

"Unearned Portion of Retainer Must Be Returned to Client." *Family Law Reporter*, 1982, 8(27):1105.

"The Unique Problems of the Previously Unmarried Stepfather." *Marriage and Divorce Today*, 1982, 8(13):1–3.

VROOM, P.; FASSETT, D.; and WAKEFIELD, R. "Mediation: The Wave of the Future?" *American Family*, 1981, 4(4):8–13.

WALDRON, J.; ROTH, C.; FAIR, P.; MANN, E.; and McDERMOTT, J. "Therapeutic Mediation Model for Child Custody Dispute Resolution." In *Reaching Effective Agreements*, edited by J. A. Lemmon. *Mediation Quarterly*, No. 3. San Francisco: Jossey-Bass, 1984.

WALLERSTEIN, J., and KELLY, J. *Surviving the Breakup.* New York: Basic Books, 1980.

WARNER, R., and IHARA T. *The Living Together Kit.* Berkeley, Calif.: Nolo Press, 1983.

WEISS, R. *Marital Separation.* New York: Basic Books, 1975.

WEITZMAN, L. *The Marriage Contract.* New York: Free Press, 1981.

"What Problems Do Your Remarriage Clients Ultimately Seek to Resolve?" *Marriage and Divorce Today,* 1983, 9(5):2.

WILKINS, R. "PC Buyer's Guide for Lawyers." *PC Magazine,* March 6, 1984, pp. 297–299.

WILSON, S. *Confidentiality in Social Work.* New York: Free Press, 1978.

WIXTED, S. "The Children's Hearings Project: A Mediation Program for Children and Families." In *Alternative Means of Family Dispute Resolution,* edited by H. Davidson, L. Ray, and R. Horowitz. Washington, D.C.: American Bar Association, 1982.

YABLONSKY, L. *Psychodrama: Resolving Emotional Problems Through Role Playing.* New York: Gardner, 1976.

ZARTMAN, I., and BERMAN, M. *The Practical Negotiator.* New Haven: Yale University Press, 1982.

Index